World of Farming

Seasons on a Farm

Nancy Dickmann

Heinemann Library
Chicago, Illinois

www.capstonepub.com
Visit our website to find out more information about Heinemann-Raintree books.

To order:
☎ Phone 800-747-4992

🖥 Visit www.capstonepub.com to browse our catalog and order online.

©2011 Heinemann Library
an imprint of Capstone Global Library, LLC
Chicago, Illinois

Edited by Siân Smith, Nancy Dickmann, and Rebecca Rissman
Designed by Joanna Hinton-Malivoire
Picture research by Mica Brancic
Production by Victoria Fitzgerald
Originated by Capstone Global Library Ltd
Printed and bound in the United States of America in Eau Claire, Wisconsin. 092014 008530RP

Library of Congress Cataloging-in-Publication Data
Dickmann, Nancy.
  Seasons on a farm / Nancy Dickmann.—1st ed.
    p. cm.—(World of farming)
  Includes bibliographical references and index.
  ISBN 978-1-4329-3939-7 (hc)—ISBN 978-1-4329-3953-3 (pb)
1. Seasons—Juvenile literature. 2. Farm life—Juvenile literature. 3. Farms—Juvenile literature. I. Title. II. Series: Dickmann, Nancy. World of farming.
  QB637.4.D53 2010
  630—dc22
                                        2009051588

Acknowledgements
We would like to thank the following for permission to reproduce photographs: Corbis pp.**7** (© Image Source), **17** (zefa Select/© Awilli), **22** (zefa Select/© Awilli); Getty Images pp.**18** (Comstock/Jupiter Images), **20**, **23 bottom** (Dorling Kindersley/Alan Buckingham); Photolibrary pp.**4** (Digital Light Source/Sergio Izquierdo), **5** (imagebroker.net/Michael Krabs), **6** (Britain On View/Chris Laurens), **8** (Reso/Diaphor La Phototheque), **9** (F1Online RF/Sodapix Sodapix), **10** (Robert Harding Travel/Ann & Steve Toon), **11** (Juniors Bildarchiv), **12** (Index Stock Imagery/Inga Spence), **13** (Neil Duncan), **14** (Tips Italia/Bildagentur RM), **15** (age fotostock/Alan Kearney), **16** (Digital Light Source/Richard Hutchings), **19** (Nordic Photos/Mikael Andersson), **21**, **23 middle** (All Canada Photos/Don Weixl), **23 top** (Britain On View/Chris Laurens).

Front cover photograph of strawberries being harvested reproduced with permission of Shutterstock (© Boris Khamitsevich). Back cover photograph of a ewe with lamb in Scotland reproduced with permission of Photolibrary (Robert Harding Travel/Ann & Steve Toon).

The publisher would like to thank Dee Reid, Diana Bentley, and Nancy Harris for their invaluable help with this book.

Every effort has been made to contact copyright holders of material reproduced in this book. Any omissions will be rectified in subsequent printings if notice is given to the publishers.

Contents

What Is a Farm?. .4

Spring. 6

Summer 12

Fall 14

Winter. 18

Can You Remember? 22

Picture Glossary. 23

Index 24

What Is a Farm?

sweet corn

A farm is a place where food is grown.

Farms change with the seasons.

Spring

plow

In spring, farmers plow the fields.

They get fields ready for planting.

In spring, farmers plant seeds.

The seeds will grow into plants.

In spring, lambs are born.

Calves are born in spring, too.

Summer

In summer, plants grow taller.

Farmers water their plants.

Fall

In fall, plants are ready to be picked.

Some farmers gather wheat.

In fall, some farmers pick apples.

hay

Some farmers make hay to feed their animals.

Winter

In winter, farmers fix their
farm machines.

Farmers make sure their animals stay warm.

seeds

In winter, farmers buy seeds to plant in spring.

20

The farm gets ready for spring.

Can You Remember?

What do farmers make hay for?

Answer on page 24

Picture Glossary

 **plow** farm tool that breaks up the ground so that farmers can plant seeds

 **season** a time of the year. Spring, summer, fall, and winter are seasons.

 **seed** plants grow from seeds. Farmers plant seeds in the ground.

Index

animals, 10, 11, 17, 19

fall, 14, 16

seeds, 8, 9, 20

spring, 6, 8, 10, 11, 21

summer, 12

winter, 18, 20

Answer to quiz on page 22: Farmers make hay so that they can feed it to their animals.

Note to Parents and Teachers

Before reading:
Ask the children to name the four seasons. Then look at a calendar together to agree when these seasons take place. What is the weather like during the different seasons?

After reading:
- As a class, make a circular picture of the seasons on a farm. Divide a large circle of paper into quarters and split the class into four groups. Give each group a season and ask them to draw pictures of what happens on the farm during that season. Have them cut out the pictures and stick them on their quarter of the circle. Then display the finished picture on the classroom wall.

- Talk about when the fruits and vegetables that grow where you live are ready to eat. Make a frieze showing each month of the year and look at books and the Internet together to find out when local foods are ready to harvest. Have the children draw these fruits and vegetables and stick them on the correct month. Talk about how some foods can be stored so we can eat them during winter.

Larry Dixon has given us an "Owners Manual" for Christians. If you aren't careful, religion can make you "weird." This book is the antidote. With incredible balance and insight, Biblical faithfulness and Christian reality (mixed with delightful humor), Dr. Dixon cuts through the nonsense and the silliness and points to what it means to live an authentic Christian life. Read it. You'll be glad you did!

Steve Brown,
Professor, Reformed Theological Seminary, Orlando
Author of *A Scandalous Freedom*

In these postmodern times, when so much writing and talk about the Christian life floats around in the flotsam and jetsam of personal feelings and emotions, it is a significant discovery to find a book so firmly anchored in the Bible and good theology. Dr. Larry Dixon is a first-rate communicator, but he is something more; he is a sound and trustworthy guide in this fine book about the Christian's life and walk.

David J. MacLeod
Dean, Department of Bible, Emmaus Bible College
Dubuque, Iowa

Experience without doctrine is dangerous, but doctrine without experience is deadening. This solidly doctrinal book is anything but dead ; it is alive with practical ways to turn our right belief into responsible behavior. Part 3, that talks about the believer's associations, is worth the price of the whole book, and has convictingly caused me to reexamine my intentional contact (or lack thereof) with unbelievers. Larry Dixon not only writes well, but he is a man who "walks the talk." And, he really IS a great tennis player, using that skill, not as an end in itself, but as a means to the end of meaningfully reaching people who need the Lord.

George W. Murray,
Columbia International University,
Columbia, South Carolina

DocWALK covers a wide range of subjects that are quite relevant to living the Christian life. Its many helpful sections include good emphases on how the Christian should use his mind and how biblical teaching should control a Christian's emotions. A wide variety of applications in the book reflect the author's breadth of knowledge on a variety of subjects. Many illustrations, both personal and non-personal, maintain a high level of reader interest.

Robert Thomas,
The Master's Seminary, Sun Valley, California

Larry Dixon gives us sound biblical teaching on the Christian life packaged with wisdom and wit. This is Bible doctrine at its best presented in a practical way that is easy to read.

Jack Fish
Professor of New Testament, Emmaus Bible College
Dubuque, Iowa

In this logical follow-up to DocTALK, Larry Dixon sets out the need for the believer to think about their faith knowing that their thoughts influence their lives, and that their walk needs to match their talk. Larry writes with the heart of a pastor and the mind of a theologian, giving careful attention to why a believer should know their faith, and how they need to live it out in an authentic way. DocWALK is a must read for any believer that is serious about their faith and is sincere in their service for our Lord.

Benjamin T. Mathew
Emmaus Bible College, Dubuque, Iowa

Dixon's "DocWALK" is both a challenge and an encouragement to believers to live out the doctrines they profess. Written clearly in a popular mode with sound exegesis and suitable, practical illustrations, the author outlines the areas of performance in which doctrinal certainties enable the Christian to live and serve both church and community in the Name of God. Highly recommended for better doctrinal understanding and practical application of the great truths to particular situations.

Thomas V. Taylor,
Biblical Theological Seminary, Hatfield, Pennsylvania

What a delightful read! I couldn't put it down. I can't imagine a more enjoyable way to learn theology than with humor, simplicity, and practical application. Larry has the rare gift of making theology a joy. I heartily recommend DocWALK.

Ken Daughters
President, Emmaus Bible College
Dubuque, Iowa

DOCWALK

Putting into practice what you SAY you believe

LARRY DIXON

CHRISTIAN FOCUS

Other works by Larry Dixon:
"DocDEVOS," "DocTALK,"
"The Other Side of the Good News: Contemporary Challenges to Jesus' Teaching on Hell,"
and "Heaven: Thinking Now about Forever."

Dr. Dixon's website is www.theoprof.com

ISBN 1-84550-052-0

10 9 8 7 6 5 4 3 2 1

Published in 2005
by
Christian Focus Publications, Geanies House, Fearn,
Tain, Ross-shire, IV20 1TW, Scotland.

www.christianfocus.com

Printed and bound by
CPD, Wales

Cover Design by Alister MacInnes
Cartoons © Copyright Ron Wheeler

Unless otherwise stated, Scripture quotations are taken from
The Holy Bible, New International Version © 1973,1978, 1984 by International
Bible Society, or from the King James Version (KJV)

Contents

Foreword 9
Introduction 11

PART 1

Chapter 1: "The Believer's Acceptance" 17
Chapter 2: "The Believer's Authority" 35

PART 2

Chapter 3: "The Believer's Anatomy: 'If I Only Had a Brain...'" 53
Chapter 4: "The Believer's Anatomy: 'The Heart of the Matter...'" 73
Chapter 5: "The Believer's Anatomy: 'Problems with My Want to...'" 87
Chapter 6: "The Believer's Anatomy: 'From Hell: The Tongue!'" 103
Chapter 7: "The Believer's Anatomy: 'I'm to Present *My* Body?!'" 119

PART 3

Chapter 8: "The Believer's Associations: 'Who You Callin' a *Pagan*?'" ... 135
Chapter 9: "The Believer's Associations: 'Goin' to the Chapel
            and We're...'" 155

PART 4

Chapter 10: "The Believer's Attitudes" 177
Chapter 11: "The Believer's Actions" 201
Chapter 12: "The Believer's Assurance" 217
Chapter 13: "The Believer's Anticipation" 247

Dedication

This work is fondly dedicated to Mr. Tom Taylor, my former seminary professor, gifted mentor, and friend. Tom, thank you for your input in my life and ministry. Your infectious humor and commitment to "building up the saints" inspires me (and numerous others) to "serve the Lord with gladness." (I still think we'll get to have our table tennis match in glory!)

Foreword

Contemporary Christian literature, other than the fiction market, tends to develop particular themes in which some books are written polemically (to make us decide on a doctrine) and others are written rebukingly (to make us see the errors in some parts of our ways) and yet more are written devotionally (to warm our hearts with the Lord) while a few are written just to entertain us (to make us feel good). In his sequel to the earlier book *DocTALK*, Dr. Dixon has succeeded in using all four of these motifs in a most profitable way. He begins by a reminder of sound doctrine underlying the life of the Christian and then prompts us to think of some of the practices of life that do or do not conform to this foundation. He maintains our interest with meaningful and often amusing illustrations and personal accounts in which he is not always the hero, thereby allowing us to identify with him in the positions he affirms. Throughout the book he encourages a warm love for the Lord and His will.

Dixon does these things without a lot of fanfare or excessive claims for infallibility. One cannot help but be encouraged at the positive tone the book assumes and the challenge that it offers that our "walk" should be an accurate and meaningful expression of our belief. Unlike the common axiom "clothes make the man", Dixon regularly asserts that doctrine should make us what we ought to be. It is doctrine in practice, however, not merely a creedal affirmation. The four parts of the book are cleverly arranged to cover the believer's life beginning with the believer's acceptance and concluding with the believer's actions. There is no hidden agenda in the book and no threatening mailed fist. It provides genuine spiritual insight combined with meaningful application. His friendly style and approach to the subject will maintain interest and any serious reader will find helpful and encouraging food for thought.

Thomas V. Taylor, STD
Professor Emeritus,
Biblical Theological Seminary,
Hatfield, Pennsylvania

Introduction

DocWALK is a logical follow-up to *DocTALK*,[1] our survey of all ten areas of Christian doctrine. In *DocTALK* our concern was right belief. What are Christians supposed to believe about the doctrine of Christ, the doctrine of sin, the doctrine of the Holy Spirit, the doctrine of the church? In this text our concern is right behavior. The late Dr. Francis Schaeffer said, "There is only one command for those who do not believe in Christ – and it is this: *Watch those who do!*" We are a watched people and we had better be a well-behaved people. C. S. Lewis put it this way: "When we Christians behave badly, or fail to behave well, we are making Christianity unbelievable to the outside world."[2]

I understand that the U.S. Forest Service received the following actual comments from backpackers after wilderness camping trips: "Trails need to be reconstructed. Please avoid building trails that go uphill." "Too many bugs and spiders.

---

[1] *DocTALK: A Fairly Serious Survey of All That Theological Stuff* (Fearn, Ross-shire, Great Britain: Christian Focus Publications, 2002).

[2] C. S. Lewis, *Mere Christianity* (New York: Macmillan, 1972, 16th printing), Bk. IV, Ch. 10, p. 176.

Please spray the area to get rid of these pests." "Chairlifts are needed so we can get to the wonderful views without having to hike to them." "A McDonald's would be nice at trail head." "Too many rocks in the mountains." And my favorite: "The coyotes made too much noise last night and kept me awake. Please eradicate these annoying animals."

The Christian life often seems uphill, filled with "pests," and having too many rocks along the path. The annoyances are many and the way can be hard.

There are, of course, different ways of describing the Christian life. Some see it as a journey, some as a hike (with or without coyotes); others act as if it were a jog in the park. Some give the impression that it is a non-stop trip into the valley of the shadow of death! The Scriptures frequently describe the Christian life as a "walk." The Bible begins with Adam and Eve hearing God walking in the garden of Eden in Genesis 3:8 – and they hide from Him because of their sin. We are given the godly example of Enoch in Genesis 5 where we read that "Enoch walked with God 300 years and had other sons and daughters. Altogether, Enoch lived 365 years. Enoch walked with God; then he was no more, because God took him away" (vv. 22-24). One preacher said that Enoch's walk with the Lord was so close that one day, as they walked together, God said to Enoch, "Enoch, we're closer to my house here. Why don't you just come home with me?"

Numerous texts talk about the godly walk. Psalm 116 tells us, "Be at rest once more, O my soul, for the Lord has been good to you. For you, O Lord, have delivered my soul from death, my eyes from tears, my feet from stumbling, that I may walk before the Lord in the land of the living" (vv. 7-9). The well-known first Psalm states, "Blessed is the man who does not walk in the counsel of the wicked or stand in the way of sinners or sit in the seat of mockers. But his delight is in the law of the Lord, and on his law he meditates day and night" (vv. 1-2). Isaiah invites God's people in his second chapter: "Come, O house of Jacob, let us walk in the light of the Lord" (2:5). Isaiah cries out in the thirtieth chapter:

O people of Zion, who live in Jerusalem, you will weep no more. How gracious he will be when you cry for help! As soon as he hears, he will answer you. Although the LORD gives you the bread of adversity and the water of affliction, your teachers will be hidden no more; with your own eyes you will see them. Whether you turn to the right or to the left, your ears will hear a voice behind you, saying, "This is the way; walk in it" (vv. 19-21).

We read in Isaiah 40:28-31,

Do you not know? Have you not heard? The LORD is the everlasting God, the Creator of the ends of the earth. He will not grow tired or weary, and his understanding no one can fathom.[29] He gives strength to the weary and increases the power of the weak.[30] Even youths grow tired and weary, and young men stumble and fall;[31] but those who hope in the LORD will renew their strength. They will soar on wings like eagles; they will run and not grow weary, they will walk and not be faint.

Jeremiah declares in his sixth chapter, "This is what the LORD says: 'Stand at the crossroads and look; ask for the ancient paths, ask where the good way is, and walk in it, and you will find rest for your souls. But you said, 'We will not walk in it.'" (6:16).

The Lord Jesus says in John 8:12, "I am the light of the world. Whoever follows me will never walk in darkness, but will have the light of life." We read in John 12:35, "Then Jesus told them, "You are going to have the light just a little while longer. Walk while you have the light, before darkness overtakes you. Those who walk in the dark do not know where they are going.""

Paul challenges the Ephesian Christians in Ephesians 4:1-2, "I therefore, the prisoner of the Lord, beseech you that ye walk worthy of the vocation wherewith ye are called, With all lowliness and meekness, with longsuffering, forbearing one another in love" (KJV). We also read Paul's prayer in Colossians 1: "For this cause we also, since the day we heard it, do not cease to pray for you, and to desire that ye might be filled with the knowledge of his will in all wisdom and spiritual understanding; That ye might walk worthy of the Lord unto all pleasing, being fruitful in every good work, and increasing in the knowledge of God..." (vv. 9-10, KJV).

To walk worthy of the Lord involves knowing that we have been redeemed, ransomed, rescued and reconciled because of the atoning work of Christ. We require a trustworthy and authoritative map to guide our way. The journey will require the very best of us, utilizing every aspect of our mind, emotions, will, speech, and bodies. How we relate to those not yet on the journey as well as how we walk with those in God's family are of key importance. As we saw from the comments certain hikers made to the U.S. Forest Service, our attitudes on the journey are absolutely critical. What actions are required on the believer's journey? How may such a traveler maintain assurance in traveling in such an uncertain world? And why the journey in the first place? What is the believer anticipating as he travels life's road? Ready for the journey together?

Part One

Chapter 1

"The Believer's Acceptance"

"The redeemed are dependent on God for all. All that we have – wisdom, the pardon of sin, deliverance, acceptance in God's favor, grace, holiness, true comfort and happiness, eternal life and glory – we have from God by a Mediator; and this Mediator is God. God not only gives us the Mediator, and accepts His mediation, and of His power and grace bestows the things purchased by the Mediator, but He is the Mediator. Our blessings are what we have by purchase; and the purchase is made of God; the blessings are purchased of Him; and not only so, but God is the purchaser. Yes, God is both the purchaser and the price; for Christ, who is God, purchased these blessings by offering Himself as the price of our salvation." (Jonathan Edwards)

Psalm 116:7-9: "⁷Be at rest once more, O my soul, for the LORD has been good to you. ⁸For you, O LORD, have delivered my soul from death, my eyes from tears, my feet from stumbling, ⁹that I may walk before the LORD in the land of the living."

In one of Charles Schultz's "Peanuts" cartoons, Charlie Brown is looking over a wall with his sister Lucy. He says, "You know what I wonder? Sometimes I wonder if God is pleased with me." He then asks his sister, "Do you ever wonder if God is pleased with you?" And Lucy, patting her hair, responds with an enormous smile, "He just *has* to be!"

Our natural inclination is to think that, of course, God is pleased with us! But what automatically occurs to us is often far different than biblical truth. The Bible teaches that before a person believes in Christ, he or she is alienated from God (Col. 1:21), an enemy of God (Rom. 5:10), and under God's wrath (John 3:36). Scripture tells us that God is "angry with the wicked every day" (Ps. 7:11) and that "the wicked" includes you and me (Rom. 3:23). We do not measure up to the righteousness of God – and that should cause us to be displeased with ourselves.

It's Good to Look at the Bad News of the Good News!

How we think about ourselves must be determined by what the Word of God, the Bible, teaches. And before we can examine our new life in Christ, we must reflect upon what we were. We were "objects of His wrath" (Rom. 9:22), "separated from God" (Eph. 4:18), "lost" (Luke 15), "in our sins" (John 8:24), not measuring up to the glory of God (Rom. 3:23), spiritually dead (Eph. 2:1), deserving of God's wrath (Eph. 2:3), "walking in the darkness" (1 John 2:11), not even born yet (John 3:5), seeking to please God by our own works (John 6:28-29), etc. Need we go on?

Well, that's the bad news of the Good News. We were *not* in a spiritual state that was pleasing to God. I often hear people today use the expression, "It's all good!" I think they mean that a particular negative experience isn't all that bad, or can result in something good, or that life is too short to be down about something that happens. For the Christian, he or she can look back to their pre-conversion life and say, "It's all *bad!*"

Many in our culture are offended when we simply recite such spiritual basics of a person's *lostness*. Today people want to hear sentiments like, "I'm Okay – and You're Okay!" Or, "We are all children of God." Or, "God is too loving to send anybody to hell." Or, "Surely God will grade on the curve at the judgment. I might only squeeze by, but I'll make it!"

The biblical truth is that God is far holier than we realize. And our sin is far more repugnant than we want to admit. "Sin must either be pardoned – or punished," an old preacher (not myself) once said.

One should not be surprised at the very different reactions in present culture to Mel Gibson's *The Passion of the Christ*. Some cannot understand why such a kind-natured and soft-spoken Jewish rabbi should be tortured. Others were shocked at the cruelty of the treatment inflicted on Jesus by the Roman soldiers. Still others dismissed the film as an exercise in anti-Semitism (which it wasn't). For the believer in Jesus Christ, one common reaction to His excruciating punishment was: "That should have been me. That's what *I* deserved! He took *my* place!"

The Good News of the Good News – The *Four* R's:
The Bible is rich with metaphors and explanations of what the new believer in Jesus Christ has experienced. We will look at four of these pictures: You've been *ransomed* from your sin; you've been *redeemed* from your guilt; you've been *reconciled* from your estrangement; and, you've been *rescued* from your lostness.

Picture #1: "You've Been Ransomed from Your Sin!"
When we think of the term "ransom," we probably limit it to the capture of millionaires' children or the abduction of Christian missionaries by Communist revolutionaries in Colombia. More recently, several American contractors have been taken captive in Iraq and then beheaded, sometimes without any ransom demand made by the kidnappers.

The Bible does not limit the concept of "ransom" to the wealthy or the affluent. Mark 10:45 tells us that "the Son of Man did not come to be served, but to serve, and to give his life as a *ransom* for many." As the second Gospel account, Mark's primary emphasis is on Jesus as the perfect Servant of God. Very few discourses or speeches are found in the Gospel of Mark, for a servant is known not by his speaking but by his serving. Chapters 1–13 of Mark describe the acts of service which the Son of Man did. The last three chapters of that gospel relate Christ's primary purpose in coming: to give His life "as a ransom for many."

In the Early Church, various views were held regarding the atoning work of Christ (His death on the cross) and how it ought to be understood. One prominent view was called the "Ransom to Satan" view because some Christians thought that Jesus had to die to pay off Satan for our sins. The idea was that our sin had separated us from God, had put us under Satan's control, and now Satan had the right to demand a ransom price before he would release us.

The Bible does not teach the Ransom to Satan view. Satan is presented in the Scriptures as a usurper, a robber and a thief (John 10:10), and *God owes Satan nothing!* The primary point of the ransom image is that our salvation was *costly* (1 Peter 1:18) – and the metaphor should not be pressed beyond that emphasis.[1]

When my family and I lived in Canada, each Thursday night was special. I would drop off my daughter Amy (age ten at the time) and her friend Jean-Carla for dance lessons in the city of Winnipeg, and I would go to a table tennis club and practice my spiritual gift of ping pong. We always had fun on Thursday nights, usually capped off by a super-sized Slurpy at the local Seven-Eleven. Jean-Carla's father had abandoned the family when she was quite young. I remember one Thursday night feeling a special measure of compassion for Amy's friend and, as I dropped them off for dance lessons, I said to Jean-Carla: "Now be careful, you two. I wouldn't want either of you to get kidnaped! Jean-Carla," I said, "I'm sure I couldn't afford the massive ransom some kidnapper would demand for a great kid like *you*!" You should have seen her eyes glow, because I was telling her that she was precious and that I valued her. That's how God felt about each of us when He sent His Son as our ransom.

---

[1]If one insists on asking "To whom was the ransom paid?", the biblical answer is that God's own righteousness had to be satisfied by the death of His Son.

Hebrews 9:15 also uses the image of ransom:

> For this reason Christ is the mediator of a new covenant, that
> those who are called may receive the promised eternal inheritance
> – now that he has died as a *ransom* to set them free from the sins
> committed under the first covenant.

We have the need to be set free from our sins! And that is what
Christ's sacrifice on the cross accomplished for us.

The seminary where I teach (Columbia Biblical Seminary
and School of Missions – we have very large sweatshirts) often
has its faculty teach overseas. I've had the privilege of teaching in
India, in Moldova (a former republic of the Soviet Union), and
on the island of Sri Lanka. I've also led study tours of Germany,
Austria, and Italy. Columbia International University (which is
the corporate name of our three schools) has an official policy
should someone like myself get kidnaped. Their official position
is best summed up by the words, "God bless ya'! Tough rocks!"
That is, they will not pay any amount of ransom to rescue any
employee who gets kidnaped.

That raises some interesting questions for me: If I get
kidnaped in India, and the kidnappers demand a ransom of,
say, only the equivalent of a hundred dollars, would the school
refuse to take up a collection for me? Would no one on the
seminary faculty pass the hat for me in faculty meeting? What
if I provided my ATM pin number for them so they could take
the money directly out of my personal account? Would they
refuse to do it? What if I suggested they take it out of my future
paychecks? If the kidnappers allowed me a few moments of
internet access, could I pay them my own ransom out of my
on-line PayPal account?

Seriously, it would be incorrect to conclude from CIU's
policy that they do not value their faculty or that they would
not do anything short of paying a ransom to get one of us
released. Their point is that paying a ransom-demand facilitates
the kidnappers and only encourages them to grab others to
advance their interests

Thanks be unto God who has willingly paid the ransom price for sinners! And, according to Hebrews 9:15 ("For this reason Christ is the mediator of a new covenant, that those who are called may receive the promised eternal inheritance – now that he has died as a *ransom* to set them free from the sins committed under the first covenant"), the kidnaping which has taken place was not pulled off by some outside enemy. We can't put the blame on some counter-revolutionary party wanting to squeeze money out of us. *Our own sins* have put us in a kidnaped condition! And when you trusted Jesus Christ, the ransom got paid and you got free! (If you're not, at least inwardly, right now jumping up and shouting "WHOOPEE!", check your pulse. You might be dead).

Picture #2: "You've Been Redeemed from Your Guilt!"
When I was a wee lad, my mother used to collect S&H Green Stamps whenever she bought groceries. My job was to take those Green Stamps, lick them (you think postage stamps today taste awful?), and stick them in a redemption book. When several books were filled, my Mom and I would drive downtown to the S&H Green Stamp Redemption Center. There we could trade in those filled books for something of value, although "something of value" was a relative term (that is, my Mother would make that call). We always seemed to be redeeming those stamps for some kitchen implement, even though the store had some great toys which could be had for just a couple of books! That was my first exposure to the concept of redemption: working hard to trade for something *you* didn't want, something you didn't think you needed, leaving you with a bad taste in your mouth.

How far from the biblical doctrine of redemption my childhood experience was. We read in Galatians 3:13-14,

> Christ *redeemed* us from the curse of the law by becoming a curse for us, for it is written, "Cursed is everyone who is hung on a tree." He *redeemed* us in order that the blessing given to Abraham might come to the Gentiles through Christ Jesus, so that by faith we might receive the promise of the Spirit.

Twice we are told in this passage that we have been redeemed, a past action brought to completion by Christ Himself. The need for redemption is clear: we were under a "curse." The curse was simply that we are lawbreakers. And the Bible does not allow the game of what I call "relative guilt by comparison with others." James 2:10 says, "For whoever keeps the whole law and yet stumbles at just one point is guilty of breaking all of it."

Christ's method of redeeming us from the law's curse was neither to water down the law's demands nor to rationalize away our shortcomings. His action was to take that curse upon Himself, to become a curse in our place, specifically by dying as our substitute upon a Roman cross

The doctrine of the substitutionary death of the Lord Jesus is clearly taught throughout the New Testament, even though it offends modern sensibilities. He is the One who, "though He was rich, yet for your sake ... became poor, so that you through his poverty might become rich" (2 Cor. 8:9). We also read that "God made him who had no sin to be sin for us, so that in Him we might become the righteousness of God" (2 Cor. 5:21). Other passages tell us that He "gave Himself for our sins" (Gal. 1:4) and that "the Son of God loved me and gave Himself for me" (Gal. 2:20). We are reminded in Ephesians 5:1-2 that we are to "Follow God's example, therefore, as dearly loved children and walk in the way of love, just as Christ loved us and gave himself up for us as a fragrant offering and sacrifice to God."

In a famous passage used at many weddings, husbands are commanded in Ephesians 5 to "love your wives, just as Christ loved the church and gave himself up for her" (v. 25). First Timothy 2 teaches us that "there is one God and one mediator between God and human beings, Christ Jesus, himself human, who gave himself as a ransom for all people" (v. 5). We are also told in Titus 2 that "we wait for the blessed hope – the appearing of the glory of our great God and Savior, Jesus Christ, who gave himself for us to redeem us from all wickedness and to purify for himself a people that are his very own, eager to do what is good" (vv. 13-14). In John 10:15 Jesus says He would "lay down" His life for the sheep. Jesus Christ "laid down His life for us" and we ought to follow His example by laying down our lives for each other (1 John 3:16).

We read in Colossians 1:13-14 that God "has rescued us from the dominion of darkness and brought us into the kingdom of the Son he loves, in whom we have *redemption*, the forgiveness of sins." Biblical Christianity teaches that there is an actual, supernatural arch-enemy of the Christian whose name is Satan. He is not some cartoon-like skinny buffoon in red leotards carrying a pitchfork. He is *real* and he is the Father of lies. He despises Christians. He wants the believer in Christ to feel guilty and unforgiven. His voice whispers in the ear of the erring believer: "You call yourself a Christian and you do THAT!?" Sometimes his message is: "You've got to WORK HARD for God to love YOU!" And he relishes taking the Christian's attention off faith in Christ alone when he argues: "Surely Christianity CAN'T really mean that Christ's sacrifice for you was ENOUGH! Can it?"

Satan encourages us to feel guilty about those things that are neither here nor there as far as God is concerned (see Rom. 14). He also works hard at getting us to *not* feel guilty about violating clear biblical standards, and we cooperate with him when we drag out our excuses and our "explanations." He's into guilt when it serves his purposes – and he's into rationalizing self-defense and relativism when these keep us from genuine repentance and confession.

We were captives in his "dominion of darkness" (see 1 John 2:9-11). The Apostle Paul actually says of the Ephesian Christians, "For you were once darkness, but now you are light in the Lord. Live as children of light..." (Eph. 5:8). It's one thing to be in the darkness; it's another to walk in the darkness. But the worst is *to be* darkness! And that's where Christ's rescue comes in!

Not only have we been rescued; we've been *relocated*, Colossians 1 tells us. We've been moved from the dominion of darkness to "the kingdom of the Son He loves." What a great transition! It is in that Son that we have *redemption*.

Redemption is not in a religious system, but in a Person, the Son of God. Colossians 1 beautifully explains *redemption*, a powerful theological term, with the parallel expression "the forgiveness of sins."

The believer in Jesus Christ has been *forgiven!* I once heard of a man who said, "I don't mind forgetting and forgiving. It's just that I don't want the other person that I *forgave* to *forget* that I have *forgiven!*" God righteously forgives us in Christ. In the redemptive work of Christ, Paul says, God "did it to demonstrate his justice at the present time, so as to be just and the one who justifies those who have faith in Jesus" (Rom. 3:26).

A German proverb says, "If God were not willing to forgive sin, Heaven would be empty." There was no other way for God to justly forgive our sin other than by means of the death of Christ. Oswald Chambers says,

> Forgiveness, which is so easy for us to accept, cost the agony of Calvary. It is possible to take the forgiveness of sin, the gift of the Holy Ghost, and our sanctification with the simplicity of faith, and to forget at what enormous cost to God it was all made ours. Forgiveness is the divine miracle of grace; it cost God the cross of Jesus Christ before He could forgive sin and remain a holy God.[2]

In his *Foundations of Faith*, J. C. Ryle put it this way:

> Forgiven souls *are humble*. They cannot forget that they owe all they have and hope for to free grace, and this keeps them lowly. They are brands plucked from the fire – debtors who could not pay for themselves – captives who must have remained in prison for ever, but for undeserved mercy – wandering sheep who were ready to perish when the Shepherd found them....[3]

---

[2] Oswald Chambers, *My Utmost for His Highest, The Golden Book of Oswald Chambers* (Uhrichsville, OH: Barbour and Company, 1963), p. 241.

[3] J.C. Ryle, *Foundations of Faith: Selections from J.C. Ryle's "Old Paths"* (South Plainfield, NJ: Bridge Publishing, 1987), p. 62.

Picture #3: "You've Been Reconciled from Your Estrangement!"
The third picture in Scripture which explains what happened
to you when you trusted Jesus Christ as your Savior is that of
reconciliation. Now I know that *reconciliation* is not a term you
use everyday, but it's a powerful theological expression worthy
of examination. Romans 5:9-11 says,

> Since we have now been justified by his blood, how much more
> shall we be saved from God's wrath through him! For if, when we
> were God's enemies, we were *reconciled* to him through the death
> of his Son, how much more, having been *reconciled*, shall we be
> saved through his life! Not only is this so, but we also rejoice in
> God through our Lord Jesus Christ, through whom we have now
> received *reconciliation*.

The Apostle Paul was definitely into reconciliation in this
Romans passage, wasn't he? The idea that we were enemies of
God is like a punch in the face of contemporary culture that
thinks that if there is a God, He certainly loves everyone and has
no enemies. Reconciliation implies a breach in a relationship,
an animosity caused by one or both of the parties. In our sins
we are *not* friends of God. We stand in opposition to Him and
His purposes for His creation. It took the cruel death of the
Second Person of the Trinity to bring about a peace between
the sinner and the holy Creator.

According to the Bible, we were enemies of God before
our conversion (Rom. 5:10). We were under God's wrath
(Rom. 5:9). We deserved God's judgment (Rom. 6:23). Things
were not fine. We were not at peace with God. It was not "all
good."

We sometimes hear of a married couple that are separated
from each other. There is an estrangement. The relationship
is broken. Harmony has been lost. Such a separation often
leads to a divorce, frequently for "irreconcilable differences."
Spiritually speaking, that is what our condition was before the
holy God: we suffered from "irreconcilable differences."

Thankfully, God does not wait on us to overcome those
irreconcilable differences. His mercy does not depend upon our

first getting our lives straightened out so that He can love us. He loved us even when we were His enemies. When we were in that rebellious state, that enemy condition, "we were reconciled to him through the death of his Son." And Paul makes it clear that "we have now received reconciliation."

I mentioned that I have led several study tours over to Europe. The chaperones and myself take thirty fresh high school grads and visit significant sites in Germany, Austria, and Italy. On one tour we visited a famous monastery in Maulbronn, Germany. The friar who led us around was a nice young man (some of the girls unspiritually said, "What a waste!") who seemed to love God and desired to serve Him with his life. After the tour was over, one of our students said to Brother John, "Thanks for the tour. I'll see you in heaven." To which Brother John responded, "Well, I hope so." He had no assurance of salvation, probably because he partially relied on his own dedication to spiritual things as an aspect of his salvation.[4] We can know that we have received reconciliation. And we can know for certain that we will go to heaven when we die.

The story is told of a world-famous skeptic on his deathbed. His servant said to him, "Sir, do you not think that you should make reconciliation with God before you die?" "What?" said the man. "I never knew we argued!"

Picture #4: "You've Been Rescued from Your Lostness!"

What happened to you when you became a follower of Jesus Christ? We've seen that you've been ransomed from your sin. Not only that, but you've been redeemed from your guilt. That redemption brings forgiveness. Third, you've been reconciled from your estrangement from God. You are no longer God's enemy or under God's wrath or deserving of God's judgment. The fourth image is that you've been rescued from your lostness. We read in Colossians 1:13-14 that "He has *rescued* us from the dominion of darkness and brought us into the kingdom of the Son he loves, in whom we have redemption, the forgiveness of sins."

---

[4] We discuss the doctrine of assurance in Chapter 12.

The explorer Daniel Boone was once asked if he had ever gotten lost. He replied, "No, but I was *bewildered* for three days once." Lostness is a strong biblical metaphor for the unbeliever. In Matthew 10:6 Jesus tells His disciples to go preach to the "lost sheep of Israel." Luke 15 (which we will examine shortly) tells us of the lost sheep, the lost coin, and the lost son.

In Luke 19:10 Jesus says that "the Son of Man came to seek and to save what was lost." Jesus came, as one preacher put it, to seek the last, the least, and the lost. In 1 Corinthians 15 the Apostle Paul says,

> For if the dead are not raised, then Christ has not been raised either. And if Christ has not been raised, your faith is futile; you are still in your sins. Then those also who have fallen asleep in Christ are lost. If only for this life we have hope in Christ, we are to be pitied more than all others (vv. 16-19).

In Philippians 3 Paul writes, "But whatever were gains to me I now consider loss for the sake of Christ. What is more, I consider everything a loss because of the surpassing worth of knowing Christ Jesus my Lord, for whose sake I have lost all things. I consider them garbage, that I may gain Christ." In Colossians 2 Paul writes of the false teachers who have "lost connection with the Head, from whom the whole body, supported and held together by its ligaments and sinews, grows as God causes it to grow" (v. 19).

We need to ask what we mean when we refer to people as "lost." Brian McLaren makes an excellent point in his *More Ready Than You Realize* when he writes:

> One of the more common terms used these days to label non-Christians by Christians – and in particular, by the Christians most oriented toward evangelism – is "lost people." The term comes from Jesus' stories of the lost sheep, lost coin, and lost son in Luke 15. Unfortunately, the term, which in the story means loved, precious, and sought after, can become on our lips a synonym for "impure" or "unclean." Do you feel the implied

judgment of calling someone "lost" – especially as compared to calling them "missed" or "treasured," which might be better terms to describe the sheep, coin, and son in the stories?[5]

The metaphor of lostness is a valuable one – and one which we should not lose as we reflect on where we were – and where people without Christ still are. Luke 15 makes it quite clear that "religious" people can forget the dire condition of lost people and their need to reach out to them. The late Dr. Francis Schaeffer put it this way: We Evangelicals, he said, "have in a real sense lost sense of the lostness of the lost." Jesus drives home this lesson by using three examples of lostness in Luke 15.

In the parable of the lost sheep (vv. 3-7), the shepherd has a hundred sheep and one wanders off. He does not say, "Well, I've got ninety-nine others! Why bother myself about one stupid sheep?" He leaves the ninety-nine in the open country (perhaps putting them at risk in his determination to find the one missing sheep), and goes after the one lost sheep until he finds it. Upon finding it, "he joyfully puts it on his shoulders and goes home" (vv. 5-6). He then throws a party and says, "Rejoice with me; I have found my lost sheep" (v. 6). Lostness provoked a pursuit which was followed by a party.

In the parable of the lost coin (vv. 8-10), the woman goes to a lot of trouble to find that one coin, lighting a lamp and sweeping the house until she finds it. And when it is found, she throws a party for her friends and neighbors, inviting them to "Rejoice with me; I have found my lost coin" (v. 9). Lostness causes a search to take place, followed by a celebration.

In the most extensive parable of lostness, the parable of the lost son (vv. 11-32) contains many lessons about lostness. Whereas the coin could not be blamed for getting lost and none would think to get mad at a dumb sheep for wandering off, the story of the lost son shows premeditated abandonment

---

[5] Brian McLaren, *More Ready Than You Realize* (Grand Rapids: Zondervan, 2002), p. 58. We will later notice some of the weaknesses of post-modern Christianity (such as a minimizing of theology) of which McLaren is a leading spokesman.

of his place in the family. His moral culpability is revealed as he essentially says to his father, "As far as I'm concerned, you're as good as dead. I would like my inheritance now – in tens and twenties – if you don't mind." Not only does he turn his back on his family, but he quickly departs town and systematically does all he can to debauch himself. His resources eventually run out, hunger sets in, and somehow he comes to his senses.

With a repentant heart he chooses to go back to his father, preparing a speech of contrition which he will deliver, a simple confession of twenty-eight words: "Father, I have sinned against heaven and against you. I am no longer worthy to be called your son; make me like one of your hired men" (vv. 18-19). Coins and sheep make no speeches; rebellious sons have the ability to come to their senses and come back to their father.

Like the lost coin and the lost sheep, the lost son is sought, only in this passage the father sees his son "a long way off" and is "filled with compassion for him" (v. 20). In a cultural context in which the father would have been well within his rights to count his son as *dead* (much as the younger son had counted his father as good as dead, v. 12), this father showed no such animosity. Instead he "ran to his son, threw his arms around him and kissed him" (v. 20). Such unguarded and undignified emotion must have embarrassed (and outraged) the Pharisees and teachers of the law as they listened to Jesus' story.

The father allows the son time to deliver only eighteen of his twenty-eight word confessional: "Father, I have sinned against heaven and against you. I am no longer worthy to be called your son" (v. 21). The father then throws a big party. This son had probably hocked all his possessions, and the father immediately has the best robe put on him, a ring on his finger and sandals on his feet. The fattened calf (perhaps one which had been selected and purposely well-fed in hopeful anticipation of this day) is brought out to be barbecued. "Let's have a feast and celebrate. Pass the barbecue sauce!", says the jubilant father. "For this son of mine was dead and is alive again; he was lost and is found" (vv. 23-24).

But that's not the end of the story. In fact, it seems to only be the introduction to Jesus' primary point. Unlike the story of the lost coin and the lost sheep where the accounts conclude with a party, the story of the lost son switches gears and focuses our attention on someone else: the older brother. We learned nothing of him at the beginning of the story when the younger son abandoned the family, only that there were two sons and the younger decided to leave. We do not read that the older brother strikes up a search party to go to the "distant country" to find his younger sibling (maybe he was glad he was gone). Nor do we find him next to his father, looking down the road when the younger brother walks home barefoot and destitute. And when the party gets going in earnest, the older brother is not looking over the shoulder of the caterer to make sure things are in order; he is in the field *working*. He hears the music and dancing and has to ask what the celebration is all about. A servant informs him that his younger brother is back home, safe and sound, and that their father has fired up the grill. Apparently he was not specifically invited to the party, or the father simply assumed the older brother would, of course, join in the festivities, or the father knew that the older brother did not care to hear and celebrate the good news.

Instead of joining the party, the older brother gets mad and boycotts the festivities. When the father goes out to plead with him, the older brother shockingly *rebukes* his father, then begins to list all his own acts of faithfulness and obedience. He complains that he never got such a barbecue thrown in his honor, not so much as even a young goat! "But when this son of yours who has squandered your property with prostitutes comes home, you kill the fattened calf for him!" (v. 30), he says. In other words, he tells his father that not only has the father not shown appropriate appreciation for the older brother's faithfulness, but he is going way overboard in his celebrations for the reprobate younger brother. And he reminds his father of his younger brother's abominable conduct: squandering the father's property with *prostitutes!* The older brother does not only feel slighted and taken for granted, he is repulsed by his father's extravagant excitement about the squanderer's return home. Such action on the father's part, in the opinion of the older son, is a moral and religious *outrage!* Interestingly, the older brother does not refer to the prodigal as "my brother," but as "this son of yours" (v. 30).

However, the older brother does not get the last word. The father who has temporarily left the party which he was throwing for his recovered son says, "My son, you are always with me, and everything I have is yours. But we had to celebrate and be glad because this brother of yours was dead and is alive again; he was lost and is found" (vv. 31-32). The father is indicating that the older brother's problem is not what the father did not give *him*, but what the father graciously gave the repentant "squanderer."[6] The father indicates that the only appropriate response to the younger brother's return was to throw a huge party. "We had to celebrate and be glad!" In a bit of a dig the father reminds the older brother that "this brother of yours" was dead and is alive again. He "was lost and is found."

Although it is generally true that a parable has one primary point, and we need to be careful not to make a parable into an allegory by finding spiritual meaning in every detail, this third story of lostness certainly has at least two points. The first is the eagerness of the father for the return of the lost son. The second is the callousness of the older brother who not only refused to join the party, but felt he needed to set his father straight as to the inappropriateness that such a celebration should be held at all.

Both the story of the lost sheep and the story of the lost coin conclude with similar words. Regarding the lost sheep we read, "There will be more rejoicing in heaven over one sinner who repents than over ninety-nine righteous persons who do not need to repent" (v. 7). Concerning the lost coin we are

---

[6] In this regard, compare this text to Jesus' story of the gracious employer in Matthew 20:1-16. There we read of a gracious landowner who pays the same wage to workers signed up at the last hour that he paid to those who started working much earlier. The early workers complained that they did not receive more pay than the late workers. "You have made them equal to us who have borne the burden of the work and the heat of the day" (v. 12). The landowner makes it clear that the issue is not fairness, but *generosity*!

told, "In the same way, there is rejoicing in the presence of the angels of God over one sinner who repents" (v. 10). No such expression is found at the conclusion of the story of the lost son, because the story is *about a sinner who repents* – and shows the absolute inappropriateness of the Pharisees and the teachers of the law who were muttering against Jesus, "This man welcomes sinners and eats with them" (v. 2).

When God says "Party!", we'd better party! Like the shepherd, the owner of the coin, and the prodigal son's father, God does not delight in lostness. He wants lost things and lost people *found!*

My mother-in-law, whom I love dearly, is the most organized person I know. She can perfectly tell you exactly what is in her walk-in closet, down to the last shoebox. While I don't think her condition is pathological, I do sometimes kid her and say, "You know, Mom, you never experience the joy of *finding* something that was *lost* – because you know where everything you own is. That's a sad way to live your life!" She laughs at me, and then changes the subject.

God delights in finding that which is lost, and the Good News of the Gospel is that you've been rescued from your lostness. God is holding a party in heaven because He just "had to celebrate and be glad" (Luke 15:32) because you came home!

One could ask a question of the older brother, "Who was *really* the 'lost' son?" The younger brother who abandoned his family and squandered his father's wealth, or the older brother whose "faithfulness" to his father made him callous, uncaring, self-righteous, and unwilling to join the party? Who was the real prodigal – the one who left (and came back) or the one who stayed, thinking he had no reason to repent, and in the process lost his heart?

Chapter 2

"The Believer's Authority"

"Whatever keeps me from my Bible is my enemy, however harmless it may appear to be. Whatever engages my attention when I should be meditating on God and things eternal does injury to my soul. Let the cares of life crowd out the Scriptures from my mind and I have suffered loss where I can least afford it. Let me accept anything else instead of the Scriptures and I have been cheated and robbed to my eternal confusion." (A. W. Tozer)

"Thy word is a lamp unto my feet and a light unto my path" (Ps. 119:105).

If you as a believer have been accepted by God, ransomed from your sins, redeemed from your guilt, reconciled from your estrangement from God, and rescued from your lostness, then where do you go from here? What is to be the *source* of your marching orders?

Here Evangelical Christians emphasize the Bible, the Word of God, as their first and final authority for their lives. We are to be the "people of the Book." Before we look at five pictures or images of the Scriptures (presented in the Bible itself), it is necessary to recognize and reject three superstitious views of God's Word.

"Very Superstitious" ♫ ♩

Christians frequently treat the Bible as a magic book, and such superstitious views impede the serious study of the Word of God. Sometimes the Bible is viewed as if it were *a religious rabbit's foot*. Today's generation may find it hard to believe that many people used to carry their keys on the severed foot of Bugs Bunny, but actual rabbits' feet used to be quite popular as key chains. These rabbit's feet were considered good luck (for all but the rabbit). When we treat the Bible as if it were a good luck charm, we move from biblical Christianity to pagan superstition.[1]

When I was in seminary, one of my fellow students worked a second shift job in downtown Philadelphia. A committed believer, he carried his New Testament with him, even on the job. Making a delivery late one night to a run-down neighborhood in South Philadelphia, Steve was stabbed by a mugger. He survived his injury, but his compact New Testament did not save him from harm. The Bible is not a talisman. Stories of servicemen in the military being saved by their New Testament inevitably involve a New Testament with a steel cover!

Christians are warned in numerous Scriptures to have nothing to do with astrology (Lev. 19:26; Deut. 18:10-12; Isa. 47:13-14; Jer. 10:2; etc.). Yet we sometimes treat the Bible as if it were some kind of *holy horoscope*. A horoscope is an attempt to predict something about a person's future based on that person's birthdate and the "alignment" of the stars. Just to show how foolish such "readings" are, I've taken the following from my local newspaper:

ARIES (March 21–April 19): "Look inward to discover the truth about what's going on in your personal life. If you can't

---

[1] See Israel's treatment of the ark of the covenant as a good luck charm in 1 Samuel 4-5.

be completely honest with yourself, you will never be honest with those around you."

TAURUS (April 20–May 20): "Partnerships and love are in a high cycle – take advantage of this and make your move."

GEMINI (May 21–June 20): "Don't make a rash decision that you will end up paying for."

CANCER (June 21–July 22): "The future looks bright, so stop being so negative."

LEO (July 23–Aug. 22): "You may find yourself taking care of other people's business. Do the job quickly and efficiently and you will be rewarded for your time, effort and kindness."

VIRGO (Aug. 23–Sept. 22): "You won't have time to think, so make sure you know exactly what you want to accomplish today."

LIBRA (Sept. 23–Oct. 22): "Sudden changes regarding your position look positive. Success is headed your way."

SCORPIO (Oct. 23–Nov. 21): "Allow yourself the freedom to work in areas where you feel most comfortable."

SAGITTARIUS (Nov. 22–Dec. 21): "You may be in trouble again if you haven't taken care of your personal obligations. Don't hide from or avoid what is rightfully up to you to take care of."

CAPRICORN (Dec. 22–Jan. 19): "You will meet someone who can change your outlook and influence your future."

AQUARIUS (Jan. 20–Feb. 18): "The time to make a change and follow through with a dream is now. Give yourself the benefit of the doubt – you definitely have the talent to do what you want."

PISCES (Feb. 19–March 20): "It may be difficult for you to handle personal matters today. You will be confused if someone tries to get you to make a decision you aren't ready to make."

What a bunch of *nonsense!* I could have written better horoscopes than that! Is it any wonder that the horoscope section occurs on the same page as the daily comics? Such bits of advice sound like someone threw "Dear Abby," The Boy Scout handbook, and the wit and wisdom of Benjamin Franklin into a kettle and stirred vigorously. Why don't they ever make really risky predictions like the following (which I made up)?

ARIES (March 21–April 19) : "Look your boss in the eye today and tell him what you don't like about his leadership. Demand that he double your salary; you're worth it!"

TAURUS (April 20–May 20): "Partnerships and love are in a high cycle! Call your old high school girlfriend (the one who was the head cheerleader and wouldn't give you the time of day when you were an acne-infested adolescent) and ask her for a date! Be bold!"

GEMINI (May 21–June 20): "Make some rash decisions today! And, if you're careful, you can pretend you didn't make them so that you won't end up paying for them!"

CANCER (June 21–July 22): "The future looks disastrous for you. Today doesn't look too good. Tomorrow's not very promising either. Stay in bed for the next week – and don't eat any delivery pizza!"

LEO (July 23–Aug. 22): "You may find yourself taking care of other people's business. Keep good records; let the boss know how others are slacking off; look for potential blackmail material."

VIRGO (Aug. 23–Sept. 22): "You're too lazy to think things through, so be ready to blame others when your plans fail. Make it look like it was everyone else's fault but yours!"

LIBRA (Sept. 23–Oct. 22): "Sudden changes regarding your position look ominous. Polish up your resume; you'll probably be fired by the end of the week."

SCORPIO (Oct. 23–Nov. 21): "Allow yourself the freedom to work in areas where you feel most comfortable. Don't worry if those areas are off-limits to you. After all, your life is being guided by the stars. Who are you to question their advice?!"

SAGITTARIUS (Nov. 22–Dec. 21): "A penny saved is a penny earned."

CAPRICORN (Dec. 22–Jan. 19): "You will meet someone who can change your outlook and influence your future. Be polite to the officer and beg him not to write that speeding ticket!"

AQUARIUS (Jan. 20–Feb. 18): "The time to make a change and follow through with a dream is certainly not now. You're too tired, too overworked, and you don't have any real goals anyway (other than reading this daily dribble)."

PISCES (Feb. 19–March 20): "It may be difficult for you to handle personal matters today. Stay in bed. Your boss will understand. If not, take a look at today's advice for *LIBRA*."

Serious Christians do not consult their daily horoscope. But sometimes we treat the Bible as if were a kind of holy horoscope. We randomly open the Scriptures (to do our "reading", hmmm...), drop our finger down on a verse, claim the promise we find, and go about our day, thinking we've "spent time with God." The expression "a verse a day keeps the devil away" characterizes this piecemeal, haphazard approach.

A third superstitious view of the Bible, I think, is what I call treating the Bible as a *fundamentalist fortune cookie*. You know, the idea is that the Bible contains trite sayings which are intended to make you feel good, kind of like that bland pastry thing you break open at the end of a Chinese meal. Have you ever really read those little white slips of paper? They say things like, "You meet beautiful person and have big success this week!" Or, "A tall, dark gentleman will have change of life very soon."

I have often thought about breaking into a Chinese fortune cookie factory. It would be great (as a Christian) to get my hands on the computer which spews out those white slips of paper and put in my own sayings. Imagine that my mission has been accomplished. A large man who has just finished his supper at the Yummi Delight Chinese Restaurant breaks open his fortune cookie and reads, "You think food bad here? If you die without Jesus, you in *big* trouble!" Or the lady who, after her Moo Goo Gai Pan is gone, reads, "You major sinner. Repent or you wind up in hell – forever!"

We trivialize the Word of God when we treat it solely as a list of proverbs, witty sayings, and happy advice. It was never intended to be so mishandled.

The True Nature of the Word of God

How *should* we treat the Word of God? It seems to me that the Bible itself presents five metaphors or pictures about its nature – and we would be wise to study them. The first picture is that the Word of God presents itself as *a hidden treasure*. We read in Psalm 119: "I rejoice in following your statutes as one rejoices in great riches" (v. 14). "The law from your mouth," says the Psalmist, "is more precious to me than thousands of pieces of silver and gold" (Ps. 119:72).

"I love your commands more than gold, more than pure gold ...," says Psalm 119:127. For many people, the "c" word (commands) is as repulsive as the other "c" word (cancer) is terrifying. They don't want to be told how to live, what to do, or what to avoid. But loving God's commands flows out of a heart which loves the God who gives those commands. Such commands are given for our benefit. As a friend of mine says, "Sin is not simply something you should not do. It is something that will hurt you and hurt you bad!"

Roger Miklos, one of the world's foremost modern day treasure hunters for a large salvage company, once said in 1978, "A very conservative estimate of the treasure still lost off the U.S. coast between North Carolina and Florida [indicates that] there is enough to put $1 million in the pocket of every man, woman, and child living in New York City." That's a lot of treasure. I only have one question: why should that money be given to *New Yorkers?!* I mean, I'm from North Carolina. Why shouldn't that money go to North Carolinians and Floridians?

When the Bible is viewed as a hidden treasure, we are not implying that much of the Bible is not valuable, or that one has to dig past all the silt to arrive at the buried gold. Not at all. The entirety of the Word of God is a treasure. Are we engaging ourselves in a hunting expedition (rather than strictly a salvage operation) to discover the Bible's value?

A second picture of the Word of God is that it is *the believer's food*. Job 23:12 tells us that Job "treasured the words of [God's] mouth more than [his] daily food." Jeremiah says, "When your words came, I ate them; they were my joy and my heart's delight..." (Jer. 15:16).

Is there anyone who you hope is a Christian so that when you get to heaven you can walk right up to them and punch them squarely in the face? What?! I have such a person in mind. His name is *Atkins*. He's the creator of the Atkins' diet and he's dead (rumor has it he died 60 pounds overweight). I hope he died as a believer, because I really want to punch him squarely in the face when I get to heaven. That man has made my life miserable. For the last six months I have been the science project of my wife, my mother-in-law, and my daughter. [I'm reminded of the late comedian Rodney Dangerfield's comment that when he dies his body is going to be donated to science *fiction!*] They have "had me on the Atkins' diet" (which, roughly translated, means "We want to starve our beloved family member to death using bacon, salad, and cardboard-tasting 'Carb-Friendly' products.").

I have lost almost thirty pounds, but that's not the point. I am now in the habit of reading the ingredients and nutritional labels of everything I ever think about putting into my mouth. Are you aware that a Butterfinger candy bar has forty-three carbs?! Did you know that a biscuit from Hardees' has enough carbs in it to power a bobsled team from the Caribbean for two weeks? If the label reads anything over about ten carbs, my gestapo force of women in my life looks at me as if I were hatching plans for World War III and says, "Don't you *even think about it!*" I really am looking forward to just one roundhouse to his jaw.

All of that to say that we become what we eat! The Germans have a saying to that effect: "*Mann ist was mann esst!*" (Roughly translated, this means "One is what one eats." But it sounds rhythmic in Deutsch and lends itself to being said by my

German mother-in-law with a guttural pronunciation which will drive a grown man to consume only asparagus and carrot juice for the rest of his natural life, until he dies with green-stained teeth but with strong rabbit-like vision).

I'm not completely opposed to being on the Atkins' diet, I'd just like to pick the Atkins I want to follow. I choose the late *Chet* Atkins' diet. That's where you can eat anything you want, never have to read how many carbs are in stuff, and you lie around all day listening to renditions of country music masterfully played on the guitar.

Alas, my life is not my own. The Bible teaches that, too. If I see the Word of God as the believer's food, then I will steadfastly avoid spiritually starving myself to death. I will not live my life based solely on second-hand meals of Bible study served me by pastors, radio preachers, or tape series. Even though I cannot see my soul, I will realize that it is nonetheless *real* and it needs to be fed. And, of course, we are not to be Greek in our view of our bodies and souls. That is, the soul is not the "real me"; the body is not "the prison house of the soul." We have been created in the image of the infinite/personal God and we are both material and immaterial. In fact, we will receive resurrection bodies and will, for all eternity, be both material and immaterial. We need the Word of God as our steady diet because it is good for our *total* lives.

A primary text which speaks of God's Word as the believer's diet is that of Hebrews 5:12-14 which says,

> [12]In fact, though by this time you ought to be teachers, you need someone to teach you the elementary truths of God's word all over again. You need milk, not solid food! [13]Anyone who lives on milk, being still an infant, is not acquainted with the teaching about righteousness. [14]But solid food is for the mature, who by constant use have trained themselves to distinguish good from evil.

The writer of Hebrews uses two images to correct these believers on how they had not moved on in the Christian life. His first image is that of students and teachers. He essentially says, "You ought to be instructors – professors – by now, but you are in need of remedial summer school!" He seems to be saying, "You've not even graduated from Christianity 101 yet!"

The second image he uses is that of milk and solid food. There was a TV ad a number of years ago by the Dairy Farmers' Association that said, "Milk does a body good!" Of course, milk can be an important part of a well-balanced diet of an adult. But something is wrong if that is the only nourishment an adult gets. A milk-only diet leads to *milque-toast* Christians. [I had to look up the term "milque-toast," by the way. It is a British dish of hot buttered toast in warm milk fed to frail people. Yuk]. Milk is great for infants. The adult who feeds only on the milk of the Word will have his or her spiritual growth severely stunted. At the risk of upsetting our Seventh-Day Adventist friends, we have been created by God as carnivores. We are to sink our teeth into the solid *meat* of the Word of God!

In using those two images in Hebrews 5, the writer is urging those Christians to move on in spiritual maturity. In fact, he goes on to say that "the mature" are those who "by constant use have trained themselves to distinguish good from evil." (v. 14). Don't miss his point: we are to *train ourselves!* We do that by feasting on the meat of the Word. In fact, such feasting develops *moral discernment* among God's people. We can know good from evil because we have been eating the right spiritual food which develops our moral muscle.

I happen to like the poem of Philip Appleman, himself no believer in Christ. Although his poem is a prayer to false gods, don't miss his last sentence. It's powerful. Ready?

> "O Karma, Dharma, pudding and pie,
> gimme a break before I die:
> grant me wisdom, will, and wit,
> purity, probity, pluck, and grit.
> Trustworthy, loyal, helpful, kind,
> gimme great abs and a steel-trap mind,
> and forgive, Ye gods, some humble advice –
> these little blessings would suffice

to beget an earthly paradise:
make the bad people good –
and the good people nice;
and before our world goes over the brink,
teach the believers how to think!"[2]

My family has recently been ministering to a young woman in our home. Beth (not her real name) had been living with her boyfriend and he had been emotionally and physically abusing her. Beth does not have a Christian background, but has been staying in our home over the last little while. We've been "sowing seeds" of the Gospel and encouraging Beth not to go back to, and certainly not live with, her boyfriend. Last night was a major victory. She was tempted to stay with him – and instead came and stayed with us (after I had a long talk with her about the kind of moral life God wants for us). Beth has no biblically-developed moral discernment, even though she acknowledges that her lifestyle is wrong. Her greatest need is salvation. And the Christian's greatest need is to feast on the Word of God so that he can make a difference in this confused, postmodern, pluralistic, anything-goes-if-no-one-gets-hurt, culture.

The third image used in Scripture of itself, it seems to me, is quite a rich one. The Bible is *a collection of case studies*. A case study is a real or fictional situation to which you or I can respond with careful analysis and well thought-out advice. The Bible is full of case studies. Although the Bible, of course, doesn't use the term "case studies," listen to Romans 15:4 –

> For everything that was written in the past was written to teach us, so that through endurance and the encouragement of the Scriptures we might have hope.

"You mean all sixty-six books of the Bible have been written to instruct *me?*," you ask. Well, Paul was probably referring to

---

[2] From his "Five Easy Prayers for Pagans," Emphasis mine. Used by permission of the author. His latest book of poetry is entitled *New and Selected Poems, 1956-1996*, University of Arkansas Press, 1996.

the thirty-nine books of the Old Testament, but the principle certainly extends to all of the Word of God. If we are allowing the Scriptures to teach us, we will develop endurance (we won't give up) and encouragement (we won't live for the approval of mere men and women) and will be blessed with hope (we will look forward to hearing our Savior say at the end of time, "Well done, good and faithful servant!").

Let me give you a list of some of my favorite biblical case studies which can be studied by the believer in Christ. Wise is the Christian who studies ...

> Joseph on the sovereignty of God (Gen. 45, 50)
> David on the steps leading to great sin (2 Sam. 11)
> Nathan on the steps in restoring a fallen believer (2 Sam. 12)
> Balaam and his matter-of-fact discussion with his donkey on doing the will of God (Num. 22)
> Three Jewish young men (Shadrach, Meshach and Abednego) on not committing idolatry no matter how many times the pagan king strikes up the band (Dan. 3)
> King Saul on God's definition of true obedience ("Goats? I don't hear any goats?!", 1 Sam. 15)
> Isaiah on God's hatred of empty ritual (Isa. 1)
> Habakkuk on the absurdity of idolatry (Hab. 2)
> Solomon on the emptiness of life without God (the book of Eccles.)

And we could go on and on. [By the way, aren't you glad that *your* life is not recorded in Holy Scripture for all future generations to analyze?]

I've often said that the stories in the Old Testament are just too good to confine to our Sunday School children. We adults need to study Enoch (Gen. 5), a man who walked with God. We need to examine Sarah's life (Gen. 18), a woman who laughed at God's promise. We would do well to think about Jacob (Gen. 32), a man who wrestled with God. And we men would particularly benefit from pouring over the life of Joseph (Gen. 39), a man who knew what to do with sexual temptation. Those four examples, by the way, are from only *one* of the sixty-six books making up the Bible.

Just to give a few more examples: We learn about the power of greed from Elisha's servant Gehazi (2 Kings 5), the power of self-deceit from King Saul (1 Sam. 15), and the power of prayer from Elijah (1 Kings 17). We get a crash course in bad spiritual counseling from Job's four friends (the book of Job). We see the disastrous effects of lying to the Holy Spirit in Acts 5, as well as the danger of false teachers in the epistle of Jude. We get a glimpse of the wonder of heaven from one who really went there in 2 Corinthians 12. We learn of what happens to those who die in their sins in Luke 16. And we learn of the purpose of tragedy in the story of the man born blind in John 9. *Case studies?* One's entire earthly life could be dedicated to pouring over these visible vignettes of God's grace and judgment and never complete the study.

We have seen that the Word of God is presented to us as a hidden treasure, the believer's food, and a collection of case studies. Notice that the Bible can also be seen as *the autobiography of God*. We don't mean that everything about God is told us in the Bible (the Bible's truth about God is sufficient, but not comprehensive). We also don't mean that God "learns" or "develops" or even "ages."

What we do mean is that the Bible discloses the mind and heart of God. We learn of His passion for lost people, for God Incarnate, the Lord Jesus Christ, cries out in Matthew 23:37, "O Jerusalem, Jerusalem, you who kill the prophets and stone those sent to you, how often I have longed to gather your children together, as a hen gathers her chicks under her wings, but you were not willing." Lost people matter to God (as we saw in our previous chapter's discussion of Luke 15). We also learn of God's care for His creation in texts like Psalm 145 ("The Lord is good to all; he has compassion on all he has made," v. 9; "You open your hand and satisfy the desires of every living thing," v. 16) and Acts 14 ("He has shown kindness by giving you rain from heaven and crops in their seasons; he provides you with plenty of food and fills your hearts with joy," v. 17). We are also informed about God's great joy and delight in those He has redeemed. For example, in Psalm 147 we read, "The Lord delights in those who fear him, who put their hope in his unfailing love" (v. 11). In Isaiah 62 we are told that "the Lord will take delight in you ... as a bridegroom rejoices over his bride, so will your God rejoice over you (vv. 4-5).

In an article entitled "Read My Lips," David McCullough makes the important point that "Nothing ever invented can give you a bigger life than a book." He continues,

> We're being sold the idea that information is learning, and we're being sold a bill of goods.... The greatest of all avenues to learning – to wisdom, adventure, pleasure, insight, to understanding human nature, understanding ourselves and our world and our place in it – is in reading books.[3]

But getting to know the God of the Bible *brings the greatest wisdom, adventure, pleasure, insight.* Beginning to study *His nature* is the key to understanding ourselves and our world and our place in it. How sad it would be to spend all of one's life reading books but miss THE BOOK!

The writer Herrick Johnson asks, "If God is a reality, and the soul is a reality, and you are an immortal being, *what are you doing with your Bible shut?*" A good question! If I want to get to know God, I will read, study, analyze, mull over, ponder, concentrate and seriously meditate on His holy Word. Could it be that one explanation for anemic Christians is that they do not have a strong enough *passion* to know God and thus do not give themselves to His Word?

The final image presented in the Bible of itself, it seems to me, is that God's Word provides *the divine agenda for the believer.* I live and die by my Daytimer. I have listed in it all my speaking engagements, family members' birthdays, critical lists

---

[3] September 2000 issue.

of what tasks I have to get done, important phone numbers, and other valuable stuff. I would be lost if I misplaced my Daytimer. If I lost my Daytimer, I wouldn't know what to do with my next week, my next month, or my next year. I'd probably walk around in circles, babbling incoherently, until pointed in the right direction and told what to do. I depend upon my Daytimer. It provides a kind of agenda for me. [Stop thinking that you're any different from me. You probably have a similar appointment book. Maybe you've even invested in a fancy PDA with bells and whistles and flashing lights. How would you feel if you lost it?]

In a much greater way, God's Word provides a divine agenda for the believer. I find out what kind of person God wants me to be, what decisions honor Him, where the pitfalls in life are, what the modus operandi of my supernatural enemy Satan is, why I need other believers, etc. More specifically, God's Word provides two overall agenda items for my life. The first is that *I am to become like the Lord Jesus Christ.* I'm told in 1 John 2:6 that "Whoever claims to live in him must walk as Jesus did." Here is the true "WWJD," although it might be better to think of it as "WDJD" ("What *did* Jesus do?"). I am to pattern my life after the Lord Jesus. I am to become like Him. When we examine the anatomy of the believer (our next five chapters), we will see how we are to follow Christ's example in our lives.

If I am to become like the Lord Jesus, I must study His earthly life (recorded in the four gospels and commented on in the book of Acts and some of the epistles). Why did He live thirty-three years on planet earth before He went to the cross to die? Part of the answer is that He has provided the example to me of how life ought to be lived. I must not let cultural distance (the fact that I do not live in the first century AD, or the fact that I am not Jewish, or the fact that my people group is not politically dominated by the Romans) inhibit me from asking how Jesus lived His life – and how I should live mine as one of His followers.

The second overall agenda the Bible provides for my life is that *I am to become useful to His kingdom.* We read in 2 Timothy 3:16-17,

[16]All Scripture is God-breathed and is useful for teaching, rebuking, correcting and training in righteousness, [17]so that the man of God may be thoroughly equipped for every good work.

How do I become "thoroughly equipped"? The answer is quite simple: I give myself to the God-breathed, usefully teaching, rebuking, correcting, training Word of God! If I want to sleepwalk through life, thinking that all is well with me and I have no major adjustments to make in my attitudes and behaviors, then I am going to need to avoid God's Word at all costs. No one likes to be rebuked or corrected, but we all need the truth the Bible gives us, and sometimes it delivers that truth like a bucket of cold water hurled into the face.

The Bible is the most practical book in the world. It is not a collection of the best human musings on religious subjects. It is the Word of God and it *qualifies us* to become useful in God's kingdom.

When we lived in Canada, I had a good friend who was an EMT (Emergency Medical Technician). Jason was about six foot eight inches tall and weighed over 300 pounds. And let me tell you, when Jason rescued you, you got rescued! I once asked him, "Jason, what should someone like me do if I come upon a serious car accident? I've not had medical training." He said, "Unless the person is bleeding to death or the car looks like it's going to explode, if you don't know what to do, *do nothing!* Call 911 of course, but more damage is done by 'Good Samaritans' who don't have the first clue about medical intervention."

I read about a man who was in a restaurant and he noticed that another man at the next table was choking. He quickly jumped from his meal, encircled his arms around the man in distress, and performed the Heimlich maneuver on him, saving his life. Unfortunately, he did not do the maneuver exactly right and damaged the fellow diner's spleen. Months later, the rescued man successfully *sued* the Good Samaritan, saying, "He invaded my privacy!"

Aren't you glad that God has invaded your privacy, saved you by His grace, and has given you an authoritative Book to guide your life? Then, may I ask you a simple question? *What are you doing with your Bible shut?*

PART 2

Chapter 3

"The Believer's Anatomy: 'If I Only Had a Brain ...'"

An English woman took her American friend to hear the great preacher Spurgeon. When the service was over they were walking away and the English woman turned to her friend and said, "What did you think of him?" The American looked up and said, "Who?" "Well, Spurgeon, of course," said the English woman. The American woman replied, "To be honest with you, I wasn't thinking of Spurgeon. I was thinking of Jesus."

"Therefore, I urge you, brothers, in view of God's mercy, to offer your bodies as living sacrifices, holy and pleasing to God – this is your spiritual act of worship. Do not conform any longer to the pattern of this world, but be transformed by the renewing of your mind. Then you will be able to test and approve what God's will is – his good, pleasing and perfect will" (Rom. 12:1-2).

We have seen that the believer in Jesus Christ has been accepted by God and now has a clear authority by which his or her life might be guided, might become more like Jesus Christ, and might become useful to God's kingdom. We now look at a five-part series I am calling the believer's "anatomy." Now don't let the word anatomy scare you. There will be no charts or diagrams which will embarrass anyone. We are simply asking, how is a Christian to use his mind, emotions, will, speech, and body to live out what he says he believes?

We Are to Love God with Our Minds

In the classic film "The Wizard of Oz," Dorothy meets the scarecrow who longs for a brain. Dorothy's poignant question to him is simply, "Why, what would you do with a brain if you had one?"[1] Great question.

Four primary truths leap out at me when I consider the Christian's use of his mind. The first is simply that God holds each of us responsible for loving Him with our minds. That concept is emphasized by Jesus when He is queried by a lawyer whose motives were diabolical. In Matthew 22 we read of the lawyer's question: "What is the greatest commandment?" Jesus answered, "Love the Lord your God with all your heart and with all your soul and with all your mind" (v. 37). As a believer I have no right to commit intellectual suicide or to somehow lock my brain in the closet when it comes to the all-important command to love God. I am to love Him with my *mind!*

It used to be said that Christians *out-thought* the world. I'm not hearing many people making that same charge these days. In his dialogue with the liberal theologian David L. Edwards, John Stott defends biblical orthodoxy in *Evangelical Essentials: A Liberal-Evangelical Dialogue.* Edwards pays Stott a high compliment in their conversation when he writes about Stott:

> It has been one of his [Stott's] great strengths that he has consistently taught a religion which claims to be true and not merely enjoyable or useful; which asks people to think, not merely to tremble or glow; which bases itself on a book which can be argued about, not on "experience" which convinces only the individual who has had it.[2]

---

[1] Someone has said, "Christians check their brains at the door of the church every Sunday, and most of them don't even bother to pick them up on the way out."

[2] David L. Edwards and John Stott, *Evangelical Essentials: A Liberal-Evangelical Dialogue* (Downers Grove, InterVarsity Press, 1988), pp. 16-17.

I love the short bit someone wrote concerning the important habit of thinking. It goes as follows:

TA - Thinkers Anonymous

It started out innocently enough. I began to think at parties now and then to loosen up. Inevitably though, one thought led to another, and soon I was more than just a social thinker.

I began to think alone – "to relax," I told myself – but I knew it wasn't true.

Thinking became more and more important to me, and finally I was thinking all the time. I began to think on the job. I knew that thinking and employment don't mix, but I couldn't stop myself.

I began to avoid friends at lunchtime so I could read Thoreau and Kafka. I would return to the office dizzied and confused, asking, "What is it exactly we are doing here?"

Things weren't going so great at home either. One evening I had turned off the TV and asked my wife about the meaning of life. She spent that night at her mother's.

I soon had a reputation as a heavy thinker. One day the boss called me in. He said, " I like you, and it hurts me to say this, but your thinking has become a real problem. If you don't stop thinking on the job, you'll have to find another job."

This gave me a lot to think about.

I came home early after my conversation with the boss. "Honey," I confessed, "I've been thinking...."

"I know you've been thinking," she said, "and I want a divorce!"

"But Honey, surely it's not that serious."

"It is serious," she said, lower lip a quiver.

"You think as much as college professors, and college professors don't make any money, so if you keep on thinking, we won't have any money!"

"That's a faulty syllogism," I said impatiently, and she began to cry. I'd had enough. "I'm going to the library," I snarled as I stomped out the door. I headed for the library, in the mood for some Nietzsche. I roared into the parking lot and ran up to the big glass doors – they didn't open. The library was closed. As I sank to the ground clawing at the unfeeling glass, whimpering for Zarathustra, a poster caught my eye: "Friend, is heavy thinking ruining your life?" it asked. You probably recognize that line. It comes from the standard Thinkers Anonymous poster.

Which is why I am what I am today: a recovering thinker. I never miss a TA meeting.

At each meeting we watch a non-educational video; last week it was "Castaway."

Then we share experiences about how we avoided thinking since the last meeting. I still have my job, and things are a lot better at home. Life just seemed, easier somehow, as soon as I stopped thinking.

The truth of the matter is that often we Christians are flat-out, let's-not-mince-our-words, *intellectually lazy!* If we've been created by the infinite/personal God, and we are made in His image (which certainly involves the idea of our being able to think), and if we have been redeemed from our sins by the sacrificial death of His Son, then we have no excuse not to give ourselves, including our minds, to loving Him.

Sherlock Holmes and Dr. Watson went on a camping trip and, as they lay down for the night, Holmes said: "Watson, look up into the sky and tell me what you see." Watson said, "I see millions and millions of stars." Holmes then asked, "And what does that tell you?" Watson responded, "Astronomically, it tells me that there are millions of galaxies and potentially billions of planets. Theologically, it tells me that God is great and that we are small and insignificant. Meteorologically, it tells me that we will have a beautiful day tomorrow." He then paused for a moment. "Holmes," asked Watson, "What does it tell you?" Holmes retorted, "It tells me that somebody stole our tent!"

Sometimes the conclusion is crystal clear, but we can't see it. Someone *has* "stolen our tent," and the tent to which I'm referring is this concept of using our minds to love God. People generally aren't too upset when Bible-thumpers speak emotionally about their "relationship" with God or when they choose to exercise their wills to serve God full-time or "waste their lives" to become missionaries. But when the Christian starts insisting that all this stuff is *true*, why, then the world gets really upset! The concept of truth and error is highly offensive to a culture which insists that all should do their own thing, that all opinions (certainly about religious issues) are equally valid, and that Christians who seek to test religions based on intellectual evidence are "intolerant" and "arrogant." Hmmm. It sounds like they are using their minds to critically evaluate and judge Christians.

If we believers are to make an intellectual impact in this world, we will have to grapple with at least two primary challenges to the Christian's use of the mind. The first challenge I call *entertainmentitus*. What I'm referring to is a disease of *epic* proportions which has already engulfed our Western society and is infecting Christian people at an alarming rate. This malady was recently expressed in a magazine ad (the magazine was called, unsurprisingly, *Entertainment*) which read:

> "THE 5 BASIC
> NECESSITIES
> OF LIFE:
> MOVIES, TV, VIDEO,
> MUSIC & BOOKS."

Not to be too critical, I enjoy entertainment like others, but is it a "basic necessity" of life? Neil Postman put it well when he wrote, "If and when American civilization collapses, historians of a future generation will look back and sneer: 'They *entertained themselves to death!*"[3]

My wife, the leader of our local Atkins' cult, teaches 9th grade English in a Christian school. She observed one young man in her classroom, his hands twitching, jerking and gesturing. He looked like his hands were having a grand mal seizure. She talked to him after class and discovered that he plays *video games* three or four hours *a day!* He was either rehearsing a famous fight sequence in his mind or he was making sure his hands and wrists and fingers were in maximum readiness for the evening's action after he got through another boring day of school.

I recently spoke for a week at a Christian camp and had some extended conversations with young people who missed their video games, their dvd's, and their Walkmen. When I assured them that life was more than the most recent invention from Sony, they scoffed. By the end of the week, many of them had not only survived seven days away from their "entertainment," but they had ridden horses, climbed mountains, investigated waterfalls, gone whitewater rafting, and even played ping pong with an aged theologian (who ate their lunch, so to speak). Combine all these "brain-rotters" with the widespread plague of *cellulitus*, and we've got a real problem. Fortunately at camp all kids had to surrender their cell phones, but have you noticed how that particular "modern convenience" seems hell-bent to ruin conversations, interrupt important meetings, and generally feed the thirty-second attention span of a generation which doesn't seem to know how to be quiet for a few minutes *and think?*

I know I'm ranting, but what about encouraging our young people to *read?* The luxury of *entertainmentitus* stands as a roadblock, generally speaking, to one's advancing in intellectual growth.

The other primary challenge to the Christian's use of his mind to love God is *rationalism*. Rationalism is defined as

---

[3] I love the comment by Groucho Marx who said: "I find television very educating. Every time somebody turns on the set I go into the other room and read a book."

allowing the human mind to be the measure of all things. That philosophical viewpoint was expressed often by some of the Deists who founded our country, but it was Thomas Paine who said, "I do not believe in the creed professed by the Jewish church, by the Roman church, by the Greek church, by the Turkish church, by the Protestant church, nor by any church that I know of. My own mind is my own church."[4]

Loving anyone involves spending significant time with them. In his very helpful book *The Purpose-Driven Life*, Rick Warren makes the point that

> The importance of things can be measured by how much time we are willing to invest in them. The more time you give to something, the more you reveal its importance and value to you. If you want to know a person's priorities, just look at how they use their time. Time is your most precious gift because you only have a set amount of it. You can make more money, but you can't make more time. When you give someone your time, you are giving them a portion of your life that you'll never get back. Your time is your life. That is why the greatest gift you can give someone is your time.[5]

How can the believer in Jesus Christ love God with his or her mind? Here are a few places to start.

(1) Spend time with God! Don't look at "devotions" or the "Quiet Time" as a religious duty, but as an opportunity to spend time with your best friend.

---

[4] Thomas Paine, *The Age of Reason*, Part First, Section I. Accessed at ushistory.org. Colson tells of a woman named Sheila who was interviewed for Robert Bellah's book *Habits of the Heart:* "I believe in God," she said. "I can't remember the last time I went to church. But my faith has carried me a long way. It's 'Sheila-ism.' Just my own little voice.'" (Charles Colson, *Against the Night: Living in the New Dark Ages* [Ann Arbor, MI: Servant Publications, 1989], p. 9).

[5] Rick Warren, *The Purpose-Driven Life: What on Earth Am I Here For?* (Grand Rapids: Zondervan, 2002), p. 127.

(2) Cultivate the habit of reading. Reading causes you to think and thinking engages you with your culture and with God's challenges for a world going to hell in a handbasket. Richard Armour has written about a library:

> Here is where people,
> One frequently finds,
> Lower their voices
> And raise their minds.[6]

(3) Believe what God tells you. I'm not talking about visions in the night or voices in your head. If you remember our previous chapter on the authority of the believer, we are to have a healthy skepticism concerning all so-called messages from God except for His Word, the Bible. Believe what the Word of God says. While some sections of the Scriptures are difficult to understand, most of the Word, if proper principles of interpretation are applied, is fairly straightforward in its meaning and application. A life of faith involves believing what God has said and doing what God wants done.

We Are to Guard Our Minds from the Thinking of the World

In asking the question, how are we to use our minds, we are to become aware of our surrounding culture which stands opposed to biblical truth and clear thinking about spiritual matters. We do not live in a spiritual vacuum. There is indeed a "spirit of the age" and we need to recognize it and intellectually engage it and steadfastly resist its seductive powers to turn us away from God's truth.

One area where this "spirit of the age" manifests itself is in education, especially the wholesale consensus that "tolerance" is the highest virtue of life. Listen to the late Allan Bloom, author of *The Closing of the American Mind*:

---

[6] Richard Armour, *Light Armour*. McGraw-Hill, 1954, p. 110.

The danger [students] have been taught to fear from absolutism is not error but intolerance.... Openness is the great insight of our times! The true believer is the real danger.... The point is not to correct the mistakes and really be right; rather it is not to think you are right at all.... The purpose of their education is not to make them scholars but to provide them with a moral virtue – openness.[7]

We Christians have no right to try to forcefully compel other religions to turn to Jesus Christ, to persecute any who are not believers, or to discriminate against those who differ with us on the essential doctrines of biblical faith. But **tolerance** (respecting the views of others and refusing to use force to drive them to our viewpoint) has degenerated into **pluralism**, a philosophical commitment which denies that anyone has absolute truth and stresses that all religious opinions (provided they don't hurt anyone) are equally valid.[8]

Some seem to treat life as a big cafeteria where there are many choices and the customer must make up his own mind whether to add to his tray the Jello with whipped creme, a cornbread muffin, or the T-bone steak (well-done). I've been in a few of those cafeterias myself (long before my life was ruined by that Atkins guy) and I've never met a cafeteria cashier who has said to me at the checkout, "Now, Sonny! You know your mother would not want you to eat *two* pieces of chocolate cake, don't you? Now go and put one of them back. And pick up a bowl of brussel sprouts instead! Go on, the line will wait for you!" Our culture insists that *we* can choose what we want in

[7] Allan Bloom, *The Closing of the American Mind* (New York: Simon & Schuster, 1988), pp. 25-26.

[8] The late comedian Bob Hope once said, "I do benefits for all religions – I'd hate to blow the hereafter on a technicality." I love Lewis' comment when he says that "...being a Christian does mean thinking that where Christianity differs from other religions, Christianity is right and they are wrong. As in arithmetic – there is only one right answer to a sum, and all other answers are wrong: but some of the wrong answers are much nearer being right than others" (Lewis, *Mere Christianity*, Bk. II, Ch. 1, p. 43).

that cafeteria of religious options and that *no one* should judge what we consume.

My analogy, of course, breaks down because Christianity teaches that other religions might have valid points, but they are not alternative paths to God. And they are not innocent entrees which may be consumed without harm. If Jesus is indeed "*the* way, *the* truth, and *the* life;" and if Jesus was right when He said "no one comes to the Father except through me" (John 14:6), then the other ways lead away from Him and away from life. So life is not a cafeteria filled with numerous nourishing options, but a kind of dangerous Wal★Mart where only one choice is healthy and the other choices are poisonous.

In guarding our minds from the thinking of the world I want to be very clear that this does not mean that we should develop godly ghettos or Christian cocoons where we isolate ourselves from the world. Jesus clearly teaches that His followers are to be "in the world" but not "of the world" (John 17:11-14). To reject the thinking of the world we need to be students who know and biblically evaluate the "spirit of this age." Although our primary attention must be given to the Word of God, I would suggest that we need to familiarize ourselves with the prevailing thought-systems and philosophies which characterize our culture. I've often said to my seminary students that, among all the other books they should be reading, they need to read a book that they know will get them hopping mad even before they get past the preface!

If we read only what we already agree with, we will not be challenged to engage our culture, nor will we understand its thinking. Some of the books that have "helped" me here, that is, books that have boiled my blood, are Charles Templeton's *Farewell to God* (which I will later discuss) and Bishop John Shelby Spong's *Rescuing the Bible from Fundamentalism*. Such books are not for the new believer, but they will challenge the maturing Christian to defend his faith and to be "ready to give an answer to everyone who asks him for a reason for his hope" (1 Peter 3:15).

Romans 12:1-2 in *The Message* reminds us that there should be noticeable differences between us and our surrounding culture:

So here's what I want you to do, God helping you: Take your everyday, ordinary life – your sleeping, eating, going-to-work, and walking-around life – and place it before God as an offering. Embracing what God does for you is the best thing you can do for him. Don't become so well-adjusted to your culture that you fit into it without even thinking. Instead, fix your attention on God. You'll be changed from the inside out.

If we are loving God with our minds we will also be vigilant in a culture which either mocks Christianity or treats it as just another option in the cafeteria of religious choices. We will present our minds as an offering to God and plead with Him to give us understanding so that we can speak the Good News of Jesus Christ into our environment. And we will be keenly aware of the seductive power of our surroundings, a power that wants us Christians to be "well-adjusted" when we really should be deeply grieved and intentionally evangelistic; a power that wants to lull us to sleep while others are on the superhighway to eternal separation from God; a power that says, "Trust yourself; trust the majority; trust your feelings," instead of guarding that "good deposit" (2 Tim. 1:14) which was given to us by the Lord Jesus Christ for our sakes and for the sake of a lost world.

We Are to Use Our Minds to Defend the Christian Faith
Someone has said, "The heart cannot rejoice in what the mind rejects as false." Believers in Jesus Christ have the responsibility to provide the best evidences they can for the truth of Jesus Christ and biblical Christianity. Apologetics, the effort to present and defend biblical truth, is the responsibility of every Christian, according to 1 Peter 3:15 –

In your hearts set apart Christ as Lord. Always be prepared to give an answer to everyone who asks you to give the reason for the hope that you have. But do this with gentleness and respect.

I love Josh McDowell's statement when he said that when he became a Christian, he did not take "a blind leap in the dark." He says, "I looked at the evidence for Jesus Christ being the Son of God, and I took a leap into the light!"

In his excellent books, *The Case for Faith* and *The Case for Christ*, Lee Strobel provides much material in helping the Christian use his mind to defend the Christian faith. In *The Case for Faith*, Strobel deals with what he calls the big eight objections to Christianity. He takes on the unbelief of Charles Templeton. Templeton was Billy Graham's close friend and became an evangelist as a young man, leading many people to Christ in his crusades. But Templeton turned from the Lord and explains why in his book *Farewell to God*. Strobel answers Templeton's objections in his *The Case for Faith* and interviewed the famous Canadian personality shortly before his [Templeton's] death from Alzheimer's.

In going over Templeton's intellectual objections to Christianity in a personal conversation, Strobel did not seem to be making much progress in answering his questions. Finally, Strobel asked Templeton, "But what about *Jesus*?" Templeton broke down and began weeping. He said, "I really miss Jesus." Templeton's unbelief in the major doctrines of the Christian faith indicate, in my opinion, that his faith was merely an environmental one.[9]

We have a responsibility to confront unbelief, to set forth the best case we can for Jesus Christ and biblical Christianity. And our evidence is *strong!* I have a cartoon in my files of one Roman centurion saying to another Roman centurion as Jesus' body is being taken down from the cross, "See – no problem!" In the next frame the two guards are standing outside Jesus' empty tomb and the one centurion says to the other centurion: "*Now* we have a problem!"

The using of our minds to defend the Christian faith does not only involve our being on the defensive as we confront

---

[9] A careful reading of Templeton's own account of his "conversion" bears this out, I think. See his *Templeton: An Anecdotal Memoir* (McClelland & Stewart, 1983).

unbelief. As God leads us, we should go on the offense and challenge those who do not believe the gospel. One scheme that some have found helpful is the following.

Let's say you have a friend who claims that he is an atheist. An atheist is someone who says categorically, "There is no God!" My suggestion is that you ask that person a series of four questions.[10] Your conversation might go something like this:

(1) "Of all the information we can ever acquire in our world, what percentage of that knowledge do you think we now have?" Let's say your atheist friend says, "Oh, I don't know. How about 50 percent? Let's say we have now acquired 50 percent of all the knowledge we could ever learn."

(2) "Okay. Of that 50 percent knowledge that we have acquired, how much of that knowledge do you possess?" "Oh, I don't know," your friend says. "I made pretty good grades in school. In fact, my mother was very proud of me." "I'm sure she was," you say. Your friend says, "I guess maybe I know 10 percent of that knowledge. Yea, 10 percent!"

(3) "Okay. Here's my next question: Is it possible that outside your 10 percent (of that 50 percent) knowledge that there *might* be evidence that God exists?" Your friend responds, "Well, I guess *it's possible*."

(4) You then say, "Congratulations! You've moved from the category of being an atheist to the category of being an agnostic (someone who says he does not know if God exists). I have only one more question for you. Are you ready for it?" "Sure," your friend says.

(5) "Here it is. What *kind* of agnostic are you?" "What do you mean what 'kind' of agnostic am I? You mean like Republican or Democrat?," your friend asks. "No, no," you say. "There are two kinds of agnostics. The first is the one I call the *apathetic agnostic*. This is the person who says, "There may be evidence that God exists, but I'm really not interested in discovering what it may be." The second kind

---

[10] This approach is discussed in *DocTALK* as well.

of agnostic I call the *eager agnostic*. This is the person who says, 'If there is evidence that God exists, I want to hear it. Please share it with me!' What kind of agnostic are you?"

By the way, this particular logical scheme can be used against the Christian, as we will see in just a few moments. But first, let me deal with the question how you and I should work with someone who says, "I guess I'm an *apathetic agnostic*. There might be evidence that God exists, but I really don't care. Just leave me alone and don't bring up this Christianity stuff anymore!" To that person, I would suggest, there are several aspects of your response to him.

First, grant his request. Let him know that you are not going to try to manipulate conversations around to spiritual things. You will not be trying to force a discussion of Christianity down his throat. [I have one friend who suggests that on rare occasions, you might want to say the following to a family member or friend who asks you never to bring up Christ to them again: "If that's the way you feel, then would you bow in prayer with me for just a minute?" Your friend or family member bows. "Dear Lord, this person has said that he or she never wants to talk about you or Your Son ever again. I ask in Jesus' name that You leave them alone – forever!" That's pretty drastic, but it does illustrate the fact that we cannot and should not try to force the gospel down people's throats].

You might even say to your unsaved friend or family member, "It will be up to you to bring up spiritual questions from this point on. Let me assure you that I will be happy to meet with you at any time, day or night, if you have questions about the gospel that I can answer. Now, what do you think about the Yankees' chances of getting to the World Series this year?"

The second bit of advice is that we should pray even more consistently and strategically for that person. They can't stop us from praying for them. And our prayers should focus on asking God the Holy Spirit to bring conviction of sin into their lives.

The third bit of advice is that you and I should do our very best to live out the Christian life before them. Someone has said,

"You can't argue with a changed life." First Peter 3 indicates that we will get opportunities to share our faith as observers notice that the way we react to the circumstances of life is dramatically different than how Joe Pagan or Jane Cynic responds.

Now, I mentioned that this particular logical scheme (of turning an atheist into an agnostic) can be used against the Christian. The unbeliever may ask the Christian the same questions ("How much knowledge have we gained? How much of that knowledge do *you* know? Isn't it possible that outside your realm of evidence there might be evidence that God *doesn't* exist?"), but I think that should be welcomed and not avoided. Those questions bring the Christian to the place of providing *evidence* for faith and *reasons* to believe, and that is exactly what we want!

We Are to Set Our Minds by the Word of God

Not only are we to love God with our minds, guard our minds from the thinking of the world, and use our minds to defend the Christian faith, we also are to have our minds transformed by the Word of God. The Apostle Paul writes in Colossians 3:1-3,

> Since, then, you have been raised with Christ, set your hearts on things above, where Christ is seated at the right hand of God. Set your minds on things above, not on earthly things. For you died, and your life is now hidden with Christ in God.

When we speak of "setting" our clocks, we mean adjusting them to the correct time. What makes us think that our lives need less adjustment than our clocks? But how do we adjust our lives? The answer is quite simply that we allow the Word of God to focus our thinking on the things that really count in life. Paul explains this process in our passage above. We recognize that we have been raised up with Christ. Our life is a new life and we are one with Him. We are to consciously choose to set our *hearts* on things above because that is where our Savior is! His priorities are to be *my* priorities. And we are set our *minds* on things above, not on earthly things. Please notice: our hearts are to be set, in a sense, *geographically* (where Christ is) and our minds are to be set *strategically* (that is, we are to consciously choose to focus on things above, not on earthly things).

One obvious implication of such thinking is that the Word of God, the Bible, is to be the Christian's final authority. A. W. Tozer puts it quite clearly when he writes,

> Whatever originates outside the Scriptures should for that very reason be suspect until it can be shown to be in accord with them. If it should be found to be contrary to the Word of revealed truth, no true Christian will accept it as being from God. However high the emotional content, no experience can be proved to be genuine unless he can find chapter and verse authority for it in the Scriptures. "To the word and to the testimony" must always be the last and final proof.[11]

In our Christian sub-culture which seems to extol voices and dreams, the challenge to be biblically-literate believers seems mundane and taxing. Why study a *verse* when one can wait on a *voice*? Instead of working hard at *exposition* of the Scriptures, many opt for their *experiences*. Rather than giving themselves to careful *observation* of a biblical passage, many prefer their own *opinions* as to what they think a text means.[12] Setting our minds by the Word of God involves labor – and we should never underestimate our proclivity to intellectual inertia! I'm reminded of a famous preacher (I think it was Donald Grey Barnhouse) who was asked by a young man after his sermon, "Mr. Barnhouse, how long did it take you to gain such insight into the Scriptures?" Barnhouse responded, "Five minutes – and twenty-five years!"

I have a confession to make: I sometimes read Ellery Queen mystery stories. I know. I know. But I can stop anytime. I read

---

[11] A.W. Tozer, *Man, the Dwelling Place of God* (Harrisburg: Christian Publications, 1966), p. 125.

[12] I am a fan of the detective show *Monk*. In one episode, Captain Stottlemeyer says about Monk's powers of observation: "How does he do it? I have two eyes. I see everything that he sees. But I don't see what he sees."

one short story (written by Isaac Asimov I believe) a while back in which the writer described one of his characters as "an honest young man who seemed to have been marinated in integrity from an early age." What a great phrase. We are to *marinate our minds* in the truths of Scripture. Paul emphasizes in 2 Timothy 3:16-17,

> Stick with what you learned and believed, sure of the integrity of your teachers.... There's nothing like the written Word of God for showing you the way to salvation through faith in Christ Jesus. Every part of Scripture is God-breathed and useful one way or another – showing us truth, exposing our rebellion, correcting our mistakes, training us to live God's way. Through the Word we are put together and shaped up for the tasks God has for us. (2 Tim. 3:16-17, *The Message*).

Please notice that Scripture has not been given simply to lead us to salvation. I suspect that 80 percent of the Bible has been given to *teach us how to live*! The Bible's practicality rests in the fact that it has been God-breathed. Of course our Creator is going to know what we need in our lives. We need to be shown truth, to have our rebellion exposed, to have our mistakes corrected, to have our lives trained to live God's way. *The Message's* rendering of the last verse indicates that it is through the Word that we are "put together" and "shaped up" for the tasks God has for us. Confusion about our purpose in life, uncertainty as to how we can serve God, puzzlement about our place in the cosmos, are solved by giving ourselves to God's Word.

Hebrews 4 speaks directly to this issue of setting our minds by the Word of God:

> [12]For the word of God is alive and active. Sharper than any double-edged sword, it penetrates even to dividing soul and spirit, joints and marrow; it judges the thoughts and attitudes of the heart. [13]Nothing in all creation is hidden from God's sight. Everything is uncovered and laid bare before the eyes of him to whom we must give account.

The Bible is not a dead book! It is alive and active. And it is *sharp*. My wife and I recently had one of her former high school students over to our house to demonstrate the cutlery that he was selling. The brand of knife he sells is extremely pricey and has a patented serrated edge which is guaranteed to stay sharp for all eternity! He tested it against the knives we had in our kitchen drawers. We had to saw for several minutes with our knife to cut through a length of rope. With his knife one could simply pull it over the rope and the rope was severed quickly and effortlessly. I didn't have the heart to ask him when I might need to cut a rope in the kitchen in preparing a meal, but I listened patiently to his presentation. He then took out "an ordinary penny" and proceeded to cut it in half with his super-knife! I was impressed. If I ever come across a recipe which calls for a severed rope and half a penny, and if I ever decide to actually do my own cooking, his super-expensive, incredible sharp, space-age knife will come in handy.

Our salesman explained that dull knives hurt people. I think sharp knives hurt people too, but that's not the point. The point is that the Word of God is *sharp*. Surgeons need sharp scalpels, and our God is the Master Surgeon. The Word's penetrating ability exposes us, opens us up, so that our thoughts and our attitudes become apparent. Apparent to whom? Certainly not to God; He already knows us from the inside out! Perhaps it is for our benefit so that we know where we need to focus our attention in cooperating with God's work in our lives.

We have seen in our study that we are to love God with our minds. We are to guard our minds from the thinking of the world. We are to use our minds to defend the Christian faith. We are to set our minds by the Word of God. Our minds indeed do matter to God – and they ought to matter to us.

I heard the story of a magician who liked to close his act with the famous guillotine illusion. He picked someone out of the audience to be his assistant and said to her, "You hold the bucket to catch the head." He then put a cabbage head in the stocks and dropped the guillotine. The cabbage head was neatly sliced in two, and his assistant caught the remains in the basket.

He then asked for another volunteer to come forward. He put her head in the stocks, the audience gasped, and he dropped the guillotine. Of course the volunteer was not injured, but the "assistant" (whose eyes had been closed) whispered to the magician, "What shall I do with the head?" A good question, don't you think?[13]

---

[13] When my family and I moved back to the States from Canada, one of my funnier Canadian friends said he would miss me. And then he said, "Are you aware, Larry, that by your leaving Canada and moving back to the States you are raising the intellectual level of *two* countries?

Chapter 4

"The Believer's Anatomy: 'The Heart of the Matter...'"

Two women were talking. One said, "I've broken up with Joe, and cancelled our engagement." Her friend said, "What happened?" "Well, my feelings changed for Joe." The friend asked, "Well, did you give the two-carat engagement ring back to him?" "Oh, no," replied the woman, "my feelings haven't changed about the engagement ring!"

"... it would seem that Our Lord finds our desires, not too strong, but too weak. We are half-hearted creatures, fooling about with drink and sex and ambition when infinite joy is offered us, like an ignorant child who wants to go on making mud pies in a slum because he cannot imagine what is meant by the offer of a holiday at the sea. We are far too easily pleased." (C. S. Lewis)

"Guard your heart – for out of it flow the issues of life!" (Prov. 4:23).

What is the place of emotions in the Christian life? Emotions like sadness, joy, despair, surprise, irritation, anger, confusion, grief, happiness, love, frustration, anxiety, fear, or discouragement?

Some of these emotions, we must admit, are always sinful. *Anxiety*, for example. We are told that we are to

> Be anxious for nothing, but in everything by prayer and supplication let your requests be made known to God. And the peace of God which passes all understanding shall guard your hearts and minds in Christ Jesus (Phil. 4:6-7).

Some of us have enough credits in worry that we have earned a master's degree in that emotion. But worry is always sin.

Despair is an emotion which takes our eyes off the Lord Jesus and His sovereignty – and fixes them solely on our circumstances and our human resources. It is always wrong to despair, but we fall into that emotion at times, don't we? We believers sometimes share the pessimism of the unbeliever Bertrand Russell when he expressed his belief that

> ... all the labours of the ages, all the devotion, all the inspiration, all the noon-day brightness of human genius, are destined to extinction in the vast death of the solar system and that the whole temple of Man's achievement must inevitably be buried beneath the debris of a universe in ruins.... Only within the scaffolding of these truths, only on the firm foundation of unyielding despair, can the soul's habitation henceforth be safely built.[1]

Someone has said, "The young man who has not wept is a savage, and the old man who will not laugh is a fool." Ecclesiastes 3:4 tells us that there is a "time to weep and a time to laugh." Is *happiness* always a right emotion? Of course not. Sometimes we might be happy over the misfortune of others. And if *peace* is an emotion, are we always right when we feel *peaceful*? Like Jonah, we might very well be out of the will of God in our *peace!*

The larger question, of course, is what is the place of our emotions in the Christian life? A popular song of a past decade

---

[1] Bertrand Russell, "A Free Man's Worship" in *Mysticism and Logic and Other Essays* (London: Longmans, Green and Co., 1921), pp. 47-48.

had the line, "Feelings, nothing more than feelings...." Debbi Boone rocked the Christian world years ago when she sang a secular tune with the lyrics, "How can it be wrong when it feels so right?" We groaned, because her Christian testimony and our understanding of the secondary role of emotions (to biblical morals) took a body blow with those lyrics.

Frequently, we Christians have portrayed our emotions, or our feelings, as the caboose on the believer's train. The first car is named FACTS, the second car FAITH, and, bringing up the rear, is FEELINGS. Our decisions need to be made as a result of our obeying God's Word, whether we do that out of our mind, emotions, or will. There are times when we exercise our will – and we are wrong! It is certainly dangerous to make our decisions only when we *feel* a certain way, but we dare not forget that God wants our hearts as well as our heads and our wills.

An interesting historical aside to be considered is that theologians in the Middle Ages were concerned to protect God from the idea of change, so they developed a doctrine they called the "impassibility" of God. By that term they meant that God is not susceptible to passions; He is *impassive*. They felt that emotions imply instability, fluctuation. And so they thought that God was without emotions. One wonders what Bible they were reading. As Philip Yancey has pointed out in his *Disappointment with God*, the God of the Bible is an incredibly *passionate* God! He, as it were, wears His emotions on His sleeve. It is not more spiritual to be emotionally neutral or emotionally dead, for that is not the picture of God which we get from Scripture.

There are many reasons why we Christians minimize the place of emotions in the Christian life. One is that we often find our emotions unreliable and changing. *We* are indeed susceptible to the weakness the theologians of the Middle Ages were trying to protect God from: we are unstable; our emotions fluctuate.

Another factor may be that we over-focus on the intellectual side of Christianity. I'm reminded of the man who said to his bride at the altar, "Listen, Sweetheart, I'm only going to say this once. I'm not one for flighty, emotional expressions of endearment. I'm committed to rational thought and deliberate, well-reasoned decisions. Now, listen carefully. Are you listening? I think intellectually we make a good pair. You help me to use my mind, and that's good. Here it is. I love you. There. I said it. Now don't expect me to ever say it again." I think the bride should take her bouquet, bash him across the head with it, and storm out of the wedding ceremony. We are not simply brains attached to the top of our necks.

A third reason why we minimize our emotions may be that we live under a grit-your-teeth-and-just-do-it kind of discipleship. We go through the motions and leave behind the emotions. Christianity is not simply clenching one's fists and doing what needs to be done out of sheer will-power. What about one's *heart*?

A fourth reason may well be that we have overreacted to our culture which says, "Follow your heart!" One contemporary song touches on this theme by saying, "Follow your heart – but what if it *lies*?" Jeremiah 17:9 says, "The heart is deceitful above all things and beyond cure. Who can understand it?" While we are not to follow our hearts, we also must not forsake our hearts!

A final reason that occurs to me why we minimize our feelings may be that giving our hearts over to the Lord means relinquishing control. Deuteronomy 6:5 says, "Love the Lord your God with all your heart...." 1 Samuel 13:14 tells us that "the Lord has sought out a man after his own heart...." 1 Samuel 16:7 says that "The Lord does not look at the things man looks at. Man looks at the outward appearance, but the Lord looks at the heart." David charges his son Solomon with the words, "serve God with wholehearted devotion and with a willing mind, for the Lord searches every heart and understands every motive behind the thought." The Psalmist prays, "Give me an undivided heart, that I may fear your name" (Ps. 86:11). "I run in the path of your commands, for you have set my heart free," the Psalmist says in Psalm 119:32. Proverbs 4:23 gives the profound advice, "Above all else, guard your heart, for it is the wellspring of life." Proverbs 23:26 says, "My son, give me your heart and let your eyes keep to my ways."

God wants our hearts, as imperfect as they may be. He made us as emotional creatures. We honor Him as we use our emotions for Him and for His purposes. The Bible is an immensely practical book which can be studied, particularly in this area of how we live out our emotional lives. Much can be learned as we examine the case studies of biblical characters, what they cared about, what got them upset (notice the life of Jonah here), how they *felt* about issues in life, etc. Studying the emotional lives of Old Testament (as well as New Testament) individuals would be a profitable study.

Our Emotional Example: The Lord Jesus
However, our approach will be to follow what we read in 1 John 2:6 which says of the Lord Jesus, "Whoever claims to live in Him must walk as Jesus did." The Christian's emotional life should be patterned after the earthly life of the Son of God. He is our model.

If you really believe what I wrote in the preceding paragraph, then you need to ask a number of questions. What got Him angry? What brought Him joy? What grieved His heart? If the Lord Jesus Christ is to be our model for our emotions, then we need to study His reactions to the circumstances of life and the actions of others around Him. We will find that He was a man of grief, anger, and joy.[2]

A Man of Grief and Anger
In Mark 3:1-6 we read,

> [1]Another time he went into the synagogue, and a man with a shriveled hand was there. [2]Some of them were looking for a reason to accuse Jesus, so they watched him closely to see if he would

---

[2] Liberal theologians often argue that God was a God of wrath and vengeance in the Old Testament, but God is a God of love in the New Testament. This is a greatly skewed view of God and does not bear up under close scrutiny.

heal him on the Sabbath. ³Jesus said to the man with the shriveled hand, "Stand up in front of everyone." ⁴Then Jesus asked them, "Which is lawful on the Sabbath: to do good or to do evil, to save life or to kill?" But they remained silent. ⁵He looked around at them in anger and, deeply distressed at their stubborn hearts, said to the man, "Stretch out your hand." He stretched it out, and his hand was completely restored. ⁶Then the Pharisees went out and began to plot with the Herodians how they might kill Jesus.

There is much to learn from this text about the emotions of the Lord Jesus – and how we can pattern our lives after His. This seems to have been a "set-up" situation, for it was unlikely that the Jewish leaders would have had a man with a shriveled hand sit on the front row of the synagogue. But it appears that he had the best seat in the house. We are told that some of them were looking for a reason to accuse Jesus, and so they watched Him.

When key theological issues were at stake, Jesus was not reluctant to do what needed to be done. He publically called out the handicapped man, commanding him to stand up in front of everyone. In Jewish culture, physical handicaps were often thought to be the judgment of God upon a sinner (compare John 9), and this may have been a hard thing for the man with the deformed hand to do. As the man stood there, Jesus posed a profound question to the religious leaders, a question they should have been able to answer with hardly a moment's thought: "Which is lawful on the Sabbath: to do good or to do evil, to save life or to kill?" Such an either-or question really should have been a theological piece of cake for them, but they were no dummies. They could see that Jesus, whom they thought they had on the defense, was on the offense – and that *they*, not He, were on trial!

What kind of answer could they give to such a straightforward, basic-as-Bible 101, moral question? They could have said, "Well, normally we should do good on the Sabbath, but in this circumstance – and certainly not with this man with the shriveled hand – you'd better not heal him on the Sabbath!" Or they could have said, "We'll get back to you on that question, Jesus. We need to do a little research on Sabbatarian morality and what one can or cannot do on this special day." They give neither response. The text says, "they remained silent." They had been silent from the moment Jesus entered, and they remained silent when He addressed this piercing question directly to them.

The Bible indicates in Hebrews 5:14 that "Solid food is for the mature, who by constant use have trained themselves to distinguish good from evil." Although these religious teachers didn't have the book of Hebrews, they should have remembered their Old Testament Sabbath School lessons about doing good to others (Ps. 106:3; Prov. 3:27; 14:22; Isa. 56:1-2; etc.). The last thing they should have done was to respond to Jesus' question with *silence!*

Please notice Jesus' emotional response in the face of uncaring, hypocritical, legalistic silence. We read that "He looked around at them in anger ... deeply distressed at their stubborn hearts...." Christ's anger is combined with His distress or grief at their stubborn hearts.

G. Walter Hansen puts it well when he writes,

> I am spellbound by the intensity of Jesus' emotions: not a twinge of pity, but heartbroken compassion; not a passing irritation, but terrifying anger; not a silent tear, but groans of anguish; not a weak smile, but ecstatic celebration. Jesus' emotions are like a mountain river cascading with clear water. My emotions are more like a muddy foam or a feeble trickle.[3]

Jesus is our example of how anger can be godly. When anger is combined with grief at the hard-heartedness of others (or ourselves), there's a high likelihood that it is righteous anger.

Another example of the *grieving* of the Lord Jesus is seen in John 11. There we read,

---

[3] G. Walter Hansen, "The Emotions of Jesus," *Christianity Today*, vol. 41, No. 2, Feb. 3, 1997, pp. 43-46.

³²When Mary reached the place where Jesus was and saw him, she fell at his feet and said, "Lord, if you had been here, my brother would not have died." ³³When Jesus saw her weeping, and the Jews who had come along with her also weeping, he was deeply moved in spirit and troubled. ³⁴"Where have you laid him?" he asked. "Come and see, Lord," they replied. ³⁵Jesus wept. ³⁶Then the Jews said, "See how he loved him!"

In a rich context in which Jesus actually allows time for His good friend Lazarus to die (so that Christ would be glorified by raising him back to life), Jesus identifies with a grieving family (and professional mourners) and *weeps*.

When I was a young boy, I was in a church where I could earn a free trip to camp if I memorized fifty Bible verses. Can you guess what the first verse on my list was? That's right – John 11:35 "And Jesus wept." The text is clear that Jesus sees Mary's grief; He observes the professional mourners' weeping, and He is "deeply moved in spirit and troubled." After He finds out where the body of Lazarus has been laid we read that "Jesus wept."

Charles Spurgeon once wrote,

We should weep, for Jesus wept. Jesus wept for others. I do not know that He ever wept for Himself. His were sympathetic tears. He embodied the command, "Weep with them that weep" (Rom. 12:15). He has a narrow soul who can hold it all within the compass of his ribs. A true soul, a Christlike soul, lives in other men's souls and bodies as well as in its own. A perfectly Christlike soul finds all the world too narrow for its abode, for it lives and loves; it lives by loving, and loves because it lives. Think of other weepers and have pity upon the children of grief.⁴

How little weeping we believers do! It takes a lot for today's hardened, cynical, medicated people to shed tears over anything of any major consequence. When we do weep, it is often for the

---

⁴ Charles Spurgeon, From a sermon entitled "The Power of Christ's Tears." No further information available.

wrong reasons. I'm reminded of the story of the lawyer who was pulling out of a parking place in his brand-new BMW. A car zipped by, tearing off his door in the process. A policeman who saw the accident quickly came to the aid of the lawyer. "Are you okay, sir?" asked the cop. "Oh, my Beemer. My beautiful Beemer!", wailed the attorney. "Sir," the officer said, "you lawyers are so materialistic! I can't believe it! You haven't even noticed that your left arm was *ripped off* by the car which hit you!" "Oh, my Rolex!" said the lawyer. "My *beautiful* Rolex!"

Let's think about Spurgeon's comment for a few moments. If Jesus wept, *we* ought to weep. And He wept for *others*. Do we? Psalm 126:5-6 teaches us that "Those who sow in tears will reap with songs of joy. He who goes out weeping, carrying seed to sow, will return with songs of joys, carrying sheaves with him."

Did Jesus ever weep for Himself? Spurgeon says no. On the surface, Jesus' experience in the Garden of Gethsemane seems to suggest that He was shedding tears for Himself. A closer examination of that text (Matt. 26:36-45; Mark 14:32-42; Luke 22:39-46), however, indicates that He was weeping for *us*, for the price that had to be paid that we could be righteously forgiven for our sins.

I love Spurgeon's comment that "he has a narrow soul who can hold it all within the compass of his ribs." Do we pour out our souls in intercessory prayer for others (as our Savior in John 17)? Or are we so caught up "in the terrible squirrel cage of self" that we present only our own needs and problems to God? A man was telling his pastor about his many struggles to live out the Christian life. He looked up from his coffee and saw tears streaming from his pastor's eyes. "Why are you crying, Pastor?" "Why, Bill," the pastor said, "I'm crying over your sins."

Perhaps part of the reason we do not weep for others is that we do not consistently *pray* for others. We find life so fast-paced and prayer often appears as a last resort to many of us. Maybe we're not so sure that prayer accomplishes all that much. But it does and we need to pray – and weep – for others. The book of

Ecclesiastes tells us that there is "a time to mourn" (Eccles. 3:4). Jesus Himself taught that "blessed are those who mourn, for they shall be comforted" (Matt. 5:4). A watching world needs to see Christians weep for we take sin and its many tragic consequences seriously. Someone named Isaac of Nineveh once wrote: "Whoever can weep over himself for one hour is greater than the one who is able to teach the whole world; whoever recognizes the depth of his own frailty is greater than the one who sees visions of angels."

A Man of Joy

A simple reading of the entire Bible demonstrates that the Creator experiences the full range of emotions. We are told that "He is angry with the wicked every day" (Ps. 7:11). We learn in Zephaniah 3:17 that

> The LORD your God is with you,
>   he is mighty to save.
> He will take great delight in you,
>   he will quiet you with his love,
> he will rejoice over you with singing.

Wow! How can any believer not be encouraged by those lines?! "He will rejoice over you with singing"! God *sings* over His people! His singing is not some funeral dirge, lamenting how we are often disobedient and not living as He wants us to. His singing in this text is a singing of *rejoicing!* He rejoices over us. We read of the Lord Jesus in Hebrews 12,

> Let us fix our eyes on Jesus, the author and perfecter of our faith, who for the joy set before him endured the cross, scorning its shame, and sat down at the right hand of the throne of God (v. 2).

What a mixture of emotions! The Lord Jesus "endured the cross, scorning its shame," at the same time that He anticipated that joy which was set before Him. What was that joy? Certainly that joy was His looking forward to all who would have their sins forgiven because of the work which He would accomplish on the cross.

We saw in chapter one how God rejoices over a lost one who has been found (Luke 15). In fact, that text uses words in the parable of the lost sheep like "*joyfully* puts it [the lost sheep] on his shoulders" (v. 5). The shepherd invites his friends to "*Rejoice* with me..." (v. 6), and concludes by saying, "in the same way there will be more *rejoicing* in heaven over one sinner who repents than over ninety-nine righteous persons who do not need to repent" (v. 7). Concerning the lost coin, the woman invites her friends to a party when the coin is found saying, "*Rejoice* with me; I have found my lost coin" (v. 9). That story concludes with the words, "In the same way, I tell you, there is *rejoicing* in the presence of the angels of God over one sinner who repents" (v. 10). The story of the prodigal son is full of rejoicing! The father says when the son returns, "Let's *have a feast* and *celebrate*" (v. 23). We read, "so they began to *celebrate*" (v. 24). The older brother hears "*music and dancing*" (v. 25). His refusal to party with the family is sternly met by the father's words: "we had to *celebrate* and *be glad*" (v. 32). [God's parties are not *optional!* He who does not party with God is partying against God.][5]

Our God is a God who *rejoices!* His primary delight is over sinners who repent. Perhaps our churches experience little rejoicing because they experience few new conversions to Christ.

We also learn in Scripture that God is pleased at the obedience of His children. The Apostle Paul says, "we make it our goal to please him, whether we are at home in the body or away from it" (2 Cor. 5:9). Our God is a God who can be pleased.

Elton Trueblood in his classic book *The Humour of Christ* says that we miss His humor for at least two reasons. First, we have made the *sad* story the *whole* story. As "the man of sorrows," Jesus came to die for our sins, for that was His primary mission. But He was also a man of joy. One need only

---

[5] Tony Campolo's *The Kingdom of God Is a Party* (W Publishing Group, 1992) is worth reading in this area.

look at His many interchanges with His disciples, His use of parables and observations to illustrate the truths of God, and His confrontations with the religious leaders of Israel to see that His sense of humor was very much intact. Sometimes His humor was appropriately biting, such as when He calls the Pharisees "whitewashed tombs" in Matthew 23. He says they look beautiful on the outside, but on the inside are full of the bones of the dead and everything unclean (v. 27). To suggest that those who did everything they could to avoid being around dead bodies were actually walking funeral homes was the highest insult Jesus could have given them! That may not sound very humorous to us, but it is an ironic statement to shock the Pharisees into a realization of their hypocrisy and wickedness.

Sometimes His humor was a kind of twinkle-in-the-eye variety. In Matthew 14's account of the feeding of the 5,000, we read,

> [15]As evening approached, the disciples came to him and said, "This is a remote place, and it's already getting late. Send the crowds away, so they can go to the villages and buy themselves some food." [16]Jesus replied, "They do not need to go away. You give them something to eat."

The disciples could hear the crowds' stomachs rumbling in stereophonic, high-fidelity, 32-bit digital sound. They appeal to Jesus to dismiss the crowds so they can go and buy their own meals. Sometimes the stories of the Bible are way too familiar to us in the sense that we miss the wonder, the drama, of the moment. The disciples are surrounded by thousands of men, women, and children. They've had it up to here (picture me with my hand, palm downward, touching the top of my forehead) with people – and they want the meeting concluded, over, *finito*! They are peopled out. Instead of Jesus doing the "reasonable" thing and encouraging the people to go buy food for themselves (after all, the disciples did not have much money), He says to the disciples, "They do not need to go away. *You* give them something to eat"! Somehow the disciples had the ability to feed this massive crowd, and they didn't know it.

Trueblood also suggests we miss the humor of Christ because we are too far removed from the culture of Jesus' day. We do not live in a world of parables. We are too busy for stories which illustrate biblical truth (or so we think). Jesus tells many parables which have an element of humor to them. He speaks of an unjust judge who must be nagged to death before he does what is right (Luke 18:1-7), of a wedding celebration where the guests are expected to fast instead of feast! (Matt. 9:14-15), and of the dramatic parable of the Pharisee and the tax collector where we learn that an elaborate, self-righteous prayer of a professional religionist pales in comparison to the heart-felt, human petition of a lowly tax-collector (Luke 18:9-14). There is purposeful humor in most if not all of the parables of Jesus, because everyone loves a good story.

Philip Yancey criticizes what he calls the image of a "Prozac Jesus," arguing that the gospels give the opposite picture of the Lord. They clearly "depict him performing his first miracle at a wedding, giving playful nicknames to his disciples, and somehow gaining a reputation as a 'gluttonous man and a wine-bibber.'"[6] We must ask, how has the church lost the humor of its Savior? When we fail to see Christ's humor, we lose a major part of His humanity.

One writer has said that we "Christians owe it to the world to be supernaturally joyful!" Yet joy often seems to be the farthest emotion from us. We are right to focus on Christ's sacrificial death for us, but, beloved, He did not stay in the grave! If Jesus Christ is the model for our emotional lives, then we need to study His life, become thoroughly acquainted with His world (so that we can understand His reactions), and seek to respond to daily life as He did.

---

[6] Philip Yancey, *The Jesus I Never Knew* (Grand Rapids: Zondervan, 1995), pp. 86-87.

Chapter 5

"The Believer's Anatomy: 'Problems with My Want to....'"

"We ought to stamp out of our vocabulary the nonbiblical and misleading expression 'finding God's will'." (Bruce Waltke)

"My teaching is not my own. It comes from him who sent me. Anyone who chooses to do the will of God will find out whether my teaching comes from God or whether I speak on my own" (John 7:16-17).

Many of us suffer from the fear of really giving our wills over to the Lord. As a teen, I was petrified that if I completely turned over my will to the Lord, He would send me to a place where I would have to eat what human beings were never intended to eat! Or, worse, *be eaten!*

The more I think about that struggle now, the more I realize that I suffered from a very poor view of God's *goodness.* I actually thought that if I said to the Lord, "Okay, Lord. I'm Yours. Every part of me. I will do anything, go anywhere You want me to ...", my prayer would have been interrupted by the crash of lightning, the sound of thunder, and a voice from heaven which would say, "AHA! *NOW* I'VE GOT YOU! HA, HA,

HA! YOU'RE *MINE!* I'M GOING TO SEND YOU TO...."
And my mind would begin to list God-forsaken lands (known
only to National Geographic researchers) where I would have
to live out my days being miserable for Jesus.

My struggle with the concept of God's goodness, however, is
not the same as coming to grips with God's supposed "safety."
He is good, but He is not safe.[1] Such struggles might, at times,
cause God to laugh, but I suspect He more often weeps as His
children think they know better than He does. Submitting to
God's will is not a once-for-all decision, but a lifetime of many
crisis points and *choices* to live the way He wants us to.[2]

This chapter will be an extended discussion of the believer's
will, but will begin with a survey of a number of biblical texts
on *God's* will. When we think of the will of God, it may appear
to be something mysterious, unsearchable, as hard to grasp as
the vast distances of the galaxies.

But when we search the Scriptures, we find God's will clearly
spoken of over and over again. The book of Revelation speaks

---

[1] This fact is presented in "The Lion, the Witch, and the Wardrobe,"
C. S. Lewis' children's story (*The Chronicles of Narnia*, New York: Scholastic,
1995 reprint, pp. 79-80). In that story, Jesus is represented as Aslan, a great
lion. The children in the story are shocked to realize that they must meet
Aslan. "Ooh!" Susan says, "I'd thought he was a man. Is he – quite safe?
I shall feel rather nervous about meeting a lion." "That you will, dearie, and
no mistake," said Mrs. Beaver [the animals talk in these stories], "if there's
anyone who can appear before Aslan without their knees knocking, they're
either braver than most or else just silly." "Then he isn't safe?" said Lucy.
"Safe?" said Mr. Beaver. "Don't you hear what Mrs. Beaver tells you? Who
said anything about safe? 'Course he isn't safe. But he's good. He's the King,
I tell you."

[2] Lewis put it well when he said, "Good and evil increase at compound
interest. That is why the little decisions you and I make every day are of
such infinite importance. The smallest good act today is the capture of a
strategic point from which, a few months later, you may be able to go on
to victories you never dreamed of. An apparently trivial indulgence in lust
or anger today is the loss of a ridge or railway line or bridgehead from
which the enemy may launch an attack otherwise impossible" (Lewis, *Mere
Christianity*, Bk. III, Ch. 9, p. 117).

about creation and says, for "by thy will they were created and have their being" (4:11).

Let's look at other primary passages on God's will. In John 7:16-17 the Lord Jesus says,

> My teaching is not my own. It comes from him who sent me. Anyone who chooses to do the will of God will find out whether my teaching comes from God or whether I speak on my own.

Here we learn that the Christian's ability to understand the teaching of Christ depends upon that believer's *choice* to do "the will of God." Our will must be submitted to His will.

The Apostle Paul says to the Ephesian elders "I have not hesitated to proclaim to you the whole will of God" (Acts 20:27). We can be selective in teaching God's will, but Paul wasn't.

The Third Person of the Trinity, the Holy Spirit, assists us with God's will. We read in Romans 8: "He who searches our hearts knows the mind of the Spirit, because the Spirit intercedes for God's people in accordance with the will of God" (v. 27).

We learn that Paul was called to be an apostle of Christ Jesus "by the will of God ..." (1 Cor. 1:1). We are told in 1 Thessalonians in as straightforward manner as words allow that "It is God's will that you should be sanctified" (4:3).

We learn in 2 Corinthians 8 that God's will involves not only submitting to Him but giving ourselves to God's people. Paul speaks of the Corinthians who "went beyond our expectations; having given themselves first of all to the Lord, they gave themselves by the will of God also to us" (2 Cor. 8:5). Giving ourselves to other believers (in service, in prayer, in support) must not happen legalistically. It must be a matter of the heart – a heart which has first been given to the Lord.

What would you have done if you had been a slave in New Testament times? Seek to escape your master? Complain about the life of a slave? Start a union for slaves? Paul advises those who are believers: "Slaves, obey your earthly masters with respect and fear, and with sincerity of heart, just as you would obey Christ. Obey them not only to win their favor when their eye is on you, but as slaves of Christ, doing the will of God from your heart" (Eph. 6:5-6). Paul, despite critics like Charles Templeton and Bishop John Spong, is not supporting or defending slavery, rather he is giving godly advice on how slaves can be witnesses for their Savior. In fact, he intimates that all believers are *slaves of Christ* and should live in such a way that others will see us doing the will of God from our hearts.[3]

We learn from Colossians that we can pray that others will "stand firm in all the will of God, mature and fully assured" (4:12). When fellow believers fall, falter, respond in spiritually immature ways, or seem uncertain and wavering, it may well be that the body of believers has not "wrestled (like Epaphras) in prayer" for them that they would "stand firm in all the will of God, mature and fully assured" (Col. 4:12). We need each other – and we desperately need each other's prayers, especially when it comes to the will of God.

Doing God's will involves *perseverance*, according to Hebrews 10: "You need to persevere so that when you have done the will of God, you will receive what he has promised" (v. 36). Doing His will is not always simple or easy. Nor should we expect it to be. Perhaps part of our "struggle" with the will of God is not an issue of perception (understanding what His will is), but perseverance (giving ourselves wholeheartedly to *doing* what He calls us to do).

As we continue our brief survey of biblical texts having to do with the will of God, we are told in 1 Peter 4 that there is a clear choice for the believer to make every day: "they do not live the rest of their earthly lives for evil human desires, but rather for the will of God" (vv. 1-2). First John 2 says that "whoever does the will of God lives forever" (v. 17).

The man who was born blind in John 9, an unlikely source of theological truth, lectures the religious leaders of Israel with the basic idea that "God does not listen to sinners [but] to the

---

[3] See the fine study of servant leadership by Don N. Howell, Jr., *Servants of the Servant: A Biblical Theology of Leadership* (Eugene, OR: Wipf & Stock, 2003).

godly person who does His will" (v. 31). The last thing these religious teachers wanted was for Jesus to be called a godly person who was doing the will of God!

Rather than God's will being something mysterious, Paul says to his hearers that "The God of our ancestors has chosen you to know his will ..." (Acts 22:14). The Jews were those who knew God's will (Rom. 2:17-18), but needed to be reminded that no one (ultimately) is "able to resist his will" (Rom. 9:19-20).

Paul declares in Ephesians 1 that "He made known to us the mystery of his will according to his good pleasure ..." (v. 9). This same God is he who "works out everything in conformity with the purpose of his will" (Eph. 1:11). But we grow in an understanding of God's will as others pray for us, as Paul prayed for the Colossians, "We continually ask God to fill you with the knowledge of his will through all the wisdom and understanding that the Spirit gives ..." (Col. 1:9).

We also need to realize that we have a supernatural enemy, Satan, who sets traps for us. Paul says to Timothy that those who oppose the gospel have been taken "captive to do his [the devil's] will" (2 Tim. 2:25-26).

The Holy Spirit distributes gifts "according to his will" (Heb. 2:3-4) and provides all that we need for living a life of obedience to God. In fact, the writer to the Hebrews powerfully makes this point when he states,

> May the God of peace, who through the blood of the eternal covenant brought back from the dead our Lord Jesus, that great Shepherd of the sheep, equip you with everything good for doing his will, and may he work in us what is pleasing to him, through Jesus Christ, to whom be glory for ever and ever. Amen (13:20-21).

We need to be equipped by God to do His will, and His desire is to give us "everything good" for accomplishing that! We need both to be equipped and for God to "work in us what is pleasing to him ..." Even our prayer lives need to be conditioned by His will, for 1 John tells us that "This is the confidence we have in approaching God: that if we ask anything according to his will, he hears us. And if we know that he hears us – whatever we ask – we know that we have what we asked of him" (5:14-15).

I once read a Christian pamphlet which said that we are wrong if we condition our prayers with the expression "if it be Thy will." The writer was trying to make the case that we should pray in faith and that such an expression ("if it be Thy will") comes out of doubt. You know, sometimes I think there *might be* a time for burning books and pamphlets – and I would have this one at the top of the pile! What a bunch of nonsense! A simple look at Jesus' own prayer in the Garden of Gethsemane where He *twice* prays such words (Matt. 26:39 and 42) shows how silly such a position is. We often don't know God's exact will – and we are always better off in such circumstances to pray "if it be Thy will"!

We learn from Matthew 7 that it will be those who *do* the will of God who will enter heaven (v. 21), from Matthew 12 that doing the will of the Father means that one is Christ's brother and sister and mother (vv. 48-50), and from Matthew 6 that the disciple's prayer should be "Thy will be done on earth as it is in heaven" (v. 9).

We have Jesus as our example that we should give ourselves (not simply our sacrifices and offerings) to the Lord:

Therefore, when Christ came into the world, he said: "Sacrifice and offering you did not desire, but a body you prepared for me; with burnt offerings and sin offerings you were not pleased. Then I said, 'Here I am – it is written about me in the scroll – I have come to do your will, O God'" (Heb. 10:5-7).

We read much the same in the Old Testament book of Micah:

With what shall I come before the Lord
and bow down before the exalted God?
Shall I come before him with burnt offerings,
with calves a year old?

Will the Lord be pleased with thousands of rams,
with ten thousand rivers of oil?
Shall I offer my firstborn for my transgression,
the fruit of my body for the sin of my soul?
He has showed you, O man, what is good.
And what does the Lord require of you?
To act justly and to love mercy
and to walk humbly with your God (6:6-8).

What a powerful passage! What does God want from us? The answer is simply: *us*! It is not your sacrifices but your *self* that God wants.

Although there is much more to say about this subject,[4] here is a list of ten truths which ought to guide us concerning the subject of God's will:

(1) The will of God is something that we can choose to do (John 7:16-17). In fact, choosing to do God's will will lead to a knowledge of the truth. Obedience precedes knowing!

(2) The Spirit of God intercedes for the people of God according to the will of God (Rom. 8:27). We are not in this alone!

(3) We are to do the will of God from our hearts. God is not interested in conformity without conviction! (Eph. 6:5-6).

(4) We are to stand firm in all the will of God, growing in maturity and assurance (Col. 4:12).

(5) God's will is our sanctification, our becoming like Christ (1 Thess. 4:3).

(6) Perseverance is required to do the will of God (Heb. 10:36).

(7) The one who does the will of God will live forever! (1 John 2:15-17).

(8) We can pray that God would fill one another with the knowledge of His will (Col. 1:9).

(9) God longs to "equip us to do His will" (Heb. 13:20-21).

(10) Above our sacrifices, God wants our*selves* (Heb. 10:5-7).

---

[4] I highly recommend the book *The Will of God as a Way of Life* by Gerald Lawson Sittser (Grand Rapids: Zondervan, 2000).

Might it not be said that the will that is really mysterious, the will that is hard to understand, is not God's will – but *our* will? That is, why is it so difficult for us to trust God, to obey God, to live the way God wants us to live? The biblical answer is that we are sinners, and our sin has affected all aspects of our personality. We do not feel as we ought for our emotions have been tainted by sin. We do not think as we should because our minds are fallen. And we do not *choose* as we can because our wills have been perverted by sin. I suspect that the many times that I have thought of God's will as mysterious were simply a smoke screen keeping me from giving in to His will.

Finding the Will of God: A Pagan Notion? by Bruce Waltke[5] makes some critical points: First, the language we often use about finding the will of God is almost void of biblical warrant and is, in fact, more closely related to pagan notions of the secret, arbitrary, wistful, and often scheming will of the gods. Waltke says, "We ought to stamp out of our vocabulary the nonbiblical and misleading expression 'finding God's will.'" We do not "divine" the will of God. Such divinations have always been placed in the darkest categories of biblical sin. We must remember the principle of Deuteronomy 29:29 that the secret things are God's. What God wants us to know, He has revealed.

Second, rather than "the will of God," Waltke suggests we should speak about the "guidance" of God. Christians will know themselves to be in the will of God when they are in an obedient, growing relationship with Him, a relationship that opens them up to the guidance of God. The teachings and examples of Scripture give us the plan for walking with God.

Third, Waltke points out that biblical study, prompt obedience to what God has revealed and commanded, counsel from those wiser in the faith than us, discernment and sense regarding circumstances (which God providentially uses), and our own giftedness are the outline for walking in the guidance of God in true relationship with God.

[5] Grand Rapids: Eerdmans, 2002, reprint.

Fourth, Waltke rightly insists that God has given us a program of guidance that involves getting to know Him through His Word. It is through His Word that He shapes our character. God has called us to draw close to Himself and to live holy lives. Waltke insists that there is no mystery to his will.

If Waltke has demystified the concept of the will of God, John Boykin has challenged the believer to take personal responsibility for his life. Our life is made up of the choices we make, he writes in his book *The Gospel of Coincidence*. He critiques the viewpoint that suggests we are victims in decision-making.

> My favorite absurdity comes from a renowned historian who, describing the origins of World War I, wrote that "planning for war assumed its own momentum until 1914, military expediency dominated the decision-making process, and war declared itself."! Whatever happens is the direct result of decisions people make and things people do. Decisions affecting your circumstances are not necessarily all made by you, by anyone available for you to argue with, by anyone recently, or by any one person alone – but they are all made by people. And groups of people are nothing but people, whether they are a congress, a mob, or a refreshments' committee.[6]

We choose to become the people we want to be. And our choices flow out of the priorities we set for our lives.[7]

---

[6] John Boykin, *The Gospel of Coincidence: Is God in Control?* (Grand Rapids: Zondervan, 1986), p. 23.

[7] Lewis says, "... every time you make a choice you are turning the central part of you, the part of you that chooses, into something a little different from what it was before. And taking your life as a whole, with all your innumerable choices, all your life long you are slowly turning this central thing either into a heavenly creature or into a hellish creature: either into a creature that is in harmony with God, and with other creatures, and with itself, or else into one that is in a state of war and hatred with God, and with its fellow-creatures, and with itself. To be the one kind of creature is heaven: that is, it is joy and peace and knowledge and power. To be the other means madness, horror, idiocy, rage, impotence, and eternal loneliness. Each of us at each moment is progressing to the one state or the other" (*Mere Christianity*, Bk. III, Ch. 4, pp. 86-87).

A mother asked her son to clean his room. He said no. She said yes. He was only six, but the mother wanted to know why he refused to do what he was asked. She said, "Son, are you too tired to clean your room?" "No, Mom," he said. "Well, do you not think your room needs cleaning?" "No, Mom, I know it needs to be straightened up." "Well, Son, what is the problem?" The son responded, "Mom, I just don't *want* to clean my room. I guess I have a problem with my 'want-to'!"

Often our doing the will of God boils down to using our wills to do His will! Let's ask two questions as we conclude this chapter: How do you know when you are *not* doing the will of God and how do you know when you *are* doing it? It seems to me that there are five warning signs that you are not doing the will of God. The first sign is if your love for the Word has become cold. James 1 challenges the Christian:

> [22]Do not merely listen to the word, and so deceive yourselves. Do what it says. [23]Those who listen to the word but do not do what it says are like people who look at their faces in a mirror [24]and, after looking at themselves, go away and immediately forget what they look like. [25]But those who look intently into the perfect law that gives freedom and continue in it – not forgetting what they have heard but doing it – they will be blessed in what they do.

The one who refuses to look into a mirror is probably the one who does not want the truth of what he or she looks like. Not doing God's will has a chilling effect upon one's love for God's Word.

The second warning sign that you are not doing the will of God is very similar to the first and it is that you are unable to defend your position or behavior from Scripture. Not only has your love of Scripture become cold, but you find yourself *using* Scripture to justify yourself or your actions. Some Christian men have been known to justify their dictatorial role in the family by quoting Ephesians 5:

^{22}Wives, submit yourselves to your own husbands as you do to the Lord. ^{23}For the husband is the head of the wife as Christ is the head of the church, his body, of which he is the Savior. ^{24}Now as the church submits to Christ, so also wives should submit to their husbands in everything.

The context, of course, is the loving leadership of the husband who is to care for his wife as Christ cared for the church by giving Himself up for her. Sacrificial love, not selfish domination, is the thrust of Ephesians 5.

A third sign that you are not doing the will of God is that you have no desire to be around Christians who may disagree with you. I once preached a sermon to a youth group that was entitled "How to Be a Mediocre Christian." I explained that the word mediocre literally means "half-way up a rocky mountain," and that there are some serious decisions a complacent Christian needs to make if he wants to remain mediocre. One of those decisions was to stay away from other Christians who are growing – they might rub off on you! You should have seen the looks on the faces of those teens. They thought I had lost my mind. I hope all of them got below the surface of my message and decided to follow the Lord with enthusiasm!

There's an interesting play on words in 1 John that illustrates this point. 1 John 2 says:

^{18}Dear children, this is the last hour; and as you have heard that the antichrist is coming, even now many antichrists have come. This is how we know it is the last hour. ^{19}They went out from us, but they did not really belong to us. For if they had belonged to us, they would have remained with us; but their going showed that none of them belonged to us.

John is speaking of those Christians who chose to no longer be part of the Christian community. He says, "They went out from us, but they didn't really belong to us. For if they had belonged to us, they would have remained with us." He is really saying, "They proved they were not really 'with' us because they are no longer 'with' us." Sticking with God's people is a sure sign that one wants to grow in the Christian life. Are you "with" me?

A fourth warning sign that you are not doing the will of God is that you cite your experience or the opinions of others as your authority for your life or behavior. Perhaps the clearest example of this attitude is reflected in the statement by the psychologist Carl Rogers who said,

> Experience is, for me, the highest authority ... No other person's ideas, and none of my own ideas, are as authoritative as my experience. It is to experience that I must return again and again, to discover a closer approximation to truth as it is in the process of becoming in me. Neither the Bible nor the prophets, ... neither the revelation of God nor man – can take precedence over my own direct experience.[8]

What a foolish position! We should grant an unquestioning authority to our own experience?! But what if we are self-deceived? What if we interpret our own experience incorrectly? God's Word must not be supplanted by our own subjective experiences.

A fifth sign is that your highest goal in life is not how to become more like the Lord Jesus Christ. Romans 8:29 says, "For those God foreknew he also predestined to be conformed to the likeness of his Son, that he might be the firstborn among many brothers and sisters." I am either co-operating with that conforming process or I am not. The Christian life is to be lived proactively, intentionally, and strategically as we give ourselves to the Word of God.

The second question to be asked is how do you know when you *are* doing the will of God? First of all, let me emphasize that doing the will of God is more vital than the popular concept of being "in the will of God." The Psalmist David clearly declares,

---

[8] Carl Rogers, *On Becoming a Person* (Boston: Houghton Mifflin, 1961), pp. 23-24.

"I delight to do your will, O my God; your law is within my heart" (Ps. 40:8). An internal motivation to please God is a certain sign that one is doing the will of God.

Second, you are doing the will of God when you are obeying the Word of God. This involves determined, systematic, personal exposure to the teachings of the Scriptures. I recently read of a man who bought a brand-new, leather-bound Bible. He asked the salesman, "How do I keep the leather in good shape over the years? What would you recommend as a leather treatment?" The salesman said, "Believe it or not, the best treatment for this Bible's leather cover is the oil found in human hands. Use it often!"

Third, you are doing God's will when you are striving to be like the Lord Jesus Christ. We must get beyond the faddishness of the WWJD trinkets and really ask how the Lord Jesus is our model for this earthly life. Serious study of texts like Philippians 2 ("Let this mind be in you which was also in the Lord Jesus ...") is the only way we can be assured we are being molded after the example of our Savior.

Fourth, you are doing God's will when you've come to peace with the peace issue. What do I mean by that statement? Well, the *presence* of some kind of peace does not automatically mean that you are doing the will of God. Jonah, the reluctant missionary, seemed to have been at peace when he was sound asleep in a ship headed in the opposite direction of God's clearly declared will (see Jonah 1:3). And the *absence* of peace does not imply that one is not in the will of God or not doing the will of God. John the Baptist is our example here. He was in prison for standing up to the immoral King Herod, and seemed to have had doubts as to whether Jesus was the true Messiah. He sent two of his disciples to interrogate Jesus and Jesus told John's disciples to look at the evidence of His miracles. Jesus then said, "Blessed is anyone who does not stumble on account of me" (Matt. 11:6). The presence or absence of peace may be a supplemental indication of your being in God's will, but it alone should not be finally determinative.

Fifth, you are doing the will of God when you are actively participating in your sanctification. We clearly read in

1 Thessalonians 4:3 that "It is God's will that you should be sanctified." If my becoming like Christ is the will of Almighty *God*, then who am I to stand in the way of God? Rather than standing in the way of God, I should join Him in whatever steps it takes for me to become like His precious Son.

If you're not sure where to start in this cooperative process, may I recommend 2 Peter 1?

> [5]For this very reason, make every effort to add to your faith goodness; and to goodness, knowledge; [6]and to knowledge, self-control; and to self-control, perseverance; and to perseverance, godliness; [7]and to godliness, mutual affection; and to mutual affection, love. [8]For if you possess these qualities in increasing measure, they will keep you from being ineffective and unproductive in your knowledge of our Lord Jesus Christ. [9]But if any of you do not have them, you are nearsighted and blind, and you have forgotten that you have been cleansed from your past sins.

We are to "add" to our faith. These moral qualities ought to be ours "in increasing measure." If these are not being developed in my life, then I will be "ineffective and unproductive in my knowledge of our Lord Jesus Christ" (v. 8). Jesus is drafting co-laborers; He is not into hangers-on! The Christian who does not have these qualities – and, presumably, shows no interest in developing them – is "nearsighted and blind, and [has] forgotten" that he has been forgiven!

In short, you are doing the will of God when, in obedient submission, you give Him your will, trusting Him in every stage of life. I recently found myself behind a car with the bumper sticker which read, "TRY JESUS!" I'm sure the driver's invitation was well-meaning, but I was reminded of a song by the 1970's rock group Abba entitled "Take a Chance on Me!" What an insult to the living God! Is He really only one choice among a myriad of options that people can "try"? Should we take Jesus for a test drive? Do we "take a chance" on GOD?!

What arrogance for a lost world to suggest that we should "try" Jesus! Instead, we should fall on our faces and call Him

"Lord and God" – and then submit our wills to His. Let's start a new fad. All of us should plaster a bumper sticker on our cars which reads, "Fall on your face and give your life, your *will*, to Jesus Christ, the Lord of the Universe!" Let's just make sure that we follow our own advice.

Chapter 6

"The Believer's Anatomy: From Hell: The Tongue!"

"The problems of the world could be solved overnight if men could get victory over their tongues." (Billy Graham)

"Words and magic were in the beginning one and the same thing, and even today words retain much of their magical power. By words one of us can give to another the greatest happiness or bring about utter despair.... Words call forth emotions and are universally the means by which we influence our fellow creatures. Therefore let us not despise the use of words...." (Sigmund Freud)

"For out of the overflow of the heart the mouth speaks" (Matt. 12:34).

Why don't we take the danger of the tongue more seriously? One reason may be that we underestimate its harmful effects, except when it is used against us! Proverbs 15:28 says, "The heart of the righteous weighs its answers, but the mouth of the wicked gushes evil." That same Old Testament book reminds us that "He who guards his lips guards his life, but he who speaks rashly will come to ruin" (Prov. 13:3).

We all have probably experienced the powerful positive use of words, words to encourage, to uplift, to motivate, to congratulate. Sydney Harris has said, "We are the most impressionable creatures on God's green earth, and a kind word can set us up for a whole week." Proverbs 12:25 says, "An anxious heart weighs a man down, but a kind word cheers him up." Although this chapter is mostly about the destructive effects of the tongue, there are many biblical passages which challenge us to use our words in ways which do not unnecessarily wound. Ecclesiastes 5:2 challenges us: "Do not be quick with your mouth, do not be hasty in your heart to utter anything before God. God is in heaven, and you are on earth, so let your words be few."

I don't know about you, but as a minor example of the destructiveness of our words, I am shocked at the acceptability of profanity in our culture. I just looked at two cartoons, appearing on the same day, in our local paper. Sarge of "Beetle Bailey" is at a driving range and he says, "I give up! I just can't hit the &#^@%@ ball!" Obviously the &#^@%@ symbols represent rather colorful language. He winds up crushing the range bucket, and gets charged for it by the range attendant. I guess one would expect Sarge to use such words, but were they really necessary? But what really concerned me was a strip named "Funky Winkerbean." In it, a female who wants Funky to be interested in her romantically sees that he has arrived to take her on a date. She says, "Funky's here ... I think I've managed to hide everything that could scare him off...." In the last frame, she is reaching for her little baby daughter and says, "And if you scare him off, Sweetie ... that's just too &#^@%@ bad!" Amazing. What a role model.

Another reason we may not take the danger of the tongue more seriously is that we simply are not biblical in our thinking about the power of our words. Jesus teaches in Matthew 12:

[33]"Make a tree good and its fruit will be good, or make a tree bad and its fruit will be bad, for a tree is recognized by its fruit. [34]You brood of vipers, how can you who are evil say anything good?

For out of the overflow of the heart the mouth speaks. [35]Good people bring good things out of the good stored up in them, and evil people bring evil things out of the evil stored up in them. [36]But I tell you that people will have to give account on the day of judgment for every empty word they have spoken. [37]For by your words you will be acquitted, and by your words you will be condemned."

Note Jesus' words: "For out of the overflow of the heart the mouth speaks." The *source* of our words is our heart, and if our heart is evil, our words will be evil. Our words are not simply verbal pollution that will dissipate over time. We will be held accountable for what we say. Jesus says, "People will have to give account on the day of judgment for every empty word they have spoken" (v. 36).

If we were more biblical in our thinking about the power of our words, we would take verses like Colossians 4:6 seriously: "Let your conversation be always full of grace, seasoned with salt, so that you may know how to answer everyone." I'm not one for using much salt. In fact, I'm amazed when I watch people in a restaurant salt and pepper their food without first tasting it! But salt in biblical times was both a preserving as well as a flavoring agent,[1] and we need to sprinkle our conversation liberally!

Earlier in Colossians Paul had written:

[16]Let the message of Christ dwell among you richly as you teach and admonish one another with all wisdom through psalms, hymns and songs from the Spirit, singing to God with gratitude in your hearts. [17]And whatever you do, whether in word or deed, do it all in the name of the Lord Jesus, giving thanks to God the Father through him.

Our words can be powerful as we teach and admonish each other. Our weaponry of wisdom includes psalms, hymns, and songs from the Spirit. As we thankfully sing to God, we build

---

[1]See our discussion of the Christian as salt and light in Chapter 12.

one another up. Paul's great summary of the Christian life gives equal attention to our words and our works as he writes, "And whatever you do, whether in word or deed, do it all in the name of the Lord Jesus, giving thanks to God the Father through him."

A third reason why we may not take the danger of the tongue more seriously seems to be that we value works over words. We say, "Actions speak louder than words," and that is often true. But our actions, our works, are not immune from being done hypocritically, legalistically, or with mixed motives. Biblically, we need to value both works and words.

The Positive Power of Words

What are some ways in which our words may be used positively? Although he said much that conflicted with biblical Christianity, the father of psychiatry Sigmund Freud rightly declared,

> Words and magic were in the beginning one and the same thing, and even today words retain much of their magical power. By words one of us can give to another the greatest happiness or bring about utter despair.... Words call forth emotions and are universally the means by which we influence our fellow creatures. Therefore let us not despise the use of words....[2]

We might not think of words as having "magical power," but we know that the Son of God, the Second Person of the Trinity, came into His world as "the Word" (John 1:1, 14). He is the One who has correctly *exegeted* (explained) the Father to us (John 1:18). The job of explaining God and His truths to a needy world is now ours.

The first way in which we may use our words positively is that we can encourage each other in hard times. Proverbs 12 says, "An anxious heart weighs a man down, but a kind word cheers him up" (v. 25). We have the power, through words, of building one another up, of strengthening one another,

---

[2]Sigmund Freud, *A General Introduction to Psychoanalysis* (New York: Pocketbooks, 1935), pp. 21-22.

to remain steadfast when life seems to have its grip on one's throat.

We err, by the way, when we think that we can only encourage by speaking. It seems to me that the Bible gives a great deal of attention to four friends who lectured when they should have listened. I am speaking, of course, of Job's companions, Eliphaz, Bildad, Zophar, and Elihu, who thought that *words* would straighten out Job's faulty theology. The only thing they did right, I would suggest, was that they sat *silent* with him for seven days on the ash heap at the beginning of Job's trials (Job 2:11-13). It was when they felt that they had to correct Job's erroneous view of God's ways that they moved from silence to sermons, from listening to lecturing. And they, with the best of intentions, issued him a multi-chaptered *spiritual mugging*. [We learn in Job 42:7, by the way, that God did not agree with most of their spiritual counsel, calling it "folly."]

Sometimes simply *listening* is the best counsel one may give. Might a watching world be a more receptive world if we Christians were listening more and talking less?

"A word aptly spoken is like apples of gold in settings of silver," the writer of Proverbs tells us (Prov. 25:11). That same writer also says, "Better is open rebuke than hidden love. Wounds from a friend can be trusted, but an enemy multiplies kisses" (Prov. 27:5-6). One aspect of encouraging one another in hard times involves speaking hard words when they are needed. Notice that Proverbs contrasts "open rebuke" with "hidden love." All of us want to be loved; we all would like to think that we never need correction. But the truth of the matter is that we all stray; we all take detours away from God's truth. We need others to help us in our course correction.

A godly friend is someone who cares too much about you to let you slide away from the Lord. He or she will take great risks and intervene when such involvement is called for.

I remember once reading an article which argued vehemently against the spanking of children. While I believe that controlled spanking is one legitimate form of discipline, I was struck (no pun intended) by the writer's statement that "Afterall, hitting is hitting!" I thought about that. And I decided that I disagree. There are different kinds of hitting. Let's shift the analogy. Is it fair to say that cutting other people is always wrong, because, afterall cutting is cutting? No, of course not. There can be good cutting and bad cutting. A surgeon wielding a scalpel is hardly in the same category as a mugger with a knife!

All of that to say that wounding another person might be the very best thing that one could do! The text says, "Better is open rebuke than hidden love. Wounds from a friend can be trusted, but an enemy multiplies kisses" (Prov. 27:5-6). There are times when a friend needs to wound another friend so that healing can come.

The second way we may use our words positively, I would suggest, is that we can remind each other of God's promises in the Word. Hebrews 3:13 commands us that we should "Encourage one another daily, as long as it is called Today, so that none of you may be hardened by sin's deceitfulness." The writer of Hebrews has an interesting way of saying, "Encourage each other *now!*" He says, "Encourage one another daily, as long as it is called Today...." Well, "today" is called "today" until one uses the term "tomorrow" (which I guess would be another "today," wouldn't it?).

Because we Christians don't take the Bible very seriously, this point of reminding each other of God's promises in His Word might not sound revolutionary. But what if we *did* take the Word of God seriously? Rather than treating the Bible merely as a Christian fashion accessory, what if we really believed what it said – and looked for opportunities to share its truths with the rest of God's family? I am not suggesting that we become skilled in shooting what a friend of mine calls "Bible bullets," firing verses which are supposed to immediately solve the hurting Christian's problem and bring blessed "happiness." I mean that we would grow not only in our knowledge of the Word, but also in our application of it to ourselves and our suffering brothers and sisters.

We "know" the verses, but what would it mean to a Christian who thinks he has been forsaken by the Lord to share with him the truth of Hebrews 13 where the Lord promises, "Never will I leave you; never will I forsake you" (v. 5). The context of that promise concerns keeping one's life "free from the love of money and be[ing] content with what you have, because God has said, 'Never will I leave you; never will I forsake you.'" The more I think about it, perhaps Hebrews 13:5 should be shared not so much with someone feeling forsaken by God, but with someone who is trying to fill his life with stuff instead of the Savior! How would it help a sister in Christ who feels that all of life is against her and that God has lost control of her universe if we could talk with her about the promise in Jeremiah 29:11 where the Lord says to Israel, "'For I know the plans I have for you,' declares the LORD, 'plans to prosper you and not to harm you, plans to give you hope and a future.'" We can assure her that God's ultimate concern is not to destroy her but to use her for His glory, even in the midst of her trials. When we encounter a single dad who thinks that all the pain he went through in his divorce has been wasted and that his life can never amount to anything for Christ, we can discuss God's guarantee in James 1:2 that he should "Consider it pure joy ... whenever you face trials of many kinds, because you know that the testing of your faith produces perseverance." We should not be glib when we use such texts, but they are given to be *used!*

I am not suggesting that we write out such verses on small cards and have them in our shoulder holsters so that we can whip them out at the faintest smell of Christian trouble and plug the believer who has forgotten what God has said! Not at all. I'm talking about taking the Bible seriously so that we study and we practically discuss it with those who are in pain. When we "claim" the promises of God, expending the effort to really understand the context of what God says, it begins to dawn on us that God is much more trustable than *we* are, and that His Word is a more solid foundation than our shaky hearts (see 1 John 3:19-20).

The third way we may use our words positively is that we can pray for each other in specific terms. Perhaps you are familiar with some of the bulletin bloopers which have appeared in some churches. Two of my favorites are: "Remember in prayer the many who are sick of our church and community." And the one which reads: "Potluck supper: prayer and medication to follow." Granted, there will be times when we get sick "of" the church and I've been to some potlucks where medication was more valuable than meditation!

We are told in Ephesians 4:15 that "Speaking the truth in love, we will in all things grow up into Him who is the Head, that is, Christ." We are to speak the truth in love to each other, even to the point of rebuking when necessary as we saw in our first way of using our words positively. But what about speaking to God on behalf of others? How seriously do we take *intercessory* prayer?

I recently read the following piece by eight-year-old Danny Dutton. It was his third grade homework assignment which was to "Explain God." Danny wrote,

One of God's main jobs is making people. He makes them to replace the ones that die so there will be enough people to take care of things on earth. He doesn't make grown-ups, just babies. I think because they are smaller and easier to make. That way, He doesn't have to take up His valuable time teaching them to talk and walk. He can just leave that to mothers and fathers. God's second most important job is listening to prayers. An awful lot of this goes on, since some people, like preachers and things, pray at times besides bedtime. God doesn't have time to listen to the radio or TV because of this. Because He hears everything there must be a terrible lot of noise in His ears, unless He has thought of a way to turn it off.

Danny is certainly correct about a couple of things, isn't he? God has placed a lot of responsibility in the hands of grown-ups. His "second most important job," listening to prayers, sounds like a great challenge, as seen from an eight-year-old's perspective. There are a lot of "preachers and things" that pray at times besides bedtimes. But, praise God, He has not "thought of a way to turn it off"! God eagerly gives His full attention to His children's prayers, and especially when they pray for others.

For whom are you strategically and systematically praying? We parents pray for our children, but do we pray like the Apostle Paul for the Thessalonians? He prays,

> May the Lord make your love increase and overflow for each other and for everyone else, just as ours does for you. May he strengthen your hearts so that you will be blameless and holy in the presence of our God and Father when our Lord Jesus comes with all his holy ones (1 Thess. 3:12-13).

Or, do we merely pray for their protection and prosperity? We pray for our spiritual leaders, but do we pray for them that "they may have the full riches of complete understanding, in order that they may know the mystery of God, namely, Christ, in whom are hidden all the treasures of wisdom and knowledge" (Col. 2:2-3)? Or do we just pray that the decisions they make will go our way? We sometimes pray for the leaders of our country, but do we like Paul take that responsibility so seriously that we follow his admonition in 1 Timothy 2:

> I urge, then, first of all, that petitions, prayers, intercession and thanksgiving be made for everyone – for kings and all those in authority, that we may live peaceful and quiet lives in all godliness and holiness.

Or do we merely pray that the candidate of our choice gets elected?

You see my point? We can use our words positively to pray for others, but our prayers must be biblical. I do not mean that we must necessarily quote Bible texts in our prayers (although that would have the beneficial effect of enriching our prayers as we recite God's words back to Him), but that we take our eyes off ourselves and intercede for *others!*

Who's on your prayer list? We are to persevere in prayer, but frequently my prayers are haphazard, spur-of-the-moment affairs where, as someone said, "The hearts that go out to God seldom go out to the next pew!" I love Samuel Chadwick's statement when he said, "The one concern of the devil is to keep God's people from praying ... He laughs at your toil and he mocks at your wisdom. But he *trembles* when you pray!" Want to make the Evil One *tremble*? Then *pray* – and pray for others!

An Infernal Instrument

For the rest of this chapter we will examine one of the primary biblical texts about the power of the tongue. That text, of course, is James 3:

> [3]When we put bits into the mouths of horses to make them obey us, we can turn the whole animal. [4]Or take ships as an example. Although they are so large and are driven by strong winds, they are steered by a very small rudder wherever the pilot wants to go. [5]Likewise the tongue is a small part of the body, but it makes great boasts. Consider what a great forest is set on fire by a small spark. [6]The tongue also is a fire, a world of evil among the parts of the body. It corrupts the whole person, sets the whole course of his life on fire, and is itself set on fire by hell. [7]All kinds of animals, birds, reptiles and creatures of the sea are being tamed and have been tamed by man, [8]but no man can tame the tongue. It is a restless evil, full of deadly poison. [9]With the tongue we praise our Lord and Father, and with it we curse men, who have been made in God's likeness. [10]Out of the same mouth come praise and cursing. My brothers, this should not be. [11]Can both fresh water and salt water flow from the same spring? [12]My brothers, can a fig tree bear olives, or a grapevine bear figs? Neither can a salt spring produce fresh water (James 3:3-12).

Let's analyze this central text on the power of the tongue. Note first of all, the small size of the tongue and its great power (vv. 3-6). We learn in these verses of the tongue's great power to dictate the direction of one's life. To make this point, James uses two illustrations. Let's look at the first illustration. He speaks of how a bit in the mouth of a horse, a rather large animal, can turn the whole animal. That may well be true for all horses but Sugar, my cousin's horse which I "rode" when I was fourteen. Sugar was anything but, even though my cousin (who had no reason that I know of to want me dead) assured me that "She's a gentle mare; you'll have fun riding her!"

Well, fun *was* had – but not by me. Sugar knew right away that she had a novice on her back, looked up at me, and in horse language said, "*I'M GOING TO KILL YOU!*" My cousin had given me pre-flight instructions, even explaining the function of the bit and bridle (she almost sounded Jamesian in her assurance that all I needed to do was tug one way or the other and Sugar would instantly obey).

When my cousin let go of the reins, Sugar took off in a homicidal gallop straight for a lethal-looking set of thorn bushes. I tugged and pleaded and cajoled and screamed – and then was unceremoniously deposited into the center of those thorn-bushes. Perhaps Sugar's equestrian dentist needed to update her braces or something, but that bit did not do a bit of good. That horse went where it wanted to.

Maybe James had little to do with horses. I am sure he had never met someone like Sugar. But his point is clear: a small item, a bit, can determine the direction of a large animal. Usually.

The second illustration James uses of the tongue's great power is that of a large ship being steered by a very small rudder (vv. 4-5). I have fond memories of learning Bible verses from an old King James Bible when I was first saved. Its rendition of verse 4 is that a very small rudder can steer a very large ship "whithersoever the governor listeth"! I thought the verse had something to do with politics, but "governor" is an Old English word for a ship's pilot.

I hesitate to give the following illustration for fear that I will be thought inept with both horses and sailboats, but I'll give it anyway. When I first brought my wife-to-be home to meet my parents during Easter break from college, my older brother had just bought a beautiful small sailboat. We went out to Lake Burlington and he quietly took me aside: "Look, little brother, why don't you take Linda out on the lake in my sailboat? She'll be impressed!"

We had our Sunday best on, but I took up my brother on his offer anyway. We stepped into the sailboat, I grabbed the rope-thing that was attached to the sail-gizmo, an unusually strong wind came at us, and I thought to myself, "Let's see. Wind. Sailboat. Hmm. *Hold on tight!*" It was exactly the wrong thing to do. We (my wife-to-be, myself, and my brother's brand new boat) were upside down and began drifting toward the middle of Lake Burlington! My brother was hopping up and down on the shore yelling something. My wife-to-be was completely soaked, but doing a nice job of treading water, and I still had a death-grip on that rope thingy. Somehow we got the boat righted, sailed back to the dock, and Linda married me anyway.

It's likely that James never had any experience with small sailboats, but his point is still valid. If I had known what the right thing to do was (which was to let that rope-thing go), I probably would have sailed that boat and used the rudder to direct that boat "whithersoever the governor listeth."

James has explained the small size of the tongue and its great power to dictate direction (vv. 3-5). We next learn in this text of the tongue's great power to corrupt and destroy (vv. 5b-6). James moves from his illustrations of horses and ships to that of a great forest. When I was a young Christian we sang the song "It only takes a spark to get a fire going ..." so much that I actually thought about a career in forest fire prevention! Size does not matter here; a small campfire or a carelessly discarded cigarette have started some of the most devastating fires in human history.

James calls the tongue "a fire," elaborating that it is "a world of evil among the parts of the body." That small part can corrupt the whole person. It is a kind of built-in incendiary device: "it sets the whole course of his life on fire." And its combustion source is none other than hell itself!

James has treated the small size of the tongue and its great power (vv. 3-6). He now moves to the untamable nature of the tongue in verses 7-8. There we are told that

All kinds of animals, birds, reptiles and creatures of the sea are being tamed and have been tamed by man, but no man can tame the tongue. It is a restless evil, full of deadly poison.

James deals with these verses in two ways: In the first part of verse 8 he says that the tongue cannot be domesticated. We have obedience school for dogs, we can train Orca the Killer Whale to toss his trainer thirty feet in the air without gobbling him down when he comes down, but no such behavior modification program exists for the tongue. I must take exception to the concept that all kinds of animals have been tamed by man. Has James ever met a cat like my Buddy? This cat does what he wants when he wants to. He knows he's in a privileged position. After all he is the replacement cat for our cat Happen who was killed four days after our house burned down (no kidding). Someone has said that we humans do not pet cats; cats caress themselves on us.

In the second half of verse 8 he implies that the tongue cannot be de-fanged! I did a little research on the world's deadliest snakes, and I discovered that snake venom is divided into three categories: (1) hemotoxic (it damages blood vessels and promotes hemorrhage); (2) neurotoxic (it paralyses the heart and respiration); and (3) myotoxic (it causes severe muscular pain). These venoms have been put to use as painkillers for various chronic or terminal conditions and as coagulants for hemophiliacs.

There are many lethal snakes, but the Gaboon viper of Africa is considered the most dangerous of the African snakes. Its bite may be confused with an insect bite for it is rarely felt, but victims often die before antivenom can be given. In Australia the Inland Taipan is very rare and considered to be the most toxic of all snakes. One bite delivers enough venom to kill around 100 people! In India and other places the Saw Scaled viper is one of the smallest snakes but with a bite that is usually fatal. Cobras and the Russels viper kill close to 20,000 yearly in India. King Cobra bites can kill a full-grown elephant in less than three hours. Whether we look at the tongue as a Gaboon viper or a King Cobra or an Inland Taipan, the point is the same: it is full of deadly poison.

When we underestimate the power of our words, we fall prey to poor thinking about their impact. Someone has written the following:

> "Sticks and stones may break my bones
> But words will never hurt me!"
> That is the dumbest thing that someone said,
> Such words will ne'er convert me.
> For words can sting and words can cut
> Far deeper than a knife,
> And words can scorch and they can burn
> From grouchy husband – or nagging wife!
> They can kill a character or destroy a friend
> They can put an end to love
> They can warmly bless God and coldly curse man
> Be from the pit or from above!
> They can crush, they can bruise beyond belief,
> they can wound with devastating pain
> To deny this fact, it must be said,
> One must be truly insane!
> That organ that we call the tongue
> Is lit from the fire below.
> Its danger we often understate
> 'Tis not our friend but our foe![3]

James next considers the contradictory use of the tongue (vv. 9-10). We praise God with our tongues but curse men, made in the image of God, with the same dangerous organ. Such a disregard for God's image-bearer is wrong. Praise for God should lead to our encouraging fellow human beings. This whole concept of being made in God's image explains man's value and worth, and that value and worth is not true only of Christians. All people are made in God's image and deserve to be treated with respect and kindness.

James raises some condemning questions about the tongue, as he concludes his challenge (vv. 11-12). His first question has

---

[3] I actually wrote this.

to do with water. Fresh and salt water cannot flow from the same spring. Salt has a way of spreading throughout any quantity of water. And a spring is useless (for human consumption) if it is salty. His second question has to do with fruit and vegetables. A fig tree logically produces figs, not olives. And a grapevine bears grapes, not figs. James is obviously expecting a "no" to his three questions: "Can both fresh water and salt water flow from the same spring?" "Of course not!" "Can a fig tree bear olives?" "No, that would be just plain silly!" Can a grapevine bear figs?" "What? What's wrong with you? Don't you know your fruit?!" He concludes his questions by moving back to the water analogy: "Neither can a salt spring produce fresh water."

I recently read about the world's first successful tongue transplant. Carried out by doctors in Austria, surgeons at Vienna's General Hospital performed the 14-hour operation on a 42-year-old patient in July of 2003. A malignant tumor in his mouth had necessitated the removal of his own tongue. The leader of the surgical team, Rolf Ewers, says the patient should be able to talk and eat as normal, although his sense of taste is unlikely to be restored.

A particular problem with tongue implants is that of suppressing the immune system sufficiently so the transplant is not rejected. The mouth is a non-sterile environment due to the eating of food and poses a high risk of infection. Former tongue transplants involved the use of the small intestine because it is soft and produces mucus. Using a donor's tongue involves hooking up the nerves to the nerve stumps left in the recipient's mouth. This will hopefully lead to "total functional restoration," surgeons said.

"A lot of immunosuppressant therapy would be required to promote acceptance," said the chairman of the British Transplantation Society's ethics committee. "One would have to weigh up the benefits of a transplant with the various risks of suppressing the immune system, which raises the risk of infection, and, in the long term, of further malignancies."[4] I know that I have often needed a tongue transplant. Ah, if it were only that easy!

---

[4] NewScientist.com, posted July 22, 2003. Accessed Sept., 2004.

Chapter 7

"The Believer's Anatomy: 'I'm to Present *My* Body?!'"

H.L. Mencken once defined Puritanism as "the haunting fear that somewhere, somehow, somebody may be happy."

In the film *Chariots of Fire*, Olympic runner Eric Liddell says, "I believe God made me for a purpose, but he also made me fast, and when I run, I feel God's pleasure."

"Command those who are rich in this present world not to be arrogant nor to put their hope in wealth, which is so uncertain, but to put their hope in God, who richly provides us with everything for our enjoyment" (1 Tim. 6:17).

In discussing the place of the Christian's body, we need to keep a balance between the extremes of *materialism* and *asceticism*. Materialism teaches that only the world of matter matters. We should not let anything hinder us in our pursuit of physical pleasure. Propaganda for the materialist lifestyle is everywhere. One bumper sticker puts it: "He who dies with the most toys – wins!" I love the Christian bumper sticker which responds to that kind of thinking by saying, "He who dies with the most toys – still *dies!*"

Materialism often seems best illustrated by, are you ready for this?, beer commercials. Years ago one brand coined the expression, "You only go around once in life – You've got to grab all the gusto you can!" By "gusto," of course, they really were meaning their brand of fermented grain. A more recent series of ads shows actors doing virtually anything to protect their beers, including stealing, lying, and even risking their own (or preferably another's) life. The commercials end with the tag line: "It's all about the beer!" Materialism says it's all about the physical, the material, this life.

But as C. S. Lewis points out, materialism is too thin an explanation for our world. There is far more to our lives than merely our physical pleasures. Lewis writes, "If I find in myself a desire which no experience in this world can satisfy, the most probable explanation is that I was made for another world."[1] Our appetites are not too strong, Lewis, says, but too *weak* – and we seek to satisfy our appetites in all the wrong places.

Asceticism, on the other hand, says that only the soul matters. The body is the prison-house of the soul and should be ignored or even abused. Our twenty-first century Western culture does not appear to be caught in the throes of asceticism, to put it mildly! However, the Christian sub-culture sometimes over-reacts to materialism in ways that imply asceticism's superiority as a way of looking at the world. When we suggest that reading an hour of the Bible is better than spending that hour playing with one's grandchildren, we are moving towards an ascetic way of life. When Christians look down on art and music and culture, some of their attitude may well be from a perspective that denies beauty and goodness in the physical world. We are neither to worship nor abhor creation!

First Timothy 6 is one of my favorite passages, and provides a helpful balance between materialism and asceticism. There we read,

---

[1] C. S. Lewis, *Mere Christianity*, Bk. III, Ch. 10, p. 120.

⁶But godliness with contentment is great gain. ⁷For we brought nothing into the world, and we can take nothing out of it. ⁸But if we have food and clothing, we will be content with that. ⁹Those who want to get rich fall into temptation and a trap and into many foolish and harmful desires that plunge people into ruin and destruction. ¹⁰For the love of money is a root of all kinds of evil. Some people, eager for money, have wandered from the faith and pierced themselves with many griefs…. ¹⁷Command those who are rich in this present world not to be arrogant nor to put their hope in wealth, which is so uncertain, but to put their hope in God, who richly provides us with everything for our enjoyment. ¹⁸Command them to do good, to be rich in good deeds, and to be generous and willing to share. ¹⁹In this way they will lay up treasure for themselves as a firm foundation for the coming age, so that they may take hold of the life that is truly life.

Paul begins with a Christian motto: "Godliness with contentment is great gain" (v. 6). He then reminds Timothy (and us) that we came into this world with nothing and will leave with nothing (v. 7). Chuck Swindoll has a unique way of expressing this concept. He says you'll never see a hearse pulling a U-Haul trailer behind it! Godly contentment, Paul says, is being grateful for the basics of food and clothing (v. 8).

Sometimes we forget our material nakedness as we entered and eventually will leave this world. We can take extreme positions of either being taken up with the trappings of this life or acting as if we are "beyond" all that.

My wife and I visited Robert Schuller's Crystal Cathedral a few years ago. Because I have some theological problems with Schuller's brand of Christianity, we toured the campus with a fairly critical eye. To be perfectly honest, I made snide comments as we saw the elaborate buildings, the sculptures in the various courtyards, and the exquisite mausoleum where, as the signs advertised, burial plots were available for those who wanted to invest in them (some cost over $200,000). We could not walk through the Cathedral itself (it was closed), but, after all, it was a *crystal* cathedral, so we could look inside. In the foyer on the right there were two larger-than-life bronze statues. One was of Billy Graham, the other of Bishop Fulton J. Sheen. In the foyer on the left there were two other larger-than-life bronze statues. One was of Norman Vincent Peale and the other was of Robert Schuller himself! We were appalled.

As Linda and I continued our walking tour, we were quite critical of what we understood to be Schuller's self-centeredness and Crystal Cathedral's opulence. As I was sharing more details of the aberrant aspects of his theology, we spotted their Bookstore. Going in I headed straight for the devotional books' section. I was shocked to find three copies of my doctrinal devotional book *DocDEVOS* on the shelf, and I immediately said to my wife as we left the bookstore, "You know, Schuller's really not such a bad guy!" In my criticism of him and his campus, I found it very easy to fall into the same trap of materialism.

Those who follow get-rich-quick schemes as well as those who make it their life-goal to gradually become wealthy, Paul says, "fall into temptation and a trap and into many foolish and harmful desires that plunge people into ruin and destruction" (v. 9). The Bible is not anti-wealth; it is, however, categorically opposed to the materialistic view that one should spend one's life in the sold-out pursuit of possessions.

Perhaps one of the most misquoted biblical passages is verse 10. I have heard even reputable preachers say, "The Bible teaches that '*money* is the root of all evil'!" The text does not say that. It says, "The *love* of money is *a* root of all kinds of evil" (v. 10). And it is.

Jesus tells us in His parable in Matthew 13 that "the seed falling among the thorns refers to people who hear the word, but the worries of this life and *the deceitfulness of wealth* choke the word, making it unfruitful" (v. 22). Paul warns that in the end times, "People will be lovers of themselves, *lovers of money*, boastful, proud ..." in 2 Timothy 3:2. Hebrews 13:5 says, "Keep yourselves free from *the love of money* and be content with what you have ..."[2] Jesus, however, also advises

---

[2] Please read the immediate context to see why this is such a bad choice in life.

His followers in Luke 16 to "*use worldly wealth* to gain friends for yourselves, so that when it is gone, you will be welcomed into eternal dwellings" (v. 9). Why is the materialistic lifestyle so dangerous? Paul tells us in verse 10 of 1 Timothy 6 that "Some people, eager for money, have wandered from the faith and pierced themselves with many griefs." Straying away from spiritual reality for the sake of temporary riches is foolish and self-destructive! And those who do this commit a kind of spiritual hari-keri: they "pierce themselves with many griefs."

Paul's lecture on luxury continues in verses 17-19. He tells Timothy to warn those who are rich in this present world not to be caught up in arrogance (as if they and they alone produced wealth for themselves) or in foolish optimism (they stake all "their hope" on earthly treasures), because earthly wealth is so uncertain. Its enemies include moth, rust, fire, flood, inflation, taxes, the IRS, credit card misuse and identity theft, telemarketing schemes, expensive children, corrupt CEO's of investment companies, the deflation of currency, war, famine, pestilence, and locusts! (I took the liberty of adding a few of those to the biblical list we have in texts like Matthew 6:19-21).

Instead, the wealthy of the world, and that certainly includes you and me, must put our hope in God, "who richly provides us with everything for our enjoyment" (v. 17). The biblical position on the material world is balanced. We are not to turn away from the pleasures with which God has blessed us. You may have heard of the doctor with the stethoscope on a patient's chest saying, "You've been *enjoying* something again!" But please note Paul's language in verse 17: God is the *source* of enjoyment. That "enjoyment" includes *everything*.

Paul and Barnabas make this same point in Acts 14 where they were being worshiped by the citizens of Lystra and Derbe. They direct attention away from themselves and speak of the only true God as the One who "has shown kindness by giving you rain from heaven and crops in their seasons; he provides you with plenty of food and fills your hearts with joy" (v. 17).

Paul emphasizes in 1 Timothy 6 that God provides us with that enjoyment "richly." He is the One who lavishly provides us with everything for our enjoyment. I love how C. S. Lewis has put this point:

> I know some muddle-headed Christians have talked as if Christianity thought that sex, or the body, or pleasure, were bad in themselves. But they were wrong. Christianity is almost the only one of the great religions which thoroughly approves of the body – which believes that matter is good, that God Himself once took on a human body, that some kind of body is going to be given to us even in Heaven and is going to be an essential part of our happiness, our beauty, and our energy. Christianity has glorified marriage more than any other religion: and nearly all the greatest love poetry in the world has been produced by Christians.[3]

Paul is not against riches. He simply changes their definition. We are to "be rich in good deeds." We are to "be generous and willing to share" (v. 18). Having that perspective on our wealth will lead us to lay up treasures in heaven (v. 19). As someone has said, "You may not be able to take it with you, but you can send it *ahead* of you!"

Materialism suffers from the error of being too narrow to explain all of God's good gifts to His creation. Asceticism seems to offer the hope of escape from a greed for the material, but instead leads to an attitude of ungratefulness for those gifts which God has given to be received with *thanksgiving* (1 Tim. 4:3).

With these warnings in place about both materialism and asceticism, let us notice four truths the Bible wants us to keep in mind about the believer and his body. The first truth is simply this: The God of the Bible created the material world – including our physical bodies! Lewis again reminds us,

> There is no good trying to be more spiritual than God. God never meant man to be a purely spiritual creature. That is why He uses material things like bread and wine to put the new life into us. We may think this rather crude and unspiritual. God does not: He invented eating. He likes matter. He invented it.[4]

---

[3] C. S. Lewis, *Mere Christianity*, Bk. III, Ch. 5, p. 91.

This world did not just come into existence by itself. It has been made by the infinite personal Creator. When we act as if the soul is what really matters and that the material is really *immaterial* (if you catch my pun), we are denying this first truth that God created the physical world. When we do not show proper respect for our environment, acting as if God doesn't care how we treat His world, we are ignoring the truth of God's creation of matter. As a friend of mine puts it, "God has given us all things richly to enjoy, not all things richly to destroy!" When we seem to despise art or fail to appreciate the incredible creativity given even to those who refuse to acknowledge their Creator, we are becoming ascetic in a way which displeases God.

I mentioned earlier that I occasionally lead a study tour of Europe for high school graduates. We see many cathedrals, some simple, many ornate, even gaudy in their appearance. When I stare at the 14 carat gold vaulted ceilings with frescoes which took many years to complete, I have to admire the artists' skills. Looking at Michaelangelo's work on the Sistine Chapel causes me to wonder how many who see his artistry are drawn to a saving knowledge of Christ. Or are they simply reaffirmed in their religiosity and ritualism? I can appreciate the incredible skill and creativity required to produce such works of art, but I can too hastily say to myself, "Oh, well. All of this is going to be burnt up in the end times!" I'm not sure that kind of eschatological asceticism is honoring to God either.

When we treat our bodies as if God doesn't care what we look like, how much we weigh, whether we attempt to look the best we can, we are denying God as Creator of the physical. My wife and I watched people walk by as we shopped in our local mall and our thoroughly scientific survey concluded that eight out of ten Americans are overweight! Being overweight not only shortens our lives, it is a walking advertisement to the world that God doesn't really care about our bodies – and neither do we. But we should because the God of the Bible created the material world – including our physical bodies.

[4] Ibid., p. 65.

The second truth to keep in mind about the believer and his body is this: We must remember that God the Son, the Second Person of the Trinity, took upon Himself a real human body! We read in John 1:14 that "The Word **became flesh** and made his dwelling among us. We have seen his glory, the glory of the one and only Son, who came from the Father, full of grace and truth." One of the early heresies the Church had to fight was Gnosticism, a false teaching that said the real God would never become material. But biblical Christianity teaches that we needed a divine/human Savior who would suffer in His body the punishment our sins deserved and physically rise from the dead as evidence that His atoning work was accepted by the Father. Christianity teaches that the Second Person of the Trinity, the divine Son, at one point became fully human (but without sin or a sin nature), lived a sinless human life, died a substitutionary death on the cross, rose bodily from the grave, and ascended back to heaven. He continues forevermore as the God-man. His humanity was not a temporary condition but a permanent change in His being.

What are some of the implications of the true humanity (especially that of His having a body) of the Lord Jesus? Christians have historically fought so hard to defend the full deity of Christ that they, perhaps, have given little attention to this question. We read in Colossians 2 that "In Christ all the fullness of the Deity lives in bodily form ..." (v. 9). Jesus' body needed rest (John 4:6) and nourishment (Luke 24:41-43; John 19:28). His body could be touched (Mark 5:31; John 13:3-5), and He frequently touched others (Matt. 8:1-3; 14:31: Mark 1:40-41). He would have felt pain when He stubbed His toe. When in Joseph's carpenter shop, if Jesus got a splinter in His eye, it hurt and, like us, would have dropped everything to get it out. Although this fits under the category of speculation, it seems obvious that Jesus' muscles got sore from working with His adopted father Joseph and His legs got tired from walking. He enjoyed eating and probably had a favorite meal. If He stayed out in the sun too long, He would have gotten sunburned. When His hair got too long, He would have it cut. In His true humanity He would have experienced all the bodily functions that are part of being a physical being, yet none which would have entailed sin. When we get to heaven we Christians will see our Savior in His glorified state, but He will be recognizable and physical and, well, fully human. And we will become like Him!

We need to beware of a subtle Gnosticism in our Christian circles. I once heard a preacher use the expression "the heavenly humanity of Christ." I asked him after the church service if he remembered using that expression. "Yea, I think so," was his cautious reply. "Why do you ask?" "Well," I said, "have you been reading the writer __?" "Yes," he said, "I've learned a great deal from his commentaries." I then said to him, "Did you know that he was accused of a heresy known as Docetism, the view that says that Jesus only *appeared* to be truly human?" "No! I didn't know that!", he said a bit sheepishly. We need to be careful to defend the full humanity of the Savior.

A third truth to keep in mind about the believer and his body is that God holds us responsible for how we use our lives both physically and spiritually. One of the scarier texts in all of the New Testament is Ephesians 5 where we read,

> [28]Husbands ought to love their wives as their own bodies. He who loves his wife loves himself. [29]After all, no one ever hated his own body, but he feeds and cares for it, just as Christ does the church – [30]for we are members of his body.

Why is this passage scarey? I can hear some wives out there saying, "The way my husband treats his body, I'm not sure that's such a high standard!" You may have heard of the wife who saw her husband on the couch watching a football game on TV and eating potato chips. "You know, Honey," she said. "It just occurred to me that there are thirty pounds of you that I am not legally married to!" While husbands may not take care of themselves as much as they ought, Paul's point is that the husband should naturally think of his wife and her needs as he naturally thinks of himself and his own needs.

The Christian life is not simply mental, as if my thinking is the most important way in which I love God. It is also *physical*. How I use my body matters to God. I am not to abuse myself, nor am I to use my body any way that I see fit. On August 31, 2004, famed motorcycle builder and stuntman Indian Larry died after 8,000 people watched him crash at the Liquid Steel Classic and Custom Bike Series show at the Cabarrus Arena and Events Center in Concord, North Carolina. Featured on the Discovery Channel's Biker Build-Off series, he was performing the stunt he had become famous for and had been doing for thirty years, a stunt in which he stood on the seat of his moving motorcycle. "The bike started to wobble," said the Arena's manager, "and he was not able to regain control." Indian Larry (a.k.a. Larry Desmedt) wasn't wearing a helmet and died of his injuries.

We are not supposed to live our lives any way we choose.

Karl Wallenda was the founder of the Great Wallendas, an internationally known daredevil circus act famous for performing death-defying stunts without a safety net. Known throughout Europe for their four-man pyramid and cycling on the high wire, the act moved to the U.S. in 1928 and began working with the Ringling Brothers and Barnum & Bailey Combined Circus. In 1947 they developed the unequaled three-tier seven-man pyramid. On January 30, 1962, in Detroit, Wallenda's son-in-law Richard Faughnan and nephew Dieter Schepp were killed and an adopted son Mario was paralyzed from the waist down when the pyramid collapsed. Wallenda's sister-in-law Rietta fell to her death in 1963, and his son-in-law Richard ("Chico") Guzman was killed in 1972 after touching a live wire in the rigging. Seventy-three year-old Karl himself attempted a walk between two hotels in San Juan, Puerto Rico, on a wire stretched 37 m above the pavement. He fell to his death when winds exceeded 48 km/h.[5]

Mountain climbers and extreme sports enthusiasts who do their climbing or stunts without proper safety equipment

---

[5] Accessed at http://en.wikipedia.org/wiki/Karl_Wallenda.

are tempting God. Our lives are not our own – we have been bought with a price. Death-defying stunts and life-threatening "sports" are not honoring to God. They are *trifling* with the one earthly life which has been given to us by God's grace and are to be invested for His glory!

A Word About, Well, You Know ...

Paul minces no words in his bluntness when he writes in 1 Corinthians 6:

> [18]Flee from sexual immorality. All other sins people commit are outside their bodies, but those who sin sexually sin against their own bodies. [19]Do you not know that your bodies are temples of the Holy Spirit, who is in you, whom you have received from God? You are not your own; [20]you were bought at a price. Therefore honor God with your bodies.

Don't you love the directness, the practicality, of the Scriptures? Paul doesn't write, "Now, you Christians be nice and don't do wrong things, you know, I mean (and he whispers the next word) *sexually* with others...." He delivers a four-word barrage that simply says, "Flee from sexual immorality!" Paul may well have had the story of Joseph in mind here (Gen. 39). His admonition to RUN! is followed by a clear explanation as to why one should run: All sins are not equal in their damaging effects. Immorality – sexual sins – are those done directly against one's own person.

Occasionally we will read of countries that are legalizing prostitution as a "victimless" crime. Victimless?! Not according to Scripture. Sexual sin is a violation of one's self! Sometimes we Christians say that all sins are equal before God. Well, that's true and not true. It's true, as someone has said, that "there are no small sins before a great God." But some sins are worse than others in their effects on us (and even on God's reaction, see Lev. 18:22; Deut. 7:26; 23:18; 2 Chron. 33:2; Prov. 6:16; Jer. 32:35; etc.). Sexual self-damage is more serious than some sins we commit against others.

Paul's argument against misusing our bodies sexually involves two fundamental truths which, while not guaranteeing to keep us away from such sins, will certainly steal every excuse we can ever think of to offer! The first truth is that our bodies are the dwelling places of the Third Member of the Trinity, the Holy Spirit of God. We are indwelt, inhabited by God! Wow. That's got to mess up our minds when it comes to speaking about God's "presence." We do not "enter God's presence" when we show up at church. We take Him with us! No genuine believer can escape the Lord (see Ps. 139); one cannot flee from oneself (indwelt by the Lord)!

The Holy Spirit is in *you*, my friend, and He is simultaneously in me, and in millions of believers across this globe. My failure to understand that concept does not negate its truth. What difference does geography make with an omnipresent God? Omnipresence may be defined simply as "wherever there is a where, God is there." How, then, can we speak of the Holy Spirit being "in" you (v. 19)? Perhaps part of the problem is that we confuse spatial with relational language. I sometimes say to my seminary students: "Are you *with* me?" I don't mean geographically. I mean are they listening, am I *relating to* them? This Spirit who is in us is a gift of God.

The second fundamental concept and excuse-stealing truth Paul gives is that we do not belong to ourselves! "You are not your own; you were bought at a price" (vv. 19b-20a). What a revolutionary perspective! The great "theologian" Billy Joel was wrong when he sang, "This is my life! Leave me alone!" It isn't. Even unredeemed people don't really "belong" to themselves. They've been created by the infinite/personal Creator and ought to live their lives for Him (and they need Christ to do that). We have been made in the image and likeness of our Creator. My wife's grandfather was known to engrave his tools with the inscription: "STOLEN from George S. Tonnissen." When we behave as if we belong to ourselves, we are actually stealing from God.

Why do we not belong to ourselves? Paul does not use creation to prove that point (although he could have); he points out that "you were bought at a price." And we were not picked up at a Goodwill store for fifty cents. Our purchase price was none other than the blood of the Second Person of the Trinity! 1 Peter 1:18-19 says,

> [18]For you know that it was not with perishable things such as silver or gold that you were redeemed from the empty way of life handed down to you from your ancestors, [19]but with the precious blood of Christ, a lamb without blemish or defect.

What more reasons are needed for believers to "therefore honor God with your bodies"?

A fourth truth to keep in mind about the believer and his body is that God expects the believer to submit his or her body as a living sacrifice to the Lord! Paul writes to the Roman Christians:

> Therefore, I urge you, brothers, in view of God's mercy, to offer your bodies as living sacrifices, holy and pleasing to God – this is your spiritual act of worship. Do not conform any longer to the pattern of this world, but be transformed by the renewing of your mind. Then you will be able to test and approve what God's will is – his good, pleasing and perfect will (12:1-2).

God wants our bodies! And He doesn't want us half-dead; He wants us to offer ourselves as "living sacrifices." Note also the immediate connection between our offering our bodies to God and our refusal to continue being conformed to the thinking of this world. He wants our bodies and our minds.

I'm reminded of a famous meeting between two important Bible teachers of the last century. D. L. Moody was in London and he paid a visit to the great scholar and preacher C. H. Spurgeon. When Spurgeon answered the door, he was smoking a large Stogie. Moody, who was a large man, was appalled. He expressed his shock by saying, "*Spurgeon! How could you, a man of God, be smoking a cigar?!*" Whereupon Spurgeon poked his finger into Moody's rather ample belly and retorted, "*The same way you, a man of God, could look like that!*" How skilled we are at judging others.

PART 3

Chapter 8

"The Believer's Associations: 'Who You Callin' a *Pagan?*'"

"To tell the story of who we really are, and of the battle between light and dark, between belief and unbelief, between sin and grace that is waged within us all, costs plenty and may not gain us anything, we're afraid, but an uneasy silence and fishy stare." (Frederick Buechner)

"For John came neither eating nor drinking, and they say, 'He has a demon.' [19]The Son of Man came eating and drinking, and they say, 'Here is a glutton and a drunkard, a friend of tax collectors and "sinners."' But wisdom is proved right by her actions" (Matt. 11:18-19).

This chapter will be different from the others. I will first set out the biblical basis for the Christian's being a friend of publicans and sinners like the Lord Jesus and then follow with a first person account of what the Lord has been doing in my life over the last few years.

What Are We Afraid of?
We Christians put up unnecessary walls between ourselves and unbelievers. We think that we should have nothing to do with

the people of this world, that we certainly should not have serious relationships with them, and we're sure we have good reasons for feeling the way that we do.

Sometimes we Christians genuinely struggle with several Bible passages when it comes to our relating to unbelievers. We read in 2 Corinthians 6, for example, "Do not be yoked together with unbelievers. For what do righteousness and wickedness have in common? ..." (v. 14). We are not suggesting a permanent kind of "yoke" of believers with unbelievers. In fact, the Bible is clear that Christians should not marry non-Christians. It would also seem reasonable that Christians should not go into business ventures with those who don't know Christ.

One oft-cited text is Psalm 1:1 which says, "Blessed is the man who does not walk in the counsel of the wicked or stand in the way of sinners or sit in the seat of mockers." But this verse describes activities of getting advice for how one should live his life ("does not walk in the counsel of the wicked"), of joining sinners in their rebellion against God ("stand in the way of sinners"), and of casting one's lot with those who ridicule spiritual truth ("sit in the seat of mockers"). This text has nothing to do with our later discussion of becoming a friend of publicans and sinners.

If we ask the question what are we afraid of when it comes to being a friend of sinners, certain possibilities come to mind. Perhaps we are afraid of **contamination**. Maybe we think that if we spend time with lost people we will lose our own way in the Christian life. Their "infection" might be contagious! We might think that just as one can lose his health by touching a leper, so we might lose our holiness by associating with the lost. Perhaps we are afraid of **seduction**. They might entice us to sin, to shed our Christian convictions, to run out and commit some wicked act. Perhaps we are afraid of **inconvenience**. If we spend significant time with the lost, they might call us at all hours of the night to answer their questions, to referee family squabbles, or to even give them a ride home from a bar where they have had too much to drink! Perhaps we are afraid of **intimacy**. The closer we draw to lost people the more we will love them. And the pain of thinking that they will be eternally separated from God and His love may be more than we can bear.

Perhaps we are afraid of **exposure** or **vulnerability**. We know – even though we may try to give the opposite impression of ourselves to unbelievers – that *we* have not arrived, and that God has much to do in conforming us to the image of His Son. I think some unsaved people are kind of like a retiree who has bought a metal detector and spends his waning years combing the beach to find some lost watches or coins. The *moral* detector of our unsaved friends will always be on the highest setting. That is, they will quickly pick up on and point out inconsistencies that they see in our lives. Many Christians choose not to get close to unbelievers for this reason.

But there's a much better way. I love what one preacher said. He said that one of the best things about being a believer in Christ is that "I no longer have to defend my own goodness." When that moral detector starts its high pitch buzzing, that is, when our inconsistencies are uncovered by our unsaved friends, we should thank them for their concern, determine before God to work to remove that barrier, but not attempt to defend our mythical perfection.

Whatever excuses we might give for keeping ourselves at a distance from lost people, we are wrong. The believer is not more godly the fewer non-Christian friends he or she has – he or she is simply less like the Lord Jesus. If the unbeliever wishes to depart – let him or her depart. We must not abandon them, forsake them, or blackmail them with some kind of conditional, time-sensitive friendship.

A Catastrophic Confusion

We are very similar to the Corinthian Christians who misunderstood the Apostle Paul in his instructions about believers and unbelievers. In fact, he had to correct their wrong ideas in 1 Corinthians 5:

> [9]I have written you in my letter not to associate with sexually immoral people – [10]not at all meaning the people of this world

who are immoral, or the greedy and swindlers, or idolaters. In that case you would have to leave this world. [11]But now I am writing you that you must not associate with anyone who calls himself a brother but is sexually immoral or greedy, an idolater or a slanderer, a drunkard or a swindler. With such a man do not even eat. [12]What business is it of mine to judge those outside the church? Are you not to judge those inside? [13]God will judge those outside. "Expel the wicked man from among you" (vv. 9-13).

Let's look at this passage carefully. In verses 9-11 we see the Corinthians' **confusion**. They *thought* that Paul was telling them not to have anything to do with lost people, and consequently they isolated themselves from unbelievers. Paul's **correction** is in verses 10-11. He tells them that if he had meant that they should not be around unbelievers (and he lists several brands of sinners: the sexually immoral, those who are greedy or swindlers, those caught in idolatry), they would have to "leave this world"! God does not want His children to leave this world. Paul makes it quite clear that he was not talking about their separating themselves from unbelievers, but from one "who calls himself a brother ..." (v. 11). Paul minces no words when he says, "With such a man do not even eat" (v. 11).

To avoid any further confusion, Paul adds:

What business is it of mine to judge those outside the church? Are you not to judge those inside? God will judge those outside. "Expel the wicked man from among you" (vv. 12-13).[1]

The misunderstanding of the Corinthians had actually produced a **double victory** for Satan. His first victory was that the Corinthians' isolation from unbelievers had ruined evangelism. How could they hope to *reach* lost people when they refused to be *around* lost people? Instead of tolerating the

---

[1] It's an interesting point that the world gets mad at Christians for their judgment of them. Scripturally, we are to be judging *each other* – and not the world! Non-Christians will act like non-Christians. It's when *Christians* act like *non-Christians* that the Church should get involved.

non-Christian conduct of non-Christians, the Corinthians were *judging* them and consequently avoiding them![2]

Today's church is very Corinthian in its approach to unbelievers. Our strategies are varied: we program ourselves to death (so that we have no time for the lost); we don't hold each other accountable for developing relationships of integrity with lost people; we run our leaders to death serving *us* so they have no opportunities to get to know those who need Christ; we focus all our "outreach" strategies on those overseas (we use missions as a substitute for friendship evangelism); etc.

Satan's second victory was that the Corinthians' toleration of sinning believers had ruined discipleship. How can Christians learn to forsake sin if other believers are not getting involved in their lives? The last stage of getting involved in the lives of sinning believers (according to Matt. 18) is to treat them as unbelievers! When Paul says, "With such a man do not even eat" (v. 11), it seems that he is saying "Do not act as if their sin is unimportant. Life is not 'business as usual.' You've got a child of God who refuses to repent. Deal with him or her!" "Eating with" implies supporting those who are living in sin. In fact, Paul says that the Corinthians have an obligation to judge those inside the church. That judgment even involves *expulsion* of the wicked Christian from among the believers (v. 13).

---

[2] According to a traditional Hebrew story, Abraham was sitting outside his tent one evening when he saw an old man, weary from age and journey, coming toward him. Abraham rushed out, greeted him, and then invited him into his tent. There he washed the old man's feet and gave him food and drink. The old man immediately began eating without saying any prayer or blessing. So Abraham asked him, "Don't you worship God?" The old traveler replied, "I worship fire only and reverence no other god." When he heard this, Abraham became incensed, grabbed the old man by the shoulders, and threw him out of his tent into the cold night air. When the old man had departed, God called to his friend Abraham and asked where the stranger was. Abraham replied, "I forced him out because he did not worship you." God answered, "I have suffered him these eighty years although he dishonors me. Could you not endure him one night?" (Thomas Lindberg).

Our Business?

In reality the Corinthians had the situation completely upside-down. They were judging and isolating themselves from unbelievers, thereby ruining evangelism. And they were tolerating sinning Christians, refusing to hold one another accountable, and that was destroying discipleship.

I have great respect for Bill Hybels, pastor of Willow Creek Community Church outside Chicago. He speaks about how we Christians often try to get non-Christians to stop their bad habits. In other words, we're engaged in behavior modification – and that is not our job. He points out we Christians are not in the behavior modification business. We are in the *introduction* business. Our job with unbelievers is to introduce them to Jesus Christ. And Jesus Christ is in the behavior modification business!

The Comfort Factor

I suspect that when we try to get non-Christians to behave more Christianly, or when we avoid them altogether, the reason may simply boil down to the fact that they and their conduct make us uncomfortable. But we are not here for our comfort – we are here for them. In fact, we confuse the gospel when we imply to non-Christians that cleaning up their conduct is of first importance. They may easily conclude that Christianity is about self-improvement instead of salvation.[3]

A short biographical note: You will discover later that I have a number of non-Christian friends and believe that you should have the same. Most of my non-Christian friends drink (some heavily) and a number of them smoke. The language that I often hear on the tennis court from my friends would make a truck driver blush. Several have gone through divorces; one

---

[3] I'm reminded of the statement by Sylvia Constance Ashton-Warner, the New Zealander author and educator (1908-1984) who said: "You must be true to yourself. Strong enough to be true to yourself. Brave enough to be strong enough to be true to yourself. Wise enough to be brave enough, to be strong enough to shape yourself from what you actually are." That's not biblical Christianity!

is a known philanderer. Some regularly cheat on their income taxes. Most gossip freely about each other. The guys are almost always oggling whatever new female shows up to play on a neighboring court.

Why do I give that laundry list of my friends' sins? Because they simply represent people of this world. As Paul says in his command to the Corinthians he was "not at all meaning the people of this world who are immoral, or the greedy and swindlers, or idolaters. In that case you would have to leave this world" (1 Cor. 5:10). My job is not to abandon my non-Christian friends. My job is not to change their God-grieving, self-destructive behavior. I am not to make them feel guilty for their godless conversation or their reprobate conduct.[4] My job is to love them for Christ's sake and to try to live a Christ-like life before them. I am to strategically befriend them and pray for their salvation.

Jesus: Our Example

If we are to live our lives as Jesus lived His, then we must study how He acted around unbelievers. We read in Mark 3:

> [20]Then Jesus entered a house, and again a crowd gathered, so that he and his disciples were not even able to eat. [21]When his family heard about this, they went to take charge of him, for they said, "He is out of his mind." [22]And the teachers of the law who came down from Jerusalem said, "He is possessed by Beelzebub! By the prince of demons he is driving out demons."

Please notice that Jesus spent time with unbelievers. In fact, He spends so much time with them that His earthly family thought they had to come and rescue Him – from Himself!

Jesus' popularity is seen in this text: such a crowd gathered that Jesus and His disciples did not even have time to eat. You

---

[4] Of course, if they ask for my opinion about their conduct or habits, I will be honest with them and tell them the truth from the Scriptures. But I am here to evangelize them, not discipline or disciple them.

can imagine His Jewish mother saying something like, "You're not *eating, again?! What am I going to do with you?! Come home – let me make you some lamb!"* His family goes "to take charge of him" (v. 21). Wow. They certainly did not understand that He was God manifest in the flesh because they give the reason for their rescue attempt as "He is out of his mind." The teachers of the law were worse in their response to Jesus. They accused Him of being empowered by the Prince of demons himself in His ministry of driving out demons. But the bottom line is that Jesus spent significant time with unbelievers, regardless of how that made His earthly family or His evil foes feel.

A Partially True Charge

The primary passage we want to examine is Matthew 11. Jesus Himself responds to the criticism He has been receiving and He says,

> [18]For John came neither eating nor drinking, and they say, "He has a demon." [19]The Son of Man came eating and drinking, and they say, "Here is a glutton and a drunkard, a friend of tax collectors and 'sinners.'" But wisdom is proved right by her actions.

This text is central in deciding how we Christians ought to relate to the pagans around us. Jesus points out the difference between Himself and John the Baptist. What Jesus is saying may be summarized in chart form:

The One Attacked:	The Behavior:	The Charge:
John the Baptist	"He came neither eating nor drinking."	"He has a demon!"
Jesus	"I came eating and drinking."	"Here is a glutton and drunkard, a friend of tax collectors and sinners."

Please notice that both John the Baptist and Jesus get attacked. The attacks of the religious leaders were designed to smear the character of Jesus, discourage others from listening to Him, and justify themselves in rejecting their own Messiah.

But could someone not say, "They were wrong about John the Baptist having a demon. They were certainly wrong about Jesus being a glutton and a drunkard. Weren't they probably also wrong about His being a friend of tax collectors and sinners"? Well, the religious leaders *were* wrong about John the Baptist being demonized, but they were only *partially* wrong about Jesus. He was not a glutton and a drunkard! We are clearly told in Mark 12:37 that "the large crowd listened to him with delight."

Jesus apparently uses a common proverb when He says, "Wisdom is proved right by her actions." His emphasis seems to be "Charges are easy to make. Watch the conduct of my life!" He is responding to the religious leaders' *argumentum ad hominem*, that is, their argument against the person. They were saying, "Don't listen to John the Baptist. He has a demon!" It is interesting that the leaders *demonize* both John the Baptist and Jesus. To *demonize* an opponent means to impugn his motives, to paint his character with the worst possible brush. Politicians do this in their mud-slinging election campaigns. *We* do this when we attack another's character.

They were also saying of Jesus, "Don't listen to Him. He is a glutton and a drunkard. And not only that, He's a friend of tax collectors and sinners!" What an interesting hierarchy of character flaws. It's bad when someone is a glutton (he doesn't know when to stop eating) or a drunkard (he doesn't know when to stop drinking), and Jesus is accused of *both!* They accuse Jesus of having no control over either His appetite or His thirst. A worse sin, in their minds, worse than uncontrollable gluttony and drunkenness, was to be a friend of tax collectors and sinners. And He was that too. He had no control (apparently) over His associations.

I believe that if the Lord Jesus were on trial for the charges made against Him, to the accusation that He was a glutton Jesus would say "Not guilty!" To the charge of His being a drunkard He would say, "Not guilty!" But to the charge of being a friend of tax collectors and sinners Jesus would loudly say so that even the little old mostly deaf lady in the back of the courtroom could clearly hear Him, "Guilty! Guilty! Guilty!"

AAA Options

There really are only three options for the Christian in relating to the unsaved of the world. The first option is what I call *abandonment*. That is, the Christian doesn't relate. He expends no effort at being a friend of sinners. He might even say, "That just isn't my *calling!*" The second option is what I call *assimilation*. We give up our distinctiveness as Christians, we compromise, and we become genuinely *worldly*. Assimilation certainly doesn't help our witness. The third option is what I call *affection*. We simply become like the Lord Jesus and we begin to actually love lost people.

Working on the Friendship Factor

I have a confession to make. I collect Christian bumper stickers. Well, not exactly. I *read* Christian bumper stickers. One of my friends has a sticker on his car that reads, "GOT JESUS?" It's cute, and it appeals especially to those who come from a dairy farming background, but that's all it says. I love the older sticker that reads, "IN CASE OF RAPTURE, DRIVER WILL DISAPPEAR!" Hmmm. Most people in the world would more than likely associate the word "rapture" with romance. So the bumper sticker to them might mean, "In case of being overcome by romantic thoughts, the driver will somehow vanish." Another colleague at seminary has a 1977 Datsun whose beat-up trunk is covered with huge rust spots. His bumper sticker reads, "I LOVE TO TELL THE STORY!" Someone behind my friend's Datsun might ask, "Which story? The story of the massive rust spots?" All of this to say that our relationship with the people of this world must go beyond safe, bumper-sticker evangelism.

We must get involved with those who need Christ. 1 Corinthians 10:27 says, "If some unbeliever invites you to a meal and you want to go, eat whatever is put before you without raising questions of conscience." Although Paul's primary point has to do with whether a Christian can eat meat that had been offered to idols, let us not miss his obvious implication that non-Christians will sometimes invite Christians to their homes for a meal. Could it not be said that if we are seldom being invited to the homes of non-believers for a meal, we probably are not being a friend of sinners as Jesus was? In fact, He was invited to the home of a leper named Simon (Matt. 26:6) as well as to the home of a strict Pharisee who was also named Simon (Luke 7:36ff).

Earning the Right to Be Heard

How do we earn the right to be heard with non-Christians? Let me suggest five ideas which will help in developing relationships of integrity with those who don't know Christ. The first is simply: We listen before we speak! What makes us think we can talk to someone about *eternity* when we don't take the time to find out what they do, about their family, what they think about life?

Someone has written about one Christian:

> "His thoughts were slow,
> his words were few
> And never meant to glisten.
> He was a joy to all his friends –
> You should have heard him listen."

I am slowly learning that listening is virtually a lost art. Asking good questions of your non-Christian friends shows them that you care about *them* – and not just whether you can win them over to Christianity. I love the statement of the late Ray Charles when he said, "Most people take their ears for granted. I can't. My eyes are my handicap, but my ears are my opportunity. They show me what my eyes can't. They tell me 99 percent of what I need to know about my world. Because of my ears, I can communicate naturally and freely with people everywhere. I don't have to find an unnatural way of expressing one of the most basic human instincts God has given us."

The second idea that will help us develop relationships of integrity with non-Christians is simply that we show a genuine interest in their concerns. Some of us Christians are simply not very good conversationalists. I spoke recently with a twenty-five-year-old Christian young woman who said she was with a group of unbelievers and she didn't know what to talk about. They had no interest in her relationship with Christ; they didn't care about the issues that were most important to her. So she was fairly quiet and rather uncomfortable being with them. I suggested that she could have asked them questions about the things that matter most to them: their jobs, their relationships, their interests. Someone has said, "How shall they hear unless they be interested?" And perhaps their interest will develop as we show an interest in them and their concerns.

We honestly ask them about their jobs, their families, and their hobbies. We give them the opportunity to talk about their teenagers, their home improvement projects, their relatives.

My neighbor Phil has one of the best manicured lawns in our neighborhood. In fact, his yard won "Yard of the Month" for its beauty! I noticed a while back that he was installing a small plastic fence on the property line between his house and our driveway. When I asked him what the fence was about, he sheepishly said that it was to prevent the leaves from my decrepit Bradford pear tree from blowing into his garage. I was a bit embarrassed. I had not raked up those leaves, thinking that they could just stay there on the ground. But they were winding up in his garage. Needless to say, I apologized to Phil and raked up all those leaves that afternoon.

I have extended a number of invitations for lunch to some of my non-Christian tennis friends when they were going through tough times (a divorce, family fights, economic hard times). I promise them that I won't preach to them and that I will listen to them.

The third idea that will help us develop relationships of integrity with non-Christians is simply that we pray for them by name. The priorities of my life should show up in my prayers as a believer. If I am not presently praying for unsaved friends, then they are not a priority to me! As I'll share later, most of my non-Christian friends are tennis players. I've found that I pray for them at strange times, including during tennis matches when they are on the other side of the net! I'm not praying for athletic victory (well, maybe once in a while) but for some small step of spiritual victory in their lives.

Would you not agree that so often our mid-week prayer meetings are merely "organ recitals"? By that expression I mean that we go into great detail to pray for Christians who are suffering physically. In one church recently it seemed that all of the prayer requests concerned physical problems. One brother went into great detail about a church member who "had to have a foot of his colon removed by surgery, then he had problems with his stitches when he got home, lost several pints of blood, and had to be rushed back to the hospital, but seems to be recuperating pretty well. We need to pray for him," the brother said. Some of the requests for prayer made me feel like a third-year medical student huddled with an experienced surgeon at the foot of a patient's bed going over his hospital chart. God cares about our physical well-being, but can we talk? How about prayer requests like the following:

"Please pray for my friend Mike. His wife is a believer but he seems to have no sense of his own sin and his desperate need for Christ. Please pray that I will have an opportunity to spend time with him this weekend."

"Please remember my friend Rob in prayer. His wife Mary is an alcoholic and it's really taking a toll on the family. Please pray that they will become more interested in spiritual matters."

"My friend Tony just got separated from his wife. And their daughter Susan, who had a son out of wedlock when she was in prison for heroin possession, really needs Christ. Please pray for me that they will take my advice and meet with a Christian counselor."

We need to pray "risky" prayers, that is, the kind of prayers which will put us in the picture, where *we* have to *do something*. Or we can continue to only focus on hospital charts.

The fourth idea that should help us develop relationships of integrity with non-Christians is simply that we confess our failure to be like the Lord Jesus in this area of our lives! I'm all for church attendance (as you'll see in the next chapter), but I have a great concern for our churches. Some churches seem to believe that there should be church services every night of the week, and if you're a member, you should be at every service. I do not hold this view that the lights should be on in our churches every night of the week. When in the world would we spend time with lost people? In fact, I believe our church leaders should set the example for involvement in our communities and set believers free to get involved in some non-religious organizations (sports teams, volunteer organizations, Toastmasters' clubs, etc.).

When I first joined a local tennis team, composed mostly of unbelievers, the small group of our local church which my wife and I attended moved their meeting night to, you guessed it, the same night as our team practice. I pondered that decision pretty hard, but decided (with my wife's support) to practice tennis with my lost friends rather than fellowship on that night with my Christian family. Do you know what that small group did? They did not criticize me for not coming; *they prayed for me as I spent time with my non-Christian friends!*

Can you honestly say that you are a friend of sinners? If your answer or my answer is not an immediate "YES!", then we got some confessing to do. And, as the great "theologian" Bill Cosby says about Jello, there's always room for repentance!

The fifth idea that should help us develop relationships of integrity with non-Christians is simply that we share with other Christians those that we are befriending and strategically praying for! Again, Bill Hybels is my example here. He tells about a leadership retreat his church had where he challenged the leaders with the importance of friendship evangelism. After sharing a bit about several of his non-Christian friends, Bill said: "Okay. It's your turn. I want each of you, one after another, to quickly stand to your feet and give the first names of three non-Christians that you are seeking to befriend for Christ and for whom you are systematically praying! Ready? GO!" How would you fare with such a challenge? Hybels makes it quite clear that he wants the epitaph on his tombstone to read, "Bill Hybels. A Friend of Sinners." What will yours read?

A Personal Testimony

My family and I lived for almost ten years in Manitoba, Canada, where I taught at a small Bible college. When a seminary position opened in South Carolina, we prepared for our move back to the States. I clearly remember thanking the Lord for our years in Canada and for this new opportunity to serve Him. But I had a particular prayer request. It went something like this: "Dear Lord, we've had a great life here. But I've been surrounded by Christians: Christian neighbors, Christians at work, a Christian mailman, a strong church full of Christians. Lord, I have had almost *no* non-Christian friends. Please, Lord, give me some friends in our new home in South Carolina who don't know You."

God answered that prayer the second day after we moved. I noticed some guys playing tennis across the street and I looked at my wife with that look that she immediately understood and she said, "Go. GO! Don't worry. I've got plenty of boxes to unpack." I met Mark and Phil that day, two guys desperately in need of Christ.

I was soon asked to join a mixed doubles' tennis team. "Mixed doubles?" I thought to myself. "Isn't that like kissing your sister?" Anyway, my wife Linda doesn't really play tennis. She gave me her blessing and Angela and I became part of a team which won it all. When I say "won it all," I mean *all*. We won the Columbia City tournament, the South Carolina state tournament, the Regional tournament, and the Sectional tournament. At my age one doesn't win many tournaments in anything, so forgive my excitement here.

I have shared some of my experiences with that team in a message I preach called "A Weekend with Pagans." I believe we suffer from either thinking that we are more godly the fewer non-Christian friends we have, or from staying so busy with

Christian meetings that we only have the left-overs to offer them. I know of at least one Christian who brags that the doors of his church are open every night of the week. His friend said to him, "Bill, that's just wrong! When do your church people ever have time to rub shoulders with unbelievers?!"

Let me summarize some of what I learned as I spent time with about eleven other people who gave no indication that they were believers in Jesus Christ.

1. We are here for them! A lot of time we Christians act as if we are here for us! In Matthew 9:10 we read that Jesus had dinner at a local IRS agent's home. We are here for the sick (although it seems that we spend most of our time with the "healthy"). My family and I have come to a conclusion. When we have non-Christians in our home who smoke, we do not ask them to go outside. We don't give them a lecture on the dangers of second-hand smoke. We simply provide an ashtray (by the way, we don't own an ashtray. We provide an old coffee cup). Recognizing that we are here for them will cost us. In one tournament I had to pay for a fairly expensive meal for myself. Linda was not able to be at that tournament. But I wanted to go out to dinner with my friends.

2. They are people like us! That may seem like a simple conclusion, but that weekend made me aware that unbelievers need approval, friendship, the basics of a good marriage, respect. We Christians break out in a cold sweat when we think about beginning a conversation with the lost about spiritual things. Why don't we start a conversation about things in general?

In one of the tournaments, I had a conversation with a hotel service person. I'm not sure how the conversation started. How often do we look right past "such people"? She told me that she had been divorced twice. She said her second husband beat her and would greet her when she came home from work with a loaded shotgun and the words, "I'm going to kill you!" She told me that he ruined her credit. All I did was ask her how she was, you know, breakfast conversation. But I listened to her answer.

She said that she had kids to support and when she was broke, she began calling local churches to ask if they would help. Every one of them told her, "Yes, we help with such matters. But we only help those who are members of our congregation." In the middle of her sharing all this with me, she caught herself and said, "Oh, I shouldn't be telling you all this!" At the end of our conversation, I felt I needed to ask her a question. We hadn't even exchanged names, but I felt God wanted me to say to her, "Thank you for telling me your story. I'm so sorry about your experiences with those churches. I'm glad things are going better for you. But may I ask you, what are you doing about the hole in your heart?" She said, "Oh, it's still there. And I'm still looking to find the right answer." I wish I could tell you that she got saved, and everyone eating their morning donuts in that breakfast area trusted Christ, but that's not what happened. I was sowing seeds as a Christian who really listened to her and her problems and tried to show her the love of Christ.

3. We Christians have so much in life! We can talk about the fundamental differences which Christ has made in our lives without becoming preachy. My team often asked me, "Larry, why don't you drink?" You need to know that I didn't turn religious on them. I answered them by saying, "If I drank alcohol, I would probably lose my lunch on the court – and that wouldn't be a good thing!" Instead of making my non-drinking a barrier, I made light of it without condemning them. My unsaved team members are not lost because they drink; they are lost because they don't know Christ. As someone has said, "Christ has not called me to be a mother to the world, but a witness." At one tournament, our captain (who always had a fifth of Bourbon in his hotel room) drank too much at dinner. He asked me to drive him and his wife back to the hotel. Perhaps we Christians ought to apply to become the designated drivers of the world.

4. We must give ourselves to relationship-building, instead of evangelism by straffing. We need to understand that there are specific steps in building relationships with unbelievers.

What makes us think that we can simply hop-scotch into the most intimate issues of their lives? At one tournament, I had breakfast with one of the couples. Before I realized it, they were in the middle of a year-long fight! Although they wanted me to take sides, God gave me the wisdom not to. I did, however, share about how my wife and I have enjoyed over thirty years of marriage together – and that we would love to have them over to our home sometime to talk about what we are learning about getting along together. Unfortunately, they moved out of state before we could get together with them. We Christians need to see our relationships with non-Christians as long-term. We need to take specific steps to get to know them, to begin to love them, and to develop trust with them. How about having lost people over to your house to play games, to watch the Superbowl, or to work on Creative Memories albums together?

5. It is critical to pull our own weight! Sometimes we Christians are just flat-out *cheap!* Do I hear an "Amen!"? Did you know that the most dreaded day of the week for waiters and waitresses is ... *Sunday!* Can you guess why? Christians are notoriously lousy tippers. Some, in fact, will leave a little gospel tract entitled "A Tip for You" *instead of* a tip! Don't do that. If you leave a tract, double your tip! During one of our tournaments, my partner Angela asked me one morning at breakfast, "So, Larry, what did you bring for some of our team meals?" I didn't remember being asked to bring anything. I said to her privately, "I didn't know I was supposed to bring anything. Can I contribute some money to help pay for our food?" She said, "No, that's okay. I was just teasing you." But what if I hadn't offered to do my part financially? Pulling our own weight means we don't take advantage of unbelievers because we are Christians. We don't ask for special deals from retailers because we are believers. We don't assume that they will cover all the expenses on trips.

Our tennis pro was once talking with a number of the players I am befriending when I was not with them. He reminded them that if they had a non-member play on the courts, they would have to pay $5 per person. Someone said, "Larry has his friend Mike play each week – and Mike's not a member!" The pro said, "Yes, he does. But Larry pays that $5 every time he and Mike play." Boy, was I glad that I had paid that fee!

Well, those are a few of the lessons that God made very vivid to me during that mixed-doubles season. But I do want to tell you one more story before this chapter is done. In the third round of the playoffs, our whole team was meeting in the captain's hotel room. He had his fifth of Bourbon flowing freely, the TV was blaring, others were downing their beers, and the conversation turned to the sexual escapades of then-President Bill Clinton. The guys were playing "Can you top this?" in terms of filthy jokes about Clinton making the rounds over the internet. I was tempted to leave that hotel room and all that garbage, but something encouraged me to stay. One of the women players, Sue-Chin, turned to me while all this stuff was going on and asked me, "Larry, I know you believe the Bible. But do you believe in *Christians?*" As a Korean her English wasn't too good, but I knew we needed to talk. So we sat in a corner of that hotel room among all that sinful nonsense and talked about the gospel and her background and how Christians will often fail, but Jesus will never let us down. I was glad I was there. By the way, did I mention that we won it all?

Chapter 9

"The Believer's Associations: 'Goin' to the Chapel and We're ...'"

"Oh, the comfort, the inexpressible comfort, of feeling safe with a person; having neither to weigh thoughts nor measure words, but to pour them all out just as they are, chaff and grain together, knowing that a faithful hand will take and sift them, keep what is worth keeping, and then, with the breath of kindness, blow the rest away." (Dinah Maria Mulock Craik)

"Christians, like snowflakes, are frail, but when they stick together they can stop traffic." (Vance Havner)

The early Christians "devoted themselves to the apostles' teaching and to fellowship, to the breaking of bread and to prayer" (Acts 2:42).

Don't you just love it when someone in the world says something incredibly profound, wonderfully Christian, although there is no evidence of that person having a relationship with the Lord Jesus Christ? I'm thinking of a great statement by George Bernard Shaw when he said,

This is the true joy of life: the being used up for a purpose recognized by yourself as a mighty one; being a force of nature instead of a feverish, selfish little clot of ailments and grievances, complaining that the world will not devote itself to making you happy.[1]

I'm not sure when he said that, or where he said that, but I'm glad he said it. Rick Warren uses that quote in his powerful book *The Purpose-Driven Life*. Shaw agrees with the concept of living life on purpose. In fact, he says that your life purpose should be "a mighty one."

Of course, we Christians see ourselves not as a "force of nature," but as co-laborers with Christ (1 Cor. 3:9; 2 Cor. 6:1), as God's army of infiltrators whose mission is to continue the work begun by the Lord Jesus (John 17:11, 15-20). That's a mighty purpose and a whole lot better than merely being a force of nature!

What concerns me about Shaw's quote is the last half, for I believe that often the Christian conducts himself as little more than "a feverish, selfish little clot of ailments and grievances, complaining that the world [or the church] will not devote itself to making [him] happy." Perhaps we've been blinded by our "inalienable right to the pursuit of life, liberty, and, especially, *happiness*," but what about **holiness**? Happiness, biblically speaking, was never intended to be sought as an end in itself. It is evident from Scripture that happiness or joy is a by-product of holiness (see Ps. 1, for example).

But how does the Christian get holy? Judging by what appears to be the Christian status quo, holiness comes by attending church meetings, volunteering to teach the sixth-grade girls' class, and maybe going on one short-term missions team to Venezuela in one's lifetime. Rituals, not relationships, seem to be the key to Christian growth. In this chapter I want to suggest that individual holiness is developed in Christian friendships as we practice the four priorities of the Early Church.

---

[1] Quoted in Rick Warren's *The Purpose-Driven Life*, p. 33.

A Focus on Friendship

Someone has written the following graduation address that, apparently, was never given. It's a bit lengthy, but I think you'll enjoy it.

Ladies and gentlemen, wear sun screen. If I can offer only one tip for the future, sun screen would be it. The long-term benefits of sun screen have long been proved by scientists whereas the rest of my advice has no basis more reliable than my own meandering experience. I will dispense this advice now. Enjoy the power and beauty of your youth. Oh, never mind. You will not understand the power and beauty of your youth until they're faded. But trust me. In twenty years you'll look back at photos of yourself and recall how fabulous you really looked at the time. You are not now as fat as you imagined. Don't worry about the future. Or, worry, but know that worrying is as effective as trying to solve an algebra equation by chewing gum. Real troubles are apt to blindside you at 4 pm on an idle Tuesday. Do one thing daily that scares you. Don't be reckless with other people's hearts. Don't put up with people who are reckless with yours. Floss! Remember compliments. Forget insults. Keep old love letters. Throw away old bank statements. Stretch. Don't feel guilty if you don't know what you want to do with your life. Some of the most interesting 40-year-olds I know *still* don't know what they want to do with theirs. Be kind to your knees. You'll miss them when they're gone. Read the directions even if you don't follow them. Do not read beauty magazines – they will only make you feel ugly. Get to know your parents. You never know when they'll be gone. Be nice to your siblings. They're the best link to your past and the people most likely to stick with you. Understand that friends come and go, but with the precious few you should hold on. The older you get the more you need the people who knew you when you were young. Accept these certain truths. Prices will rise. Politicians will philander. You too will get old. And then you'll fantasize that when you were young, prices were reasonable, politicians were noble, and children respected their elders. Respect your elders. Don't expect anyone else to support you. Maybe you have a trust fund. Maybe you'll have a wealthy spouse. But you never know when either one might run out. Don't mess too much with your hair or by the time you're forty, it will look eighty-five. Be careful whose advice you buy, but be patient with those who supply it. Advice is a form of nostalgia. Dispensing it is a way of fishing the past from the disposal, wiping it off, and recycling it for more than it's worth. But trust me on the sun screen.

When it comes to how to live the Christian life, advice is all around. Some of it is good; much of it seems unnecessary. But what makes us think that we can live the Christian life in isolation? We need the other members of the Body of Christ.

There's Not a Friend Like the Lowly Jesus (Who Needed Friends Himself)

The Lord Jesus is our example in this area of relationships. He desired the companionship of His disciples. In John 6 Jesus makes some incredible statements about Himself which cause many to turn away. He sadly addresses the Twelve in verse 67 and asks, "You don't want to leave me, too, do you?"

I used to teach New Testament Greek in our seminary. What is helpful about the Greek of verse 67 ("Do you want to leave me, too?") is this: Jesus' question is a construction in Greek that implies that He is looking for or expecting a "NO!" answer. "You're not going to leave me too, are you?" Jesus was hoping for, anticipating, the answer: "No, Lord. Of course not!" And he gets that in spades from Simon Peter who responds: "Lord, to whom shall we go? You have the words of eternal life. We have come to believe and to know that you are the Holy One of God" (v. 68).

The Lord Jesus in His perfect humanity needed the companionship of His disciples. What makes us think that we need one another less than He did?

May I suggest that there are a number of barriers[2] which we must overcome if we are to have the Christian relationships

---

[2] Some of those barriers include our mobile society, our over-emphasis on the vertical versus the horizontal, a failure to forgive one another, a basic misunderstanding of fellowship, etc.

which we need. We will examine only two of these at this time: the barrier of busyness and the "I-have-no-need-of-thee" syndrome.

The Barrier of Busyness

The first barrier is simply the busyness of life. To really get into another's life, you must have shared experiences. We have been sucked into a way of living which moves us, gasping, from one event to the next. We are being consumed by carpooling, wearing out our kids and ourselves by shuttling them from one activity to a music lesson to a hotly-contested soccer match. And we wonder why we're *pooped!* You may have heard the story of Mr. Smith, the harried executive, who said to his administrative assistant, "Ms. Jones, do you know where my pencil is?" She said, "Mr. Smith, it is behind your ear." He retorted, "Ms. Jones, you know I am a busy man. *Which* ear?!"

In his book *Faster: The Acceleration of Just About Everything*,[3] James Gleick makes the point that we suffer today from what he calls "hurry sickness." We believe that we possess too little time (which, of course, is a myth). We must slow down the RPM's of our lives if we expect to develop and maintain Christian friendships.

The "I-Have-No-Need-Of-Thee" Syndrome

A second barrier we must overcome in order to develop solid friendships is the "I-have-no-need-of-Thee" syndrome. We simply do not make the cultivation of Christian friendships a priority in our lives. But how important, really, are our relationships with other believers? Isn't "Just Jesus and Me" (the name of an old praise chorus) enough? Do I really *need* other believers?

The New Testament epistle of 1 John unequivocally declares our need for our brothers and sisters in Christ in what I call a spiritual surprises fashion. Let us briefly notice nine passages in 1 John which challenge the "I-have-no-need-of-Thee" syndrome.

---

[3] New York: Pantheon, 1999.

For example, we read in 1 John 1:3, "We proclaim to you what we have seen and heard, so that you also may have fellowship *with us*. And our fellowship is with the Father and with his Son, Jesus Christ." One would have expected John to say that he was writing this letter that its readers might have fellowship with *God*, or with *Jesus*, but he writes "that you also may have fellowship with *us*"! We were never designed for fellowship only with God. In fact, we read in Genesis 2:18 (after Adam had been created in the perfection of the Garden) that "The Lord God said, 'It is not good for the man to be alone. I will make a helper suitable for him.'" Before sin entered God's good creation, God Himself declared Adam as lonely and needing a human counterpart. We were never created to live only with God; we need human companionship.

A second text in 1 John indicating our need for one another is 1:7 which says, "But if we walk in the light, as he is in the light, we have fellowship with *one another*, and the blood of Jesus, his Son, purifies us from all sin." John has been speaking about God being light and we should not walk in darkness. One would have expected him to say in verse 7, "If we walk in the light (where God is), we have fellowship with *God*"! But he didn't put it that way. Our walking with the invisible God in the light is shown by our fellowship with visible brothers and sisters.

A third text in 1 John indicating our need for one another is that of 3:10 which says, "This is how we know who the children of God are and who the children of the devil are: Anyone who does not do what is right is not a child of God; nor is anyone who does not love his brother." John sees two categories of human beings: those who are the children of God and those who are the children of the devil. The mark of the child of God is doing what is right which includes loving our fellow believers.

A fourth text in 1 John which shows the centrality of the Christian family is that of 3:14 which says, "We know that we have passed from death to life, because we love our brothers." I would have expected John to say something like, "We know that we have passed from death to life *because we have believed the gospel!*" But that is not his emphasis here. The imagery of passing from death to life is quite vivid for me, having recently watched my father pass away. There is a finality, a concreteness, to death. That same concreteness is true of first converting to Jesus Christ – and its reality is revealed by how we treat our fellow Christians.

A fifth text in 1 John emphasizing Christian relationships is 3:16 – "This is how we know what love is: Jesus Christ laid down his life for us. And we ought to lay down our lives for our brothers." I would have expected John to have said something about Christian martyrdom, the laying down of one's life for Jesus as a result of persecution. But John's concern is not to add to the list of names in *Fox's Book of Martyrs*. We prove our love for our Savior by being willing to give our lives for our brothers.

A sixth text in 1 John stressing our need for one another is 3:23 – "And this is his command: to believe in the name of his Son, Jesus Christ, and to love one another as he commanded us." The believer is under the mandate to not only believe the gospel, but also to love other believers. We do not choose between loving God and loving His children. Belief alone leaves out half of His command and is half-obedience. We must love one another.

A seventh text focusing on fellowship with other believers is 4:10-12 which says,

> [10]This is love: not that we loved God, but that he loved us and sent his Son as an atoning sacrifice for our sins. [11]Dear friends, since God so loved us, we also ought to love one another. [12]No one has ever seen God; but if we love one another, God lives in us and his love is made complete in us.

God is the initiator in the love relationship. He has proved His love for us by sending His Son as the atoning sacrifice for our sins. How should we respond to that love? One would expect John to say, "Since God so loved us, we also ought to love *God!* But he doesn't. Of course, we cannot love God in the same way He has loved us. He has no need for an atoning sacrifice for Himself – and we are certainly not in any condition to offer Him one! We respond to His love by loving one another. In fact, our loving one another is proof that God lives in us and completes His love in us.

An eighth text focusing on Christian relationships is 4:19-21 which says,

> [19]We love because he first loved us. [20]If anyone says, "I love God," yet hates his brother, he is a liar. For anyone who does not love his brother, whom he has seen, cannot love God whom he has not seen. [21]And he has given us this command: Whoever loves God must also love his brother.

Again we see that God's love is prior, that He first loved us. John minces no words when he attacks those who make a verbal profession to love God yet hate their brothers in Christ. That one, John says, "is a liar." How is he a liar? He is a liar in the sense that he *doesn't* love God, no matter how loudly he proclaims that he does. For one's love of God, the God who cannot be seen, is put to the test by one's love of his brother who is in front of one's eyes. God's command is not a multiple choice (either "A" or "B"), but a both-and (we must love God *and* our brother). Our love for the invisible God is proven by our love for our visible brothers.

A ninth and final text stressing our need to love one another is that of 5:1-3 which says,

> [1]Everyone who believes that Jesus is the Christ is born of God, and everyone who loves the father loves his child as well. [2]This is how we know that we love the children of God: by loving God and carrying out his commands. [3]This is love for God: to obey his commands. And his commands are not burdensome...

This fascinating text tells us that the new birth occurs when an individual believes that Jesus is the Christ. One who loves the father loves his child as well. Perhaps John is using a kind of play on words here. When he says that the believer "loves his child as well," does "his child" refer to Jesus or to the new believer? That is, is John saying that the one who is born of God loves God's Son Jesus? Or is he saying that the one who is born of God should naturally love God's other children, that is, our brothers and sisters in Christ? It appears that John means the latter, that is, the one who is born of God loves the children of God and proves that love by loving God and "carrying out his commands." Our loving God is shown by our loving one another and obeying the Lord.

So, to the barrier we have called the "I-have-no-need-of-thee" syndrome, John categorically declares that we were never created to live only with God; that we need human companionship; that our walking with the invisible God in the light is shown by our fellowship with visible brothers and sisters; that the mark of the child of God is doing what is right which includes loving our fellow believers; that the reality of passing from death to life is revealed by how we treat our fellow Christians; that we prove our love for our Savior by being willing to give our lives for our brothers; that only believing the gospel without loving one another is half-obedience; that our loving one another is proof that God lives in us and completes His love in us; that our love for the invisible God is proven by our love for our visible brothers; and that our loving God is shown by our loving one another and obeying the Lord. Whew!

Many other passages of Scripture challenge the prevailing attitude that we don't need one another,[4] but I believe we have made our point. The barrier of busyness and the "I-have-no-need-of-thee" syndrome must be overcome if we are to develop the kinds of relationships which foster holiness in the family of God.

The Main Thing Is to Keep the Main Thing ...
This brings us to a consideration of the issue: why the church? We're "going to the chapel and we're ..." – what? Why do we

---

[4] Especially the "spiritual gift" passages such as Romans 12, 1 Corinthians 12, Ephesians 4, and 1 Peter 4.

need to meet together as believers? What are we seeking, by God's grace, to accomplish?

Here it is that Scripture is so clear in listing the four priorities of the early church. Acts 2:42 declares that the early Christians "devoted themselves to the apostles' teaching and to fellowship, to the breaking of bread and to prayer." We will examine each of these priorities and then notice an amazing omission in that list. But first, let's not too quickly pass over the words they "devoted themselves to ...".

Have you noticed how quickly some Christians bail out of a church? There's a personality clash, a bit of a power struggle, the sermons are too long, the sanctuary is too hot (or too cold), the small groups are not "meeting my needs," the carpet is the wrong shade of fuchsia, the pastor "didn't even say hello to me last Sunday!", the parking spaces are taken up by all the visitors, there doesn't seem to be any strategy for evangelism and outreach, the music is too rocky (or too 1950s), etc.[5]

There are times when one should leave a church, such as there being no concern for carrying out the Great Commission (Matt. 28:19-20), or the leadership refuses to practice appropriate church discipline (Matt. 18; 1 Cor. 5), or there are other churches where one may better contribute to the Body, etc. But can we talk? Frequently Christians suffer from a case of what I call remedial apathy: they know what's wrong with the church; they just don't care enough to do anything about it.

Let's Hear It for *Dedication!*
The early Christians, Acts 2:42 tells us, "devoted themselves to...." They were committed to joining Jesus in the only

---

[5] Steve Brown tells about his friend Mike Glodo, the stated clerk of the Evangelical Presbyterian Church. He went to Jesus to complain about the church. "He said to Jesus, 'They are a mess. They are uncommitted, mean, and lazy. They don't care what you say or even about you and your honor. They are a stiff-necked people, and they don't deserve your love.' 'Mike,' Jesus answered, 'be careful ... she's my wife!'" (Steve Brown, *A Scandalous Freedom: The Radical Nature of the Gospel* [West Monroe, LA: Howard Publishing Co., 2004], p. 81).

building project in which He was (and is) engaged: His church (Matt. 16:18). When I was a high school student, my first part-time job was as a "carpenter's helper." That title basically meant that I did whatever the contractor told me to, usually involving getting him (and his crew) coffee, cleaning up around the building site, and staying out of their way. One of my favorite jobs was carrying bundles of shingles up on the roof. It was great exercise and it meant that the new house was nearly completed. During the framing stage, the general contractor actually let me drive some nails. I didn't hit my thumb even once!

But it's a funny thing. When the house was finished, I, a lowly carpenter's helper, stood back with the real carpenters and thought to myself, "I helped build that house!" I hadn't done much, but there was a sense of pride which I still feel today when I drive down that street. The Christian is to be *the* Carpenter's helper – and that requires dedication.

You may have heard the story about the young check-out girl at a local Wal★Mart. She seemed bored with her job, somewhat unfriendly to the customers, and was always looking at her watch to see how much longer she had to be at work. Her supervisor took her aside and said, "Becky Anne," (she was a Southern girl), "you don't seem too interested in your job here at Wal★Mart. You don't seem real motivated to contribute to our philosophy, but I'm not going to fire you right now. I want to ask you a few questions. Are you ready?" "Yessir," Becky Anne said. "Becky Anne, let's imagine that you had the power to hire any one of the following three guys you see working in a rock quarry. You interview the first guy and ask him, 'What are you doing?' He says, 'I'm moving these stupid rocks. Boy, are they heavy!' You interview the second guy, 'What are you doing?' He says, 'I'm moving this pile of dumb rocks so I can get enough money to make my truck payment.' You go to the third guy and ask him, 'What are *you* doing?' He says, *'I'm helping to build a cathedral!'* Which of those three guys would you hire, Becky Ann?" Becky Ann thought hard for a few seconds and then said, "The *cute* one, I guess!"

The early Christians were *devoted* to Christ building His church. They saw themselves as helping to erect a cathedral to God's grace. Dedication involves putting aside my own personal goals for the sake of something bigger than myself. It requires a desire to be used up for a mighty purpose. It entails being a force of God Himself, recognizing that He is pleased when I cooperate with His Son in what He is presently doing in His world. Negatively, this devotion demands that we turn away from being "a feverish, selfish little clot of ailments and grievances, complaining that the church will not devote itself to making us happy."

But what, specifically, were the areas of dedication to which the early Christians devoted themselves? Acts 2:42 makes it quite clear that those first believers "devoted themselves to the apostles' teaching and to fellowship, to the breaking of bread and to prayer." Let's examine each of these priorities and then notice an amazing omission in that list.

Priority #1: Biblical Doctrine

I have expressed my concern for the learning and enjoyment of biblical doctrine elsewhere.[6] But in our doctrinally-starved Christian sub-culture, where even some of Christianity's friends are slamming theology,[7] the early Christians remind us that they were first devoted to "the apostles' teaching." Without having a completed canon (collection of inspired books), the early Christians gave themselves to being taught by the apostles

---

[6] Please see my *DocTALK: A Fairly Serious Survey of All That Theological Stuff* (Fearn, Ross-shire, Great Britain: Christian Focus Publications, 2002). My *DocDEVOS: Ten-Minute Devotionals on the Great Doctrines of the Christian Faith* (Camp Hill, PA: Christian Publications, 2002) looks at three areas of doctrine in a kind of "Daily Bread" fashion. I have also written an in-depth treatment of the doctrine of hell entitled *The Other Side of the Good News* (Fearn, Ross-shire, Great Britain: Christian Focus Publications, 2003 reprint) and a popular discussion of the doctrine of heaven in my *Heaven: Thinking Now about Forever* (Camp Hill, PA: Christian Publications, 2002).

[7] For example, one writer says, "As the centuries have passed, the church has of necessity developed various doctrines, in most cases, to correct

what they needed to know so that they could do what Jesus wanted done. Imagine the following conversation taking place in the first century:

> "Say, Markus, did you know that the Apostle Paul is going to be speaking on the divinity of the Messiah tonight at our local synagogue?"
>
> "Really?", Markus says. "Do you want to get there early to get a good seat, Philip?"
>
> "Well, I just don't know. John Mark is over at the public square right now debating with some Stoics. And then Simon Peter is down by the lake (using his own boat as a floating pulpit, if you can believe it!) giving a lecture on the meaning of 'Upon this rock I will build my church....'"
>
> "So, which apostle are you going to go and listen to, Philip?"
>
> "Oh, I'm not sure, Markus. Maybe I'll just stay home tonight and read over my copy of Habakkuk again."

The early Christians had the Old Testament and perhaps some of Paul's epistles, but they had what we don't have today: the Apostles themselves! They could sit under the teaching of those who had been discipled by none other than the Lord Jesus Christ Himself!

When we read that the early Christians were devoted to the apostles' teaching, we are being reminded that they cared about *truth*. They wanted to know God's view of the world, of sin, of judgment, of His love in sending His Son, of His

---

tendencies toward gross misunderstandings of the essential Christian faith. However, as the centuries pass, the bulk of doctrines accumulates, like a tugboat taking barge after barge in tow as it moves upriver, and eventually, the weight of the barges plus the strength of the opposing current makes progress impossible" (Brian D. McLaren's *More Ready Than You Realize: Evangelism as Dance in the Postmodern Matrix* [Zondervan, 2002] p. 33). In the same book McLaren says, "This wonderful new situation, where the simple and basic elements of our faith suddenly become magical and valuable again, explains why I find theological quibbling over theological esoterica in such bad taste and such a sad, if not downright wicked, waste of time" (p. 95).

plans for believers and for the world, of the promised coming of the Holy Spirit, of how they ought to behave themselves in a culture which advocated either too many gods or none at all. They wanted to be prepared to be faithful witnesses of the truth in an environment which denied truth's existence or minimized its importance. In short, they wanted to know and to be what *we* ought to know and be: whole-hearted followers of the Way.

Priority #2: A Focus on Fellowship
We have discussed the need for Christian friendship at the beginning of this chapter. Here we want to emphasize that fellowship involves what we have in common *in Christ*. We must learn in our churches to tolerate and respect differences of opinion in areas such as politics, sports team affiliations, musical preferences, and even translations of the Scriptures. The unity of the local church does not necessitate uniformity. This means that when it comes to distinctive areas of doctrine, we must not all believe exactly the same thing as each other. Of course, one man's "distinctive" is another man's "essential," and focusing on the major truths which unite us will not be easy. When it comes to math, some of us Christians do division and subtraction much better than we do addition and multiplication! But we must guard our unity in the fundamentals of the Christian faith without compromise. And we must protect our right to hold different opinions on the distinctives without resorting to compulsion to conformity.

We need *fellowship* in the Body. We must spend time with each other, doing the sometimes hard work of developing relationships with one another, and talking about what we have in common in Christ. My unsaved tennis buddies actually use the term "fellowship" after a match, meaning that they're going to spend time standing around, drinking beer and talking about life.

I heard of one church where the janitor was always rushing people out of the sanctuary so that he could turn off the lights and lock up. If I were in leadership in that church,

I would fire him in a Donald-Trump-New-York minute! One sign of a healthy church is how *slowly* people actually leave the building when the formal church service is over. If they linger and talk in twos and threes, there's some serious fellowship going on.

One way to encourage fellowship in the things we have in common in Christ is to use small groups to discuss the topic of Sunday's sermon either before it gets preached (which will really keep the pastor or preacher on his toes!) or after it is given (which will test how well people were listening). Either way, there is a focus upon and discussion of the important truths which bind us together as believers.

Priority #3: What about Worship?

We learn from Acts 2:42 that the early Christians devoted themselves to "the breaking of bread." This expression could refer simply to the sharing of a common meal together, but that would seem to repeat the idea of fellowship. The early believers practiced the Agape feast which archeologists tell us was the precursor to our pot-luck church dinners (I think they have uncovered the clay equivalent of a Tupperware casserole dish). Christians shared a common meal, fellowshipped over the things they had in common in Christ, then someone would make a smooth transition and bring out bread and wine so they could celebrate the Lord's Supper together. Remembering the Lord's death until His return was one primary form of *worship* for the early Christians.

I grew up in a tradition which has very few distinguishing characteristics. The "Open Brethren" celebrate a weekly Lord's Supper, usually by a separate service dedicated to following the instructions given by the Lord Jesus in Luke 22 and repeated by the Apostle Paul in 1 Corinthians 11. That weekly service typically is not led by a minister. The men of the congregation are encouraged to come to that service prepared to share a Scripture or lead the congregation in a hymn which focuses on the sacrificial death of Christ for us. Some Brethren celebrations of the Lord's Supper are painful (for example, when there are long periods of silence[8] because the men have not prepared themselves to lead in worship, or one brother in particular waxes long on some pet doctrine, or the singing, often a capella, is so bad it would shatter a paper cup). Most I have found are encouraging and meaningful. There are many ways to worship the Lord. "The breaking of the bread" was a reminder to the believing community of the sacrifice the Son of God gave that we might be forgiven and worship God "in the beauty of holiness" (Ps. 29:2).

Priority #4: Passionate about Prayer

This fourth priority makes me extremely uncomfortable. I am not a prayer warrior. I am not a prayer conscientious objector. I am not even a prayer pacifist. I would classify myself as a pathetic, prayerless Christian who has much to learn – and much more to put into practice – about prayer.

When I was a first-year Bible college student, one of my professors gave a wonderful lecture on the Christian discipline of prayer. He was not a real approachable teacher, but I gathered my courage about me, caught up to him after class, and said, "Mr. __, I really appreciate what you said about prayer. In fact, I'm going right over to the bookstore and buy a large spiral notebook and I'm gonna' start studying all the prayers of the Bible from Genesis to Revelation!" He looked at me and said, "Hmmpf. I think you'd be better off just *praying*." And then he walked off. But he was right.

Why do I find prayer so difficult? Part of my problem is that prayer *seems* to me to be passive, a last resort alternative, the farthest thing from being proactive that I can think of. Maybe I *do* need to study biblical prayers, for I would soon learn that the prayers of God's people have stopped the rain (Elijah,

---

[8] Garrison Keillor, who himself grew up in a Brethren home, humorously describes the celebration of the Lord's Supper in his book *Lake Wobegon Days*. I listen to "Prairie Home Companion," Keillor's radio program, with mixed emotions. He is an incredibly gifted writer and humorist, but I lament the frequently risque and mocking aspects of some of his skits. In my opinion, I wish he were more "solid" in his Christian commitment.

James 5:17-18), opened prison doors (Peter, Acts 12:12ff), prevented God from wiping out a nation (Moses, Num. 11:1-3; 21:7; Deut. 9:23-29), kept God from dispensing justice to some incredibly foolish counselors (Job 42:7-9), etc.

If I look at prayer as speaking with my Best Friend, I become comfortable and ready to share my deepest secrets with Him. If I look at prayer as passing on my burden for a lost loved one, I find relief and assurance that He loves my unsaved relative more than I ever could. If I look at prayer as a reporting in for duty, I find that I become submissive to His guidance and ready to get into the battle. If I look at prayer as the means by which my life receives order and calmness, I find its effects far better than any medication our overdosed world can sell over the counter or by prescription. If I look at prayer as a primary vehicle of praising God, then I can do what ought always to be done: worship the One who gave His Son for my sins.

My problem, and yours too I suspect, is that I look at prayer wrongly. I either view it in a cosmic vending machine way (we insert prayers as if they were coins, pull the handle, and wait for God to deliver our selection), or in a monastic grit-your-teeth discipline way (we pray because God commands us to – that's all the reason we need), or as something religious to do when all our efforts at solving a problem have had little success ("Well, we'd better call God into this mess! We've done everything humanly possible!"). We seem to have God on speed dial, but His only number is 911.

When I fail to spend significant time conversing with the God I cannot see, part of my problem may be that I am walking by *sight*, and not by faith! The Christian life demands that we talk to Someone we cannot see, Someone who normally will not audibly speak back to us, Someone whom we must believe is *there*, especially when all evidences of His presence seem to be missing. We are to walk by faith, meaning that we take His promises in His written Word seriously. His Word says, "This is the confidence we have in approaching God: that if we ask anything according to his will, he hears us. And if we know that he hears us – whatever we ask – we know that we have what we asked of him" (1 John 5:14-15). I either believe that passage of His Word – or I don't.

Can we talk? Sometimes my problem is that I don't believe. I don't always believe that He has my best interests at heart. I don't always believe that He cares about my needs. I don't always believe that He answers my prayers. I don't always believe that prayer *works*. But in my saner moments, I must acknowledge that unbelief is sin, that I had better be careful in how I define "my best interests," that I often don't have a clue about how my "needs" ought to be met (or even what my real needs are), that I am sometimes so out of it spiritually that I wouldn't know an answer to prayer if it came up and bit me on my....

The first Century Christians devoted themselves to prayer. They gave themselves to systematic, strategic, heart-changing, energizing communication with the Creator. Prayer is God's gift to straighten out a messed-up Christian like me. What do you think? Am I alone in this struggle?

An Amazing Omission

In our brief examination of Acts 2:42 we have seen that the early Christians devoted themselves to (1) the apostles' teaching; (2) fellowship; (3) worship; and (4) prayer. But what about **evangelism**?! What about fulfilling the Great Commission (Matt. 28:19-20)? What about sharing the gospel with the lost?

Reading past Acts 2:42 we learn that

> [43]Everyone was filled with awe at the many wonders and miraculous signs done by the apostles. [44]All the believers were together and had everything in common. [45]They sold property and possessions to give to anyone who had need. [46]Every day they continued to meet together in the temple courts. They broke bread in their homes and ate together with glad and sincere hearts, [47]praising God and enjoying the favor of all the people. And the Lord added to their number daily those who were being saved.

God gave miraculous signs to the early church to confirm their message. And the believers practiced sharing their material goods with one another. They so connected with one another that every day they met together for common meals and worship. Their corporate prayer caused them to be held in high regard by those who looked on the Christian community. Then we read that "the Lord added to their number daily those who were being saved" (v. 47). Perhaps our failure to see others come to faith in Christ may well be because they don't see our lives being changed by God's grace and our corporate fellowship as something attractive. What they often see is our Christian churches just keeping the religious machinery humming along, going through the sanctified motions, doing the "Christian thing" without ever drawing closer to the family of God. Is it any wonder that the world isn't interested?[9]

The development of strong, trusting relationships with other believers is the place to start. They are God's instrument for making you and me holy. We need the kinds of friends Dinah Maria Mulock Craik described when she wrote:

Oh, the comfort, the inexpressible comfort, of feeling safe with a person; having neither to weigh thoughts nor measure words, but to pour them all out just as they are, chaff and grain together, knowing that a faithful hand will take and sift them, keep what is worth keeping, and then, with the breath of kindness, blow the rest away.[10]

We must get back to the four priorities of the early church. Then the world around us will sit up and take notice.

---

[9] Christian growth and evangelism are closely connected to one another. As Rick Warren says, "The church that doesn't want to grow is saying to the world, 'You can go to hell.'" (*The Purpose-Driven Life*, p. 295). A heart burdened for the lost is a healthy heart.

[10] *A Life for a Life* (London: Collins' Clear Type Press, 1900). Often misattributed to George Eliot. Accessed at GEONius.com. 11 May, 2004.

PART 4

Chapter 10

"The Believer's Attitudes"

"The longer I live the more I realize the impact of attitude on life. Attitude, to me, is more important than facts. It is more important than the past, than education, than money, than circumstances, than failures, than successes, than what other people think or say or do. It is more important than appearances, giftedness or skill. It will make or break a company ... a church ... a home. The remarkable thing is, we have a choice every day regarding the Attitude we will embrace for that day. We cannot change our past ... we cannot change the fact that people will act in a certain way ... we cannot change the inevitable. The only thing we can do is play on the one string we have, and that is our Attitude. I am convinced that life is 10 percent what happens to me and 90 percent how I react to it. And so it is with you ... we are in charge of our Attitudes." (Chuck Swindoll)

"In your relationships with one another, have the same attitude of mind Christ Jesus had:

⁶Who, being in very nature God, did not consider equality with God something to be used to his own advantage; ⁷rather he made

himself nothing by taking the very nature of a servant, being made in human likeness. [8]And being found in appearance as a human being, he humbled himself by becoming obedient to death – even death on a cross!" (Phil. 2).

How should the believer in Jesus Christ approach each new day? I'm sure, like me, you've seen some Christians who come across like they've been baptized in lemon juice. Others do not seem to be at all enthused about the Christian life. Friedrich Nietzsche said, "If you want me to believe in your Redeemer, you're going to have to look a lot more redeemed."

When we speak about attitude, we are dealing with our inner spirit, how we approach life, the expectations and responses to circumstances which ought to mark the believer. Does the world see a noticeable difference in how the Christian responds in the world versus how the unbeliever responds? We will later look at 1 Peter 3 on this crucial issue.

Granted, we all have different personalities. But I am not arguing that we all become like me, rather that we all respond to life and all it throws our way with godliness. Within our own personalities (which, after all, ought to be in the process of becoming like Christ's), we face and engage the challenges of life in ways which show Christ-like character, demonstrate God-honoring kindness and patience, and set forth before a watching world something more than merely the fact that we are "religious."

Let's Get Personal

But let's discuss the issue of *personality* for a moment. My wife (who is a high school guidance counselor) describes my personality as an "I-S-T-J." These letters come from the Meyers-Briggs Personality Test (the only Briggs I knew before my test was Briggs & Stratton, famous maker of lawnmower engines). She says that my personality is *Introverted, Sensing, Thinking, Judging*. My daughter (who is pursuing a Master's degree in clinical counseling) concurs and says that I get worn out around people, enjoy my time alone, and avoid intrusion and confusion (I'm *introverted*). She says that I am *sensing* which means that I use all my five senses, and that I prefer predictability and the status quo. I am *thinking* in the sense that I pursue objective values and appreciate theory and principles and like to avoid inconsistency and ignorance while seeking conceptual harmony, justice, and truth. I am *judging* in the sense that my primary arena is my will, for I like to take the initiative in moral issues, and can tend toward perfectionism. [Wow! Did I word all that right? Maybe I should edit that for the twelfth time?].

No wonder I'm *introverted!* I have two women who are either counselors or counselors-in-training. They analyze my every move, ambush me with Rohrshach tests, and Scotch-tape advertisements for psychotropic drugs in my *Sports Illustrated.* They say that I am *sensing.* I'm sensing that I am outnumbered by those who want to "improve" me and help me get in touch with my inner child (who is actually at recess and would prefer to be left alone, thank you). I'm told that I'm *thinking.* I guess that means that I ponder how the women in my life will re-engineer me with their psychological expertise. And they tell me that I'm *judging.* I guess that means that I am quick to confess that if there's a problem in the family, I'm probably the one who is most likely at fault! No wonder I try to avoid intrusion and confusion.

The Christian who says, "I'm just not a very happy person. I don't have to be joyful, do I?" The answer is – well, what does the Bible say about being joyful? The follower of Christ who says, "I'm a suspicious person by nature. I find trusting others very difficult," is not off the hook in terms of growing in trust toward the Lord and others.

We all have different personalities, and that makes the Body of Christ *interesting!* But within the context of our individual personalities, we need to have godly, Christ-like, biblical attitudes as we face life.[1] Five such attitudes occur to me from Scripture.

---

[1] Lewis put it as follows: "... the real problem of the Christian life comes where people do not usually look for it. It comes the very moment you wake up each morning. All your wishes and hopes for the day rush at you like wild

A Heart That Is Thankful

The first attitude which should characterize all believers in Christ is that of a thankful heart. We will draw several challenges from three passages dealing with a thankful heart.

The first passage is Colossians 3:15 where Paul says, "Let the peace of Christ rule in your hearts, since as members of one body you were called to peace. And be thankful." Please note how the peace of Christ and a thankful heart are connected with one another. I can't have peace if I am ungrateful. In fact, an ungrateful, peaceful Christian is a contradiction in terms.

This text also implies that letting Christ's peace rule in my heart and being thankful are *choices* that I make! We sometimes try to explain away the power of our choices, but *we become the people we choose to be.* As we noticed in our chapter on the will (Ch. 5), it is God's will that we become like Christ, and that involves making daily decisions to follow Him. Is it not true that we become more of the people we ought to be not by focusing on ourselves, but by giving ourselves to others? Daniel Yankelovich puts it this way:

> By concentrating day and night on your feelings, potentials, needs, wants and desires, and by learning to assert them more freely, you do not become a freer, more spontaneous, more creative self; you become a narrower, more self-centered, more isolated one. You do not grow, you shrink.[2]

Having a thankful heart involves doing a kind of spiritual inventory of God's blessings and taking the time to praise Him for His goodness to you.

Such a thankful heart does not just thank God, but reaches out to God's people in encouragement. What differences would

---

animals. And the first job each morning consists simply in shoving them all back; in listening to that other voice, taking that other point of view, letting that other larger, stronger, quieter life come flowing in. And so on, all day. Standing back from all your natural fussings and frettings; coming in out of the wind." (Lewis, *Mere Christianity*, Bk. IV, Ch. 8, pp. 168-169).

[2] Daniel Yankelovich, *New Rules: Searching for Self-Fulfillment in a World Turned Upside Down* (New York: Random House, 1981), p. 242.

it make if we regularly thanked other believers for their impact on our lives, for the ways in which they build up the Body of Christ, for their role in helping *us*?!

Our second text having to do with a heart that is thankful is Colossians 4:2 which says, "Devote yourselves to prayer, being watchful and thankful." Thankfulness is not an automatic characteristic of the Christian. It involves devotion. That devotion applies to three areas of life: (1) prayer; (2) watchfulness; and (3) thankfulness. Why do we need to be *devoted* to these three issues? Well, we do not naturally pray. We are not naturally vigilant. And we are not naturally thankful.

How do these three qualities relate to one another? Could it not be said that if I am in continuous, concentrated communication with my Lord, I will take life more seriously? I will watch for opportunities to serve Him, to submit to Him, and to share Him with others. And if I want to be a thankful Christian, I need to spend time in prayer. I dare not treat prayer as an afterthought, or as a last resort, or as a passive response to life's challenges!

C. S. Lewis gets to the heart of real prayer in his *Screwtape Letters*. As Screwtape writes his nephew demon Wormwood about how to trip up Christians, he says about prayer,

> If you examine the object to which he is attending, you will find that it is a composite object containing many quite ridiculous ingredients.... For if he ever comes to make the distinction, if ever he consciously directs his prayers "Not to what I think thou art but to what thou knowest thyself to be," our situation is, for the moment, desperate. Once all his thoughts and images have been flung aside or, if retained, retained with a full recognition of their merely subjective nature, and the man trusts himself to the completely real, external, invisible Presence, there with him in the room and never knowable by him as he is known by it – why, then it is that the incalculable may occur.[3]

---

[3] C. S. Lewis, *Screwtape Letters*, (New York: MacMillan, 25th printing, 1977), p. 22.

Our third passage on this attitude of a heart that is thankful is that of Hebrews 12:28-29 which says, "Therefore, since we are receiving a kingdom that cannot be shaken, let us be thankful, and so worship God acceptably with reverence and awe, for our 'God is a consuming fire.'" Notice that our thankfulness transcends this finite life. We are going to receive an eternal kingdom! Also notice that the level of our gratitude reveals our heart of worship: "Let us be thankful, and so worship...." Why does our worship sometimes seem so weak, so minimal? Well, we may not be so sure that our worship matters to the Lord. We might forget that God wants our hearts and not just our ceremonies. It is not beyond us to be like the Pharisee in Luke 18. There we read:

> [9]To some who were confident of their own righteousness and looked down on everyone else, Jesus told this parable: [10]"Two men went up to the temple to pray, one a Pharisee and the other a tax collector. [11]The Pharisee stood by himself and prayed: 'God, I thank you that I am not like other people – robbers, evildoers, adulterers – or even like this tax collector. [12]I fast twice a week and give a tenth of all I get.' [13]"But the tax collector stood at a distance. He would not even look up to heaven, but beat his breast and said, 'God, have mercy on me, a sinner.' [14]"I tell you that this man, rather than the other, went home justified before God. For all those who exalt themselves will be humbled, and those who humble themselves will be exalted."

Someone has said about the Pharisee's prayer that "Never were words of 'thankfulness' uttered so proudly and self-righteously!" The Pharisee represents those who are "confident of their own righteousness" and who "look down on everyone else." His prayer begins with his separating himself from others (especially "this tax collector"), runs through a laundry list of *his* religious acts of merit, and contains no request for anything from God.[4] The tax collector, on the other hand, "stood at

---

[4] Perhaps you heard the story of the young preacher at a Bible conference who was asked to open the meetings in prayer. He began, "O Thou Great

a distance", would not even look up to heaven, but beat his breast in contrition before the Lord. His prayer is eloquent in its economy of words (he prays using just seven words; the Pharisee uses thirty-three words) and honest in its acknowledgment of his need for mercy.

I'm reminded of the story of the young seminarian home for summer vacation who was asked to pray in his local church. He prayed a profound prayer, surveying most of the sixty-six books of the Bible and richly peppering his prayer with profound theological insights. After the church service, an elderly man approached him and said, "Son, that was the most eloquent prayer..." The young man's shirt buttons were ready to pop off as he listened ... "... offered to *people!*"

If I have a heart that is thankful, Christ's peace will rule in my heart, I will be devoted to watchful and thankful prayer, and my worship of the Lord will be acceptable and filled with awe.

A Mind That Is Trusting

A second attitude that should characterize the believer is that of a mind that is trusting. It is vital to point out that trusting is not the same as *gullibility*. Years ago a gospel tract came out supposedly giving the "testimony" of the conversion of Charles Darwin on his deathbed. Entitled "Darwin's Confession,"[5] it was edited by the respected Bible teacher Oswald J. Smith. The tract claims that Darwin "in the closing days of his life ... returned to his faith in the Bible." The story is that Lady Hope, a wonderful English Christian, was "often at his bedside before he died." She says he was reading the book of Hebrews, and said with agony, "I was a young man with unformed ideas.... People made a religion of [my ideas]." Darwin reportedly asked Lady Hope to speak to the servants and neighbors of Christ

---

Omnipotent, Omnipresence Spirit Who permeates our existence...." An elderly pastor interrupted him and said, "Why don't you call Him 'Father,' and *ask Him for something!*"

[5] Published by Tract Evangelistic Crusade, P.O. Box 998, Zip 85220, Apache Junction, Ariz.

Jesus "and His salvation." The tract then says that according to Richard Wurmbrand, "Darwin denied that his theories contradicted the Christian Faith. As a believer he willed his fortune to Christian Missions." The only problem with this gospel tract is that it isn't true.

Lady Hope shared her experience with the evangelist D. L. Moody and said that Darwin confessed, "How I wish I had not expressed my theory of evolution as I have done." She related how Darwin wanted to share the gospel with others. Lady Hope's story spread (with the help of Moody). Darwin's daughter Henrietta exposed the falseness of her father's "conversion" in 1922, saying,

> Lady Hope was not present during his last illness, or any illness. I believe he never even saw her, but in any case she had no influence over him in any department of thought or belief. He never recanted any of his scientific views, either then or earlier. We think the story of his conversion was fabricated in the U.S.A.... The whole story has no foundation whatever.[6]

Our problem with such stories is that we *want* them to be true. But such bogus stories do not help the Christian cause. We are not to be gullible. Nor are we to allow our hearts to be captured by anxiety.

We read in John 14:1 that Jesus said to His disciples: "Do not let your hearts be troubled. Trust in God; trust also in me." If we examine the previous chapter of John, we find that the disciples had every reason to panic. Jesus had just predicted that one of the disciples would betray Him and that all of the disciples would forsake Him! Jesus then commands His followers: "Stop letting your hearts be troubled." The Greek behind that verse indicates that their hearts were already anxious and Jesus commands them not to continue in that emotional state. What power did Jesus have to command the abandonment of anxiety? The answer

---

[6] Internet search under "Darwin's conversion."

is in His commandment: "Trust in God; trust also in me." Jesus is claiming equality with God; He is claiming divinity. He is saying, "The faith that you should already have in God – You should place in *me!*" The deity of the Lord Jesus Christ is the remedy to the disciples' panic. He has all things under control. His plans will be accomplished, despite the wholesale abandonment of Him by His followers and the particular betrayal by Judas.

The fact is that we are trusting in none other than God Himself when we trust in the Lord Jesus Christ! We read in Psalm 147 that God's "pleasure is not in the strength of the horse, nor his delight in the legs of a man; the Lord delights in those who fear him, who put their hope in his unfailing love" (vv. 10-11).

A second passage that challenges us to have a mind that is trusting is the well-known text of Proverbs 3:5-6 which says, "Trust in the Lord with all your heart – Lean not unto your own understanding. In all your ways acknowledge Him and He will direct your paths."

We are always faced with the choice: Do I choose to trust Him or myself? Trusting Him does not mean that I don't use my understanding; it means that I do not absolutely and finally stake my well-being on my evaluation of circumstances and situations. We Christians are not to live in such a way that people say of us when we walk by, "Well, there goes Gullible's Travels!" Christians are to be wise. We are not to be known as the doofuses of the world. Scripture challenges us to "test [all prophecies], hold on to what is good, reject whatever is harmful" (1 Thess. 5:21-22).

But don't we read in 1 Corinthians 13 that "love believes all things"? Yes, but the context of that statement is that love is not self-seeking; it keeps no record of wrong-doing. This does not mean that Christian love is undiscerning. Perhaps the idea is that true love gives the other the benefit of the doubt. Christians are to be "wise as serpents, but gentle as doves," we read in Matthew 10:16. We don't read that we are to be as dumb as an ox or as senseless as a turkey (I'm told that if a turkey is left outside in the rain, he will look up into the sky until he drowns!).[7]

What does it mean to "trust" the Lord? It certainly means believing what He tells me in His Word, the Bible. How easily we Christians defend the inerrancy of the Bible but do not appear to believe what it says. Defending its nature without believing its content is like sitting at a gourmet meal without picking up your salad fork. We are to believe what the Lord tells us.

Has it ever occurred to you that the Lord has no "perspective," no "opinion" of our circumstances? What the Lord declares is *reality!* He does not have a "view"; He knows and declares only *the truth.* And we are to believe Him.

Why do we Christians find it so hard to trust Him with our minds? It may be that we have not submitted our minds to His Lordship. It may also be that our perception of reality seems immediate and direct. God's declaration of reality demands that we study Scripture (so that we do not misinterpret it), wait on His Spirit for guidance (which is frequently a very difficult thing to do), and submit to the unknown (which is part of what it means to "walk by faith", 2 Cor. 5:7).[8]

When we insist that one of the attitudes that ought to mark the believer is a mind that is trusting, we are not advocating

---

[7] One turkey site on the internet [I really looked this up] says that "turkeys are extremely curious creatures by nature. Groups of domesticated turkey have been seen standing in the rain with their beaks pointed straight up toward the sky. What are they doing? According to poultry research at the University of Illinois, it is unclear. Some turkey experts speculate that these birds are curiously looking at raindrops falling from the sky. Or could they be attempting to get a drink of water? Unknown. Nevertheless, turkeys have been known to actually drown in this position. Since their nostrils are tiny oval-shaped openings which are alongside their beaks, they make the perfect receptacle for the falling rain. Not having enough sense to come in out of the rain may be an understatement in this situation." http://www.urbanext.uiuc.edu/

[8] To the watching world, the Christian often appears to be one who is "seeing things," things that aren't there. He appears as one who is "hearing things," voices that don't exist. In speaking of relating to secularists, Taylor

intellectual suicide. We read in Isaiah 1:18, "'Come now, let us reason together,' says the Lord. 'Though your sins are like scarlet, they shall be as white as snow; though they are red like crimson, they shall be like wool.'" I understand that when Jimmy Carter was President, he once said about First Lady Rosalynn Carter: "I've never won an argument with her; and the only times I thought I had, I found out the argument wasn't over yet." The Lord wants us to "reason" with Him, but not at the expense of our trusting Him!

Let's take a brief look at our third passage on having a mind that is trusting. Romans 15:13 says, "May the God of hope fill you with all joy and peace as you trust in him, so that you may overflow with hope by the power of the Holy Spirit." How do I as a Christian get joy and peace? According to this text, they come to me as I "trust in Him." Not trusting in Him brings unhappiness, anxiety, hopelessness, lack of power, etc. If I am not trusting in Him, my life should not be happy or joyful, my heart should not be at peace, and my mind should not be confident in hope. The fact that some of those conditions might be true in my life does not necessary mean that I am trusting in Him, for each can be manufactured or faked.

When believers around us do not seem to have joy, or peace, or hope, perhaps it is because we have not prayed this type of prayer for them. We're in this Christian life thing together, and we need to pray such meaty prayers for one another.

A Conscience That Is Clear Before the Lord
We've seen that we are to be in control of the attitudes we have as we deal with life and all it throws at us. The believer should be marked by a heart that is thankful and a mind that is trusting. Please notice that a third attitude should be true of

---

says, "The language of my innermost being is gibberish to their ears — literally nonsense. I see things where they are sure that nothing exists to be seen. I hear things where for them is only empty silence" (Daniel Taylor, *The Myth of Certainty: The Reflective Christian and the Risk of Commitment* [Grand Rapids: Zondervan edition, 1992], p. 47).

every Christian (regardless of individual personality): He or she should have a conscience which is clear before the Lord. Paul declares in Acts 24, "I strive always to keep my conscience clear, before God and all people" (v. 16).

The context of that statement is that Paul is on trial before Felix, being accused of "stirring up riots among the Jews all over the world" (v. 5), being a ringleader of the Nazarene sect and trying to desecrate the temple (v. 6). Paul's response is that he gladly makes his defense (v. 10) before Felix, is not guilty of any of the charges made against him, and strives always to keep his conscience clear before God and man (v. 16). As a result of Paul's defense, Felix, "who was well acquainted with the Way," adjourned the proceedings against Paul (v. 22). Felix and his wife Drusilla listened to Paul speak about his faith in Christ. Paul's discourse on righteousness, self-control, and the judgment to come apparently made Felix nervous and he dismissed Paul with the words, "When I find it convenient, I will send for you" (v. 25). Hoping for a bribe from Paul, Felix frequently sent for him and talked with him over a period of two years. Paul lived his life in such a way that his conscience was clear before God and man. So should we all live.

I understand that the Internal Revenue Service years ago received the following letter:

"Dear Sirs: I cheated on my income tax two years ago and my conscience has been tormenting me. Therefore, I am enclosing a check for $100.

Sincerely,
Tom Smith

P.S. If my conscience continues to trouble me, I will send you the rest of the money that I owe you."

How should the conscience be defined? H. L. Mencken said that "Conscience is the inner voice which warns us that someone may be looking." Some say it is the faculty by which we apprehend the will of God, designed to govern our lives. Others describe it as the sense of guiltiness before God. Another says it is that process of thought which distinguishes what it considers morally good or bad. A child was once asked the question, "What is the difference between 'conscious' and your 'conscience'?" He said, "Your 'conscience' hurts when you do something wrong and makes you 'conscious' of it." Or as another said, "'Conscious' is being aware of something; 'conscience' is wishing you weren't." "A clear conscience," says one wag, "is usually the sign of a bad memory."

We were made in God's image and have an innate (built-in) sense of right and wrong. Carl Jung helpfully says that "Through pride we are ever deceiving ourselves. But deep down below the surface of the average conscience a still, small voice says to us, 'Something is out of tune.'"[9] If reputation is how we appear to others, conscience is the generally reliable measurement of how we appear to ourselves.

C. S. Lewis affirms the universality of the conscience when he writes,

> [I want to make] two points: first, that human beings, all over the earth, have this curious idea that they ought to behave in a certain way, and cannot get rid of it. Secondly, that they do not in fact behave in that way. They know the law of Nature; they break it. These two facts are the foundation of all clear thinking about ourselves and the universe we live in.[10]

We have often heard the adage (popularized by that great "theologian" Jiminy Cricket), "Let your conscience be your guide." For many situations in life, that is good advice. However, the conscience is not perfect. Sometimes it is sensitive to things that are neither right nor wrong in themselves. One example might be of a young man who is addicted to gambling on baseball games (I'm not thinking of Pete Rose here). He gets

[9] Carl Jung, *Collected Works of C. G. Jung* (Princeton University Press, 1977), vol. 17, Paragraph 80, p. 40.

[10] C. S. Lewis, *Mere Christianity*, Bk. I, Ch. 1, p. 21.

saved and thinks that even attending baseball games is a sin. His conscience is overly sensitive to something that is neither right nor wrong in itself.

Sometimes the conscience is insensitive to things that are clearly right or wrong in Scripture. Here are some examples that come to my mind: We are commanded to share the gospel with others. Does your conscience hurt you when you make no progress in that area of Christian growth? Some Christians haven't given a thought to the use of well-written gospel tracts. They can be given to the young man who serves you at McDonald's or the woman who checks your water meter, or the toll-booth collector on the highway.[11]

It is clear from the Word of God that we are to study the Bible for ourselves. Do you feel guilty when you go for days or months at a time without investing significant energy in pouring over the Scriptures? Most Christians seem addicted to what I call a spoon-feeding frenzy: we let others do our Bible study for us and we just passively listen and take in what *they* have discovered from the Word.

The Bible is crystal clear that we are to pray for the leaders of our government. Is that a regular habit in your life? We are quick to complain when taxes are raised, when wars are fought (which we may or may not agree with), when programs are instituted or cut. But do we pray for those whom God has placed in positions of authority over us, as Romans 13 commands us? Can you even name the senators and congressmen from your state?

You may have heard the story about the two congressmen who were arguing about who was the more religious. Congressman Smith said, "Congressman Jones, you claim to be so religious. I'll bet fifty dollars you don't even know the Lord's Prayer!" "Of course I do," Congressman Jones said. "Then prove it!"

---

[11] By the way, I'm working on this area of my life. I highly recommend the American Tract Society. They've got some terrific gospel tracts. I prefer the cartoon ones by my friend Ron Wheeler (who did the cartoons in both *DocTALK* and *DocWALK*), such as "Then What?" and "How Do I Get to Heaven from Here?"

challenged Congressman Smith. "Now I lay me down to sleep, I pray the Lord my soul to keep, If I should die before I wake, I pray the Lord my soul to take!", said Congressman Jones. "I don't believe it!", Congressman Smith said as he handed over the fifty dollars, "You *do* know the Lord's Prayer!" We need to pray for those in positions of leadership over us – and feel guilty if we don't.

The Bible frequently sets forth the challenge for us to care for the poor in the world. How easily we Christians get wrapped up in our Western materialism and think only of ourselves, our families, our country, and not do anything to help the poor. We can become infected by a cynicism which says of relief agencies, "Well, they will probably waste our money and none of it will get to the needy. They're all a bunch of crooks!" We may look at the man on the exit ramp of the highway who holds up a sign saying, "I'm hungry. Please help. God bless," and think to ourselves, "If he would only get a job!" Do we feel guilty when we do nothing to help those less fortunate than ourselves? We can easily contribute to scholarships for Christian camps to pay for a week for poor children, volunteer to work at a pregnancy crisis center, or collect for the Red Cross. But we frequently don't – and we don't feel badly about it.

Am I sensitive to sin in my life? If I really believe that God is holy and that sin hurts me and grieves Him, why am I often so unconcerned about sin which I commit? Perhaps our doctrine of salvation needs to re-discover the truth of confessing and forsaking our sins. I once spoke at a church where I passed out 3x5 index cards at the beginning of the service. I said, "Now, I don't want you to write down your name, or the specific nature of the sin, but I want you to write down the date when you last confessed a known sin. Ready? Go!" I collected the cards. Some people wrote down, "This morning," or "Last week." But I got back a number of cards that read, "The last time I confessed a known sin was back when I got saved. Let's see, that was in December of 1943." Needless to say, my sermon focused on 1 John 1:9!

The Apostle Paul writes in 1 Corinthians 4:4: "My conscience is clear, but that does not make me innocent. It is the Lord who judges me." Our consciences are not to be our final guide, but, molded by the Word of God, they can be a tremendous help in sensitizing us to the emphases of Scripture. Mark Twain once said, "Good friends, good books and a sleepy conscience: this is the ideal life." Well, we've got the best Book, and we can develop good friends in the family of God. But we must have *awake* consciences that are clear before God and man.[12]

A Spirit Which Is Willing to Be Taught

With what attitude did you begin today? Could observers say that you seemed to be marked by a heart that is thankful? Would they say that you give evidence of a mind that is trusting the Lord in the circumstances of life? Hidden from the sight of observers is the third attitude of a conscience that is clear before the Lord. That attitude might be harder to discern in another, but we know ourselves. The Christian life is not a going through the motions and just doing what needs to be done. It is not some legal affair where we try not to do bad things. It is a matter of the inner person; it concerns our character and our approach to the next twenty-four hours, to the next five minutes, to right now. Attitude determines action. What we are on the inside will manifest itself in the way we behave on the outside.

The fourth attitude required of all Christians (regardless of personality type) is that of a spirit which is willing to be taught. Three passages help us here: Acts 18:24-28; Ephesians 4:20-24; and, 2 Timothy 3:14-17.

In Acts 18 we read of a young man by the name of Apollos:

> [24]Meanwhile a Jew named Apollos, a native of Alexandria, came to Ephesus. He was a learned man, with a thorough knowledge of the Scriptures. [25]He had been instructed in the way of the Lord, and he spoke with great fervor and taught about Jesus accurately,

---

[12] A profitable study can be made of 1 Peter 3:13-17 which shows that the Christian is to "keep a clear conscience" as he "gives a reason for the hope" that he has in Christ.

though he knew only the baptism of John. [26]He began to speak boldly in the synagogue. When Priscilla and Aquila heard him, they invited him to their home and explained to him the way of God more adequately. [27]When Apollos wanted to go to Achaia, the believers encouraged him and wrote to the disciples there to welcome him. When he arrived, he was a great help to those who by grace had believed. [28]For he vigorously refuted the Jews in public debate, proving from the Scriptures that Jesus was the Messiah.

Please notice that the Bible does not put a premium on ignorance. Apollos was "a learned man" (the word means erudite). He had "a thorough knowledge of the Scriptures" (v. 24).

Can we talk? There are many ways in which we Christians fail to encourage learning. I have a "Calvin and Hobbes" cartoon in my files in which Calvin and Susie are waiting for the school bus. Calvin is grumpy and says, "I can't believe I'm here waiting to go to school. What happened to summer?" Susie says, "Gosh, I couldn't *wait* for today! Soon we'll be making new friends, learning all sorts of important things, and...." Calvin's look of astonishment as he stares at the top of Susie's head causes Susie to stop in mid-sentence and ask, "What's the matter with *you*?!" He says, "Your bangs do a good job of covering up the lobotomy stitches." Sometimes we act in the church as if becoming a Christian involves committing intellectual suicide. The late Paul Little said, "God did not perform a spiritual lobotomy on you when you got saved!"

Apollos was not only a learned man, but he put into practice what he knew. He "spoke with great fervor and taught about Jesus accurately" (v. 25). He "spoke boldly in the synagogue" (v. 26). But there were limits to Apollos' knowledge. Verse 25 tells us that he knew only the baptism of John. However, we learn in verse 26 that Apollos was *open to instruction.* Priscilla and Aquila took him home and "explained to him the way of God more adequately." This quality of a teachable spirit is critical, for we all have much growing to do in our knowledge and understanding of biblical truth. "I would like to learn from you," said the young man to the master teacher. "What would you like to learn from me?" said the teacher. "I do not yet know what I need to know." replied the younger. "You have answered perfectly!" said the teacher. "Come. Let us begin our first lesson."

Apollos' teachable spirit caused him to be "a great help to those who by grace had believed," we read in verse 27. How specifically was he "a great help"? We learn in verse 28 that he "vigorously refuted the Jews in public debate, proving from the Scriptures that Jesus was the Messiah." What a tremendous learning environment: to be engaged in concentrated evangelism, using the Word of God to prove the Messiahship of Jesus to unbelieving Jews! Perhaps we often don't seem marked by a teachable spirit because we're not in the battle for men's souls!

A second text that emphasizes a teachable spirit is that of Ephesians 4 where Paul writes,

> [20]That, however, is not the way of life you learned [21]when you heard about Christ and were taught in him in accordance with the truth that is in Jesus. [22]You were taught, with regard to your former way of life, to put off your old self, which is being corrupted by its deceitful desires; [23]to be made new in the attitude of your minds; [24]and to put on the new self, created to be like God in true righteousness and holiness.

Please notice that Christianity is a way of life which must be *learned*. That teaching involves putting off the old self (v. 22), being renewed in your mind (v. 23), and putting on the new self (v. 24). That scheme of putting off-being renewed-putting on drives our attention to the fact that the Christian life does not happen to us automatically. The normal expectation for ourselves and for our brothers and sisters in Christ is that we are striving to grow.

You may have heard the story of the seventh grade teacher who was having difficulty teaching her students. They were getting poor grades. She thought maybe they were under-achievers so she decided to look at their records. Reading their files, she found that they had IQs ranging from 145 to 170! Surprised and confident that they could do better, she went to the class and demanded that they try harder. Within two weeks, the students had turned around and were getting better grades. Another teacher noticed and asked what she had done to improve them. When she explained, the other teacher said, "Keep doing what you've been doing; but those weren't their IQ's, those were their locker numbers." Sometimes our expectations of ourselves and of each other are embarrassingly low.

Our third passage is found in 2 Timothy 3 which says,

[14]But as for you, continue in what you have learned and have become convinced of, because you know those from whom you learned it, [15]and how from infancy you have known the Holy Scriptures, which are able to make you wise for salvation through faith in Christ Jesus. [16]All Scripture is God-breathed and is useful for teaching, rebuking, correcting and training in righteousness, [17]so that all God's people may be thoroughly equipped for every good work.

From this text we learn there is a need to *continue* in what we have learned (v. 14), that we should highly value Christian training in our families, and that the Word of God is multi-faceted. It is useful for teaching, rebuking, correcting, and training in righteousness!.

Do you and I have a spirit that is willing to be taught? Then we will strive to know the Word of God. We will be open to others helping us. We will use our learning to share Christ with others. We will recognize that the Christian way of life must be learned. And we will submit ourselves to the Word which equips us.

A Self That Is Humble
The fifth and final attitude which we want to examine may be the most important of all. It's hard to say which is most vital to

the Christian: a heart that is thankful, a mind that is trusting, a conscience that is clear before the Lord, or a spirit which is teachable. All these attitudes (and more) ought to mark the serious believer in Christ.

However, there is an attitude which, in some way, underlies the others, and one with which we must be extremely careful lest we become prideful! And that is a self that is humble. The great "theologian" Benjamin Franklin said, "There is perhaps no one of our natural passions so hard to subdue as pride. Beat it down, stifle it, mortify it as much as one pleases, it is still alive. Even if I could conceive that I had completely overcome it, I should probably be proud of my humility." Someone asked, "Did you hear about the man who was awarded a trophy for humility? When he stepped up to the podium to receive it, they took it away from him!"

The Scriptures have much to say on humility. For example, the Apostle Paul describes worthy living in Ephesians 4 when he writes: "As a prisoner for the Lord, then, I urge you to live a life worthy of the calling you have received. [2]Be completely **humble** and gentle; be patient, bearing with one another in love. [3]Make every effort to keep the unity of the Spirit through the bond of peace." Jesus is our great model in humility. He said about Himself in Matthew 11: "Come to me, all you who are weary and burdened, and I will give you rest. [29]Take my yoke upon you and learn from me, for I am gentle and **humble** in heart, and you will find rest for your souls. [30]For my yoke is easy and my burden is light."

But what is humility? Norman Vincent Peale said, "Humble people don't think less of themselves ... they just think about themselves less." Biblically, humility is not exalting oneself; it is not putting oneself first; it is allowing others to honor you. Jesus tells a parable in Luke 14 which illustrates the attitude of humility:

[7]When he noticed how the guests picked the places of honor at the table, he told them this parable: [8]"When someone invites you to a wedding feast, do not take the place of honor, for a person

more distinguished than you may have been invited. [9]If so, the host who invited both of you will come and say to you, 'Give this person your seat.' Then, humiliated, you will have to take the least important place. [10]But when you are invited, take the lowest place, so that when your host comes, he will say to you, 'Friend, move up to a better place.' Then you will be honored in the presence of all the other guests. [11]For all those who exalt themselves will be humbled, and those who humble themselves will be exalted."

The point is clear. We let others exalt us. We do not presume to take places of honor which we do not deserve.

I have a confession to make. I recently attended a Davis Cup tennis match (featuring Andy Roddick and Mardy Fish) between the USA and the country of Belarus. The ticket I had was for the nose bleed section. I mean my seat was so high up the players looked like ants driving forehand volleys into each other's little ant tennis courts. So I tried to get a better seat. The better seat I wanted to get was in the media section, only fifteen feet from the players themselves! Wow. However, the events' gestapo lady asked me for my ticket (which was obviously not for the media section). Fortunately, she didn't throw me out of the stadium. She, and several others around her holding $350 tickets, just looked at me with that look that said, "The *nerve* of some people – trying to sneak into the media section!"

But the story has a happy ending. My friend Mike is *with the media!* And he came to my rescue. He said to the event's gestapo lady-person, "He is with me!" And she had to let me in. I was there when Andy Roddick hit a record-breaking 155 miles per hour serve! Being invited to a better seat is far superior than trying to sneakily grab one unnoticed.

Maybe my illustration isn't such a good one. It illustrates sneakiness, not pride. And the moral of my story was not the importance of humility, but the helpfulness of having a friend in the media. But there is a similarity: I got to sit in a better seat because someone other than myself invited me there.

Martin Luther in one memorable passage addresses the issue of humility. He wrote:

If ... you feel and are inclined to think you have made it, flattering yourself with your own little books, teaching, or writing ... if you perhaps look for praise, and would sulk or quit what you are doing if you did not get it – if you are of that stripe, dear friend, then take yourself by the ears, and if you do this in the right way you will find a beautiful pair of big, long, shaggy donkey ears....[13]

The Bible teaches that the believer is to dress himself in humility. First Peter 5 states, "In the same way, you who are younger, submit yourselves to your elders. All of you, clothe yourselves with **humility** toward one another, because, 'God opposes the proud but shows favor to the **humble** and oppressed.'" (v. 5). James makes a similar point when he writes: "Do you think Scripture says without reason that he jealously longs for the spirit he has caused to dwell in us? But he gives us more grace. That is why Scripture says: "God opposes the proud but shows favor to the **humble** and oppressed" (James 4:5-6). Twice the New Testament writers quote Proverbs 3:34 when they write: "God opposes the proud but shows favor to the **humble** and oppressed." I don't know about you, but I don't want to be *opposed* by God!

A self that is humble helps us to "live a life worthy of the calling you have received" (Eph. 4:1). It is an attitude that seeks to follow the Lord Jesus who said, "Take my yoke upon you and learn from me, for I am gentle and **humble** in heart, and you will find rest for your souls" (Matt. 11). It is an attitude which does not seek to exalt oneself (Luke 14), a way of life which God opposes. An attitude of humility brings God's favor (1 Peter 5; James 4).

Like the other attitudes we have looked at, humility is not optional. It is clearly commanded in such passages as 1 Peter 3 when the often-humbled Peter writes, "Finally, all of you, be like-minded, be sympathetic, love one another, **be** compassionate and **humble**. Do not repay evil with evil or insult with insult.

---

[13] Martin Luther, *Works of Martin Luther: With Introduction and Notes, the Philadelphia Edition* (Grand Rapids: Baker, 1982), 34:285, p. 288.

On the contrary, repay evil with blessing, because to this you were called so that you may inherit a blessing" (vv. 8-9).

If the opposite of humility is pride, has pride no place in the Christian's life? Jeremiah 9:23-24 speaks about a biblical kind of boasting:

> This is what the LORD says:
> "Let not the wise man boast of his wisdom
> or the strong man boast of his strength
> or the rich man boast of his riches,
> but let him who boasts boast about this:
> that he understands and knows me,
> that I am the LORD, who exercises kindness,
> justice and righteousness on earth,
> for in these I delight," declares the LORD (vv. 23-24).

We are to boast in the Lord! We are to delight, not in our wisdom, strength, or riches, but in His attributes. That's the kind of pride which we all need to practice.

A thankful heart, a trusting mind, a clear conscience, a teachable spirit, and a humble self provide the world an undeniable advertisement of God's grace in our lives. Anybody need an attitude adjustment?

Chapter 11

"The Believer's Actions"

A pastor was making a visit to some members of his congregation. He knocked on one door, and a little 4-year-old boy came to the door and saw the pastor. He called to his dad, "Hey, Dad! That guy that works for God is here!"

"Trust in God and *do* something!" (Mary Lyon)

"Who is wise and understanding among you? Let them show it by their good life, by deeds done in the humility that comes from wisdom" (James 3:13).

When Londoner Danny Wallace's great uncle Gallus died, Danny discovered that his uncle (shortly after WWII) had wanted to start a commune where like-minded people could live, work, and play on his land. He wanted to get a hundred people to join him; alas, he got only three.

Danny says, "It was this sense of pity, coupled with the ease with which I got bored, that led me to do something I would not normally do." He placed a small, free ad in a London newspaper asking people to "join me." All they needed to do to join Danny was send him a passport photo. "Sure," Danny says, "they wouldn't know who they were joining, or what they were joining, or why they were joining ... or even what 'joining' meant ... but would that be enough to put them off? Four thousand passport photos later, I reali[zed] that was a silly question."

One problem immediately surfaced. "These people had begun to look to me as their Leader.... And they began to demand to know exactly what it was they had joined." Wallace says he, being a coward, couldn't just tell them that there was no point, that he "had made them join him on a simple whim," that "there was actually nothing that I wanted them to do. So I had to find a point to the pointlessness."

"Now, I don't know if you've ever started a cult," says Wallace, "but one of the first things you have to do is decide whether to use your powers for good, or for evil." "It's a strange thing, admitting you're a cult leader," Danny confesses. In Danny Wallace's "Join Me" cult people are encouraged to do random acts of kindness because, Wallace says,

> my cult is a cult devoted to niceness. To kindness. To improving the life of a total stranger, if only for a moment or two. I call it The Karma Army, and I encourage my followers to carry out one Random Act of Kindness for a complete stranger, each and every Friday. I call these Fridays "Good Fridays", and I ask my members to sign The Good Fridays Agreement.

He continues, "... the fact that I now have a huge group of 'joinees' who do my bidding on each and every one of these Good Fridays is as surprising to me as it must be to you."

The very moment I instructed my joinees to take to the streets and carry out Random Acts of Kindness for the benefit of strangers, in fact, they took to their task with determination and gusto. All over the country, little things were happening ... little moments of joy in towns and cities across the land. Little events that were brightening up people's lives, even if it was only for a few seconds. Pints were being bought for strangers. Shopping was being carried. Cups of tea paid for. Boxes of chocolates handed out in the streets. Flowers deposited at old people's homes. Cakes left on doorsteps. Sure, none of these events was world-changing, but they were ... well ... life-affirming, somehow. Strangers being nice to strangers. For no reason whatsoever. And it continues to this very day.

All over Britain, and, in fact, all over Europe now, thousands of people are sticking to the Good Fridays Agreement and carrying out their little acts of kindness, for no reward or personal gain other than the warm glow they get from having done one. The Karma Army is non-religious. It's non-political. It's about walking into a pub, buying a pint, putting it on a stranger's table with a nod, and walking away. It's about offering someone your *Mail on Sunday* [newspaper] when you've finished with it. It's not about being thanked, or getting any credit, or going to heaven. It's not about changing humanity; it's just about being human.

Wallace says that the Karma Army is becoming international and "that fact alone has been enough to prove one, vital universal truth to me. It's this: people are essentially good." He also believes his movement ("we're not a cult – we're a collective!") is helping to break down social barriers, especially the barrier of not helping others.

> ... my joinees - my proud and noble followers – have shown me that it's possible to break that barrier down. And not just possible, but easy. If you feel you've an excuse for doing something nice, no matter how vague or silly, then it becomes far, far easier. If you can treat it almost as a joke, almost like you're playing a cheeky prank on someone, you can be nice with almost no embarrassment whatsoever. It's like a live version [of] Candid Camera, but one in which the victim actually benefits.[1]

A Critique of "Join Me!"[2]
Sounding very much like the film "Pay It Forward," Wallace's movement has much to commend it. Doing something nice for

---

[1] Information and quotes from http://www.join-me.co.uk/story.html.

[2] One of the immediate concerns for many Christians would be the walking into a pub, buying a pint, and putting in front of some stranger.

someone else – what could be wrong with that? Doing an act of kindness for someone you do not know, with no expectation of any reciprocation, sounds eerily similar to Jesus' command in Luke 6 where He says, "If you love those who love you, what credit is that to you? Even 'sinners' love those who love them. And if you do good to those who are good to you, what credit is that to you? Even 'sinners' do that" (vv. 32-33).

The Lord knows that there is so little good will in this world, we could certainly benefit from numerous lives dedicated (at least on Good Fridays!) to doing deeds of kindness. The way some of us Christians act in the world, it would appear that Jesus has not sent us out to "bring an old man a smile" (as Wallace elsewhere describes his movement). Rather, it appears that Jesus has dispensed a misery pill to each of us and commanded us to go out and medicate the world.

However, a few items are troubling about Wallace's "Join Me" movement. First, life's purpose is not something that we must make up. Life is not pointless. The Westminster Confession asks the question: "What is the chief end (purpose) of man?" The answer given is that "The chief end of man is to glorify God and enjoy Him forever." In our high-tech, low-touch culture, it does not surprise me that many would want to join a movement to *do something*, even if they have scant details as to who, what, or why they're joining. We must have a purpose for our existence, even if that purpose is random and invented. Biblical Christianity teaches that God has not left us in the dark about life's purpose.

A second concern involves the randomness of the acts. It appears that the more random the act of kindness, the more praiseworthy it ought to be regarded. What an easy way to live one's life – to do random acts of kindness to strangers! Oh, it may cost a bit of money and creativity, but the really hard part of life is living for the welfare of those you know – and who know you! Doing a kindness to a stranger might be a lot easier

---

But if we teetotalers substituted the word "casserole" for pint, that would work, wouldn't it?

than putting up with – and being civil to – a nagging mother-in-law [I'm not speaking of my mother-in-law, mind you.]

The third concern I have has to do with the "Join Me" movement's professed avoidance of religion. One wonders what point is trying to be communicated by such random acts of kindness.[3] Wallace makes it clear that thousands of people are doing little acts of kindness,

> for no reward or personal gain other than the warm glow they get from having done one. The Karma Army is non-religious. It's non-political. It's about walking into a pub, buying a pint, putting it on a stranger's table with a nod, and walking away. It's about offering someone your *Mail on Sunday* [newspaper] when you've finished with it. It's not about being thanked, or getting any credit, or going to heaven. It's not about changing humanity; it's just about being human.

The expression "Karma Army" strikes me as somewhat troublesome. The term "karma" is used in both Hinduism and Buddhism to refer to "the sum of a person's actions in this and previous states of existence, viewed as affecting their future fate."[4] Perhaps Wallace is not Hindu or Buddhist. It is interesting that he does borrow the term "Good Friday" from Christianity. He may very well live his life as an agnostic who can't be bothered with sorting through competing religions and committing himself to any particular one.

But like death and taxes, one's religious orientation is unavoidable. One must decide what to do with the exclusive

---

[3] A good philosopher *could* make the case in a religionless worldview that "random acts of cruelty and meanness" would be as reasonable as those of kindness and goodness – and maybe more fun! Is it only fear of getting caught and being punished that prevents such groups from forming? Or is there an innate sense that we have been created by a personal-infinite God who Himself shows His kindness to us in many ways (see Acts 14:17; Rom. 2:4; 11:22; Eph. 2:7; Titus 3:4)?

[4] Highly authoritative definition from my built-in Word Perfect dictionary accessed through Windows XP.

claims of Jesus Christ in this life. As one preacher put it, "Eternity is an awfully long time to be wrong about Jesus." No one is simply "beyond all that" (even if they think they are); that is, no one is *exempt* from the central question of biblical Christianity which is: "What will you do with Christ?" Wallace's conclusion (in watching his Army do multiple acts of kindness and goodness) is that "people are essentially good." I would agree with him that our being made in the image of God prepares us to do many good – and even sacrificial – things. But the Bible teaches that we are basically sinful and need a Savior.[5]

Jesus' "Join Me" Collective

This may have seemed a long way around the barn, but Wallace's "Join Me" collective draws our attention to how the Christian life is quite different from the movement whimsically started out of boredom. We will notice those differences as we momentarily move through several key biblical passages.

In this book we have so far looked at the believer's acceptance, the believer's authority, the believer's anatomy, the believer's associations (with both non-Christians and Christians), and the believer's attitudes. We now want to consider the believer's **actions**. What should the Christian be *doing*? We've mentioned practices like Bible study, prayer, fellowship, and witnessing. But this is not a chapter on life vocations or career choices. Here we want to consider the place of good works in the Christian life. As we do we will notice that there is nothing random about the believer's actions in this world.

---

[5] One wonders if, despite the surface innocency of Wallace's movement, some of his followers will fall into the category of those on Judgment Day who will parade their good works before God as the reason they should be allowed to enter heaven (see Matt. 7:21-23). Colson quotes C. S. Lewis who wrote: "A world of nice people, content in their own niceness, looking no further, turned away from God, would be just as desperately in need of salvation as a miserable world – and might even be more difficult to save" (Colson, *Against the Night*, p. 139).

Working on Our Wobbling

Dennis Custer tells the following story of getting some new tires for his car.

> "The man mounting new tires for me," he says, "had no way of knowing that I am a mechanical engineer. As he worked, he asked, 'Do you know why I put half of the weights on the inside rim and half on the outside?' 'As a matter of fact, I do,' I replied. 'The imbalance can be resolved to a point mass located in the plane of imbalance. If an equal mass is placed at 180 degrees opposite and at an equivalent radius, then perfect balance will result. However,' I continued, 'the plane of imbalance is located somewhere between the planes of the rims. By dividing the weights between the rims, you can approximate the ideal balance.' The fellow stared at me for a moment and then said, 'Yeah, 'cause if you don't, it'll wobble.'"[6]

We wobble, don't we? When it comes to the role of works in the Christian life, we wobble from a works-have-no-place position to an overemphasis on performance and our own "goodness." We Evangelicals are very strong on biblical texts like Ephesians 2:8-9 which says, "For by grace are you saved through faith; it is the gift of God. Not of works lest any man should boast." But the text goes on to say, "For we are his workmanship, **created in Christ Jesus for good works**" (v. 10). He did not create us merely for salvation, but "for good works." It seems we've emphasized only *half* of God's desire for us: to save us apart from our works. The other half concerns God's using us (and our good works) to serve others and attract them to Him.

It is always right for the believer to do good. In facing opposition from some of Israel's leaders, the Lord Jesus said, "If any of you has a sheep and it falls into a pit on the Sabbath, will you not take hold of it and lift it out? How much more valuable is a human being than a sheep! Therefore it is lawful **to do good** on the Sabbath" (Matt. 12:11-12).

---

[6] *Readers Digest*, June 1990.

Jesus tells His disciples in Luke 6: "But to you who are listening I say: Love your enemies, **do good to those who hate you**, bless those who curse you, pray for those who mistreat you" (vv. 27-28). We might like to think that we have no enemies, but we do. In fact, Jesus emphasizes that we should do good not only to our enemies, but also to those who cannot "repay" us. He says, "If you love those who love you, what credit is that to you? Even 'sinners' love those who love them. And if you **do good to those who are good to you**, what credit is that to you? Even 'sinners' do that" (Luke 6:32-33).

The Apostle Paul warns us: "Let us not become weary in **doing good**, for at the proper time we will reap a harvest if we do not give up.[7] Therefore, as we have opportunity, **let us do good to all people, especially to those who belong to the family of believers**" (Gal. 6:9-10). Unlike many cults which focus their altruism only on themselves, Christians are to be indiscriminate in their good-deed-doing (that is, they are to serve all, while not forgetting to meet the needs of the family of God).

A Key Factor of Our Apologetics

"Who is going to harm you if you are **eager to do good**?," Peter asks in 1 Peter 3. "But even if you should suffer for what is right, you are blessed. 'Do not fear their threats; do not be frightened.' But in your heart revere Christ as Lord. Always be prepared to give an answer to everyone who asks you to give the reason for the hope that you have" (vv. 13-15).

I was a Boy Scout when I was young and it was a great time in my life. The Boy Scouts have a motto, you know, and it is "Always be prepared." They also have a kind of principle they live by that they should do at least one good deed every day. The typical good deed for the Boy Scout is that of helping a little old lady across the street. So one day, I was in my Scout uniform with my most recent merit badges expertly sewn on by my mother, and I saw a little old lady standing on a fairly busy

---

[7] Please see chapter 6 of our *Heaven: Thinking Now about Tomorrow* for a discussion of the doctrine of rewards.

street corner of my hometown. Naturally I grabbed her arm and led her briskly – but safely – across the street. Expecting her to say "Thanks!, young man," she instead looked at me a bit angrily and said, "What's *wrong* with you?! I didn't want to cross the street, Buster! I was waiting for the bus!" So I promptly took her by the right arm, sheepishly led her back across the intersection to where I had first found her, thinking to myself, *"I've taken care of two days' of good deeds!"*

I have the privilege of teaching some courses in apologetics in our university. Apologetics involves defending the Christian faith, and one of the primary texts considered in that course is this one, 1 Peter 3:15. We are always to be ready to give an answer to those who ask us the reason for our faith. The context of 1 Peter 3 is that of a Christian who gets persecuted for doing what is right – and reacting in a way unlike the world. The presumption is that our different responses will elicit questions from the unsaved world and, when they ask, we can tell them about Jesus. Our reactions – and our continuing eagerness to do what is good – will properly provoke unbelievers to ask what makes us tick. Our witness is not primarily *verbal* – our actions and our *re*actions in life ought to stimulate the non-believer to ask good questions.

We've all heard the adage that "curiosity killed the cat." May I suggest that a lack of curiosity – on the part of non-Christians – is killing the church? They need to see substantial differences in the way we live our lives in the world.[8] First Peter 3's challenge is that we would suffer patiently when wrongfully persecuted, be ready to give good reasons for our faith in Christ, and continue to do good.

Rich in Good Deeds

In a museum in Deadwood, South Dakota, there is an inscription left by a prospector years ago which reads: "I lost my gun. I lost my horse. I'm out of food. The Indians are after me. But I've got all the gold I can carry." There are some riches

---

[8] We, of course, lose our audience when we isolate ourselves from lost people. See chapter 8 on developing relationships with unbelievers.

that are not worth having. The Apostle Paul directs Timothy to challenge the wealthy in his congregation with these words:

> [17]Command those who are rich in this present world not to be arrogant nor to put their hope in wealth, which is so uncertain, but to put their hope in God, who richly provides us with everything for our enjoyment. [18]Command them **to do good, to be rich in good deeds**, and to be generous and willing to share. [19]In this way they will lay up treasure for themselves as a firm foundation for the coming age, so that they may take hold of the life that is truly life (1 Tim. 6).

Those presently rich in this world need to be reminded that there is another world – and to use their wealth for God's purposes. Both arrogance (thinking that he alone earned his wealth) and materialism (thinking that the most important thing in life is things) divert the rich person's attention from living for God. In fact, Paul says, the very ability to gain wealth is a gift from God. It is this God whose provisions for us are intended to be enjoyed.

Paul does not tell Timothy to command the wealthy to divest themselves of their riches, buy ascension robes, take their kids out of school, and wait on a high hill for the Second Coming. Rather they are instructed to "do good, to be rich in good deeds" (v. 18). That kind of spiritual wealth leads to a laying up for oneself of treasures in heaven.

The writer to the Hebrews reminds us: "Do not forget to do good and to share with others, for with such sacrifices God is pleased" (Heb. 13:16). 1 Peter 3 clearly says, "Turn from evil and **do good**; seek peace and pursue it" (1 Peter 3:11).

I understand that a young man asked an old rich man how he made his money. The old guy fingered his worsted wool vest and said, "Well, son, it was 1932. The depth of the Great Depression. I was down to my last nickel. I invested that nickel in an apple. I spent the entire day polishing the apple and, at the end of the day, I sold the apple for ten cents. The next morning, I invested those ten cents in two apples. I spent the entire day polishing them and sold them at 5:00 pm for 20 cents. I continued this system for a month, by the end of which I'd accumulated a fortune of $1.37. Then my wife's father died and left us two million dollars."

We've inherited a fortune from the Lord, including the ability to create wealth for ourselves. We must use that wealth for Him – and be "rich in good deeds."

A Visible Faith

In Matthew 5 Jesus says, "You are the light of the world. A city on a hill cannot be hidden. [15]Neither do people light a lamp and put it under a bowl. Instead they put it on its stand, and it gives light to everyone in the house. [16]In the same way, let your light shine before others, that they may **see your good deeds** and praise your Father in heaven" (vv. 14-16). We Evangelicals forget that *we* are now the light! *We* are the ones on display before a watching world. And we need to "let our light shine before others." Not so that we may get any credit but for the express purpose that "they may see your good deeds and praise your Father in heaven" (v. 16). I like the Motel 6's commercial, for it has a spiritual application here: "We'll keep the light on!"

First Peter 4:19 says, "So then, those who suffer according to God's will should commit themselves to their faithful Creator and **continue to do good.**" Unlike the "Join Me" collective, we continue to do good to serve our Creator, and not for the absurd, whimsical, happenstance basis of just being "random."

Faith's Litmus Test

James focuses his attention on the disparity between mere faith and a faith-that-works as he writes in chapter 1:

[22]Do not merely listen to the word, and so deceive yourselves. Do what it says. [23]Those who listen to the word but do not do what it says are like people who look at their faces in a mirror [24]and, after looking at themselves, go away and immediately forget what they look like. [25]But those who look intently into the perfect law that

gives freedom and continue in it – not forgetting what they have heard but doing it – they will be blessed in what they do.

We are not to be merely ears. We are to follow up our listening by our living. The mirror of God's Word tells us the truth about ourselves and urges us to act on what we learn there.

James continues his diatribe against a do-nothing faith in chapter 2 when he writes:

> [14]What good is it, my brothers and sisters, if people claim to have faith but have no deeds? Can such faith save them? [15]Suppose a brother or sister is without clothes and daily food. [16]If one of you says to them, "Go in peace; keep warm and well fed," but does nothing about their physical needs, what good is it? [17]In the same way, faith by itself, if it is not accompanied by action, is dead. [18]But someone will say, "You have faith; I have deeds." Show me your faith without deeds, and I will show you my faith by what I do. [19]You believe that there is one God. Good! Even the demons believe that – and shudder.

How absurd to do nothing when a fellow believer is standing before you naked and you can hear his hungry stomach rumbling! How empty are biblical benedictions wishing peace, warmth, and nourishment when they are unaccompanied by any deeds of kindness!

Our faith is demonstrated not by our words, but by our *works*. James illustrates this point by referring to the Jews' most precious doctrine of God: monotheism. Even the *demons* are monotheists, says James, and they have enough sense to *do something* about it. They tremble.[9]

Finally, James says in chapter 3: "Who is wise and understanding among you? Let them show it by their good life, **by deeds done** in the humility that comes from wisdom" (v. 13). We Evangelicals have felt such a need to fight for faith in Christ apart from our works that we miss the Christian life of faith *with* works.

---

[9] See our devotional "More Than Trembling Monotheists" in *DocDEVOS*.

A Brief Summary

We read in Titus 3:8, "This is a trustworthy saying. And I want you to stress these things, so that those who have trusted in God may be careful to devote themselves to doing what is good. These things are excellent and profitable for everyone." Back in chapter two Titus writes,

> [11]For the grace of God has appeared that offers salvation to all people. [12]It teaches us to say "No" to ungodliness and worldly passions, and to live selfcontrolled, upright and godly lives in this present age, [13]while we wait for the blessed hope – the appearing of the glory of our great God and Savior, Jesus Christ, [14]who gave himself for us to redeem us from all wickedness and to purify for himself a people that are his very own, eager to do what is good.

What have we learned from surveying verses on doing good? We've learned that it is always to right to do right. We're to persist in doing good. It's part of our sanctification – our becoming like Christ – to do good.[10] We're to do good to our enemies and to those who despise us. We're not to do good just to other believers. The rich are to be rich in good deeds. We're not just to turn from evil; we're to do good. Faith without works is dead. Words are cheap; actions are evidences of a genuine walk with God. John Wesley succinctly put the issue when he wrote, "Do all the good you can by all the means you can in all the ways you can in all the places you can in all the times you can to all the people you can as long as ever you can."[11]

Christians are sometimes charged with being "so heavenly-minded that they are of no earthly good." There is some merit to that charge. But a proper focus on heaven will cause us to commit ourselves to serving Christ here. Lewis hits the nail on the head when he writes,

---

[10] We read of the Lord Jesus in Acts 10:38 that He "went around doing good...."

[11] Simply *wanting* to do good is sometimes not enough. Lloyd Reeb (author of *From Success to Significance*) tells about visiting the country of Albania. Seeing a young Albanian beggar girl lying on a tattered blanket, her

If you read history you will find that the Christians who did most for the present world were just those who thought most of the next. The Apostles themselves, who set on foot the conversion of the Roman Empire, the great men who built up the Middle Ages, the English Evangelicals who abolished the Slave Trade, all left their mark on Earth, precisely because their minds were occupied with Heaven. It is since Christians have largely ceased to think of the other world that they have become so ineffective in this. Aim at Heaven and you will get earth "thrown in"; aim at earth and you will get neither.[12]

Are you aiming at heaven? Then, what on earth are you doing about it?

---

tears making clean lines down her dirty face, he wanted to *do* something. He quietly stuck some money in her filthy jacket and left. Sharing his story with a missionary, he was told, "That was the worst thing you could have done, Lloyd! You sentenced her to a life-time of street begging, for she is now branded as a very successful beggar!"

[12] C. S. Lewis, *Mere Christianity*, Bk. III, Ch. 10.

Chapter 12

"The Believer's Assurance"

A little boy was walking with his father. His father said to him: "Son, do you know where we are?" The little boy said, "No, Dad, I don't know." The father then asked, "Well, do you know how far it is to home?" "No," the little boy said, "I don't know." "Do you know the direction we ought to turn if we were going home?" asked the dad. The little boy responded, "No, Dad, I don't know." The father said, "Well, Son, you appear lost to me." The little boy responded, "How can I be lost if I'm with you?"

"I have found that petty disappointments tend to accumulate over time, undermining my faith with a lava flow of doubt." (Phillip Yancey)

"We must know where to doubt, where to feel certain, where to submit." (Blaise Pascal)

"[19]Therefore, brothers and sisters, since we have confidence to enter the Most Holy Place by the blood of Jesus, [20]by a new and living way opened for us through the curtain, that is, his body, [21]and since we have a great priest over the house of God, [22]let us draw near to God with a sincere heart in full assurance of faith, having our hearts sprinkled to cleanse us from a guilty conscience and having our bodies washed with pure water. [23]Let us hold unswervingly to the hope we profess, for he who promised is faithful" (Heb. 10).

You may have heard the story of a teacher who was having trouble with his bank. Neither the bank's accuracy nor its mode of expression lived up to his standards. The last straw arrived in the form of a letter from the bank which read: "Your account appears to be overdrawn." To this, the teacher wrote back: "Please write again when you are absolutely certain."[1]

Absolute certainty. Is it achievable in this life? Many seek to convince us (with some ironic degree of certainty) that we cannot have absolute certainty in this life. For example, in his book *The Myth of Certainty*, Dan Taylor writes:

Risk ... is indispensable to any significant life, nowhere more clearly than in the life of the spirit. The goal of faith is not to create a set of immutable rationalized, precisely defined and defendable beliefs to preserve forever. It is to recover a relationship with God.[2]

One might challenge Taylor's opposing "defendable beliefs" with "a relationship with God." He is, however, trying to take seriously the "riskiness" of life. He writes:

Faith is a quality and a choice consistent with the riskiness of the human condition. It is an appropriate response to the world as I find it. It is a superior response to cynicism or despair which use the genuine difficulty of life to deny the very real opportunity for discovering meaning in it. Faith is likewise not so weak a thing that it can exist only where there is certainty and proof, where there is no opposition either from within or without.[3]

---

[1] John J. Creedon, *Readers' Digest*, Sept., 1988, p. 158.
[2] Dan Taylor, *The Myth of Certainty*, pp. 123-124.
[3] Ibid., p. 98.

He categorically states that "My own experience is that for human beings certainty does not exist, has never existed, will not – in our finite states, ever exist, and, moreover, should not. It is not a gift God has chosen to give His creatures, doubtlessly wisely."[4] He declares (with an ironic air of certainty): "A naive conception of absolutes offers a truth packaged in an illusion accompanied by a danger. The truth, which I affirm by faith in response to evidence, is that the essential Christian claims are actually so. The illusion is that I can be certain that they are so."[5]

Having read his *The Myth of Certainty*, I would ask Mr. Taylor: Does *biblical* certainty exist? Certainty in my own conclusions is presumptive autonomy, but isn't certainty in what *God* declares a definition of *faith?* We read in Hebrews 11 that "Now faith is being sure of what we hope for and certain of what we do not see" (v. 1). It seems to me that a simple survey of the first epistle of John indicates that we can *know* certain things for certain: Our obedience shows that we have come to know Him (2:3); we can know that we are in Him if we walk as Jesus walked (2:5-6); our anointing from the Holy One assures us that we know the truth (2:20-21); we know that we are children of God and will be like Him when He appears (3:1-3); we know that we have passed from death to life because we love our brothers (3:14-15); we know what love is (laying down one's life for another) (3:16); we know that we belong to the truth (3:19-20); we know He lives in us by the Spirit He gave us (3:24b); the gift of His Spirit convinces us that we live in Him and He lives in us (4:13); we know of God's love for those who acknowledge that Jesus is the Son of God (4:15-16); He who has the Son has life and he who does not have the Son does not have life (5:11-12); we can know that we have eternal life (5:13); we both know that He hears our prayers and that we have what we have asked of Him (5:14-15); we know that we are children of God and that the whole world is under the control of the evil one and we know that the Son of God has

---

[4] Ibid., p. 94.

[5] Ibid., p. 91. Taylor implies that faith *requires* doubt (p. 81).

come and has given us understanding so that we may know him who is true (5:18-20). [John then gives one of the stronger statements of the deity of Christ in 5:20]. Whew. These are truths that the believer *knows*.

So, I appreciate some of the challenges of Taylor's book, but would emphasize the *certainty* that we can have in Christ, in God's Word, and in our assurance in belonging to Him.

A Definition of Assurance

The biblical doctrine of assurance is a fundamental teaching of Scripture which brings with it a number of benefits to the believer. But first, let's define what we mean by assurance. One dictionary definition of assurance is that it refers to "a positive declaration intended to give confidence."

That definition falls short of the biblical explanation of assurance, and actually seems like a kind of "name-it-claim-it"-type perspective: You make a positive declaration which inspires confidence. [Just a reminder: we don't get our *biblical* definitions of terms by consulting our English dictionaries. We must go to Scripture to find out what the Bible has to say about assurance.]

A brief survey of several key passages in Scripture unpacks for us what biblical assurance is. We learn, for example, that biblical assurance refers to a confidence not in ourselves, but in God's making us competent as ministers of a new covenant (2 Cor. 3:4). We are clearly commanded to put "no **confidence** in the flesh" (Phil. 3:3). It is *in Christ* that we have access to the Father, as Paul says in Ephesians 3: "In him and through faith in him we may approach God with freedom and **confidence**" (v. 12). We can pray in confidence, according to Hebrews 4, because of what our great high priest the Lord Jesus Christ has done for us:

> [14]Therefore, since we have a great high priest who has ascended into heaven, Jesus the Son of God, let us hold firmly to the faith we profess. [15]For we do not have a high priest who is unable to empathize with our weaknesses, but we have one who has been

tempted in every way, just as we are – yet he did not sin. [16]Let us then approach God's throne of grace with **confidence**, so that we may receive mercy and find grace to help us in our time of need (Heb. 4).

The believer is not to "throw away [his] **confidence**" when he undergoes persecution. He is to suffer along with those in prison "and joyfully [accept] the confiscation of your property, because you [know] that you yourselves [have] better and lasting possessions." Such confidence in the Lord "will be richly rewarded" (Heb. 10:32-36).

In our culture where a person's value seems to be based on his net worth, the challenge in Hebrews 13 reminds us about true confidence:

Keep your lives free from the love of money and be content with what you have, because God has said, "Never will I leave you; never will I forsake you." [6]So we say with **confidence**, "The Lord is my helper; I will not be afraid. What can human beings do to me?" (vv. 5-6).

Our confidence, our assurance, is not based on our performance or our faithfulness. We can be certain that we belong to Him and that He knows what He is doing with our lives. We read in 1 John:

[16]And so we know and rely on the love God has for us. God is love. Those who live in love live in God, and God in them. [17]This is how love is made complete among us so that we will have **confidence** on the day of judgment: In this world we are like Jesus. [18]There is no fear in love. But perfect love drives out fear, because fear has to do with punishment. The one who fears is not made perfect in love (1 John 4).

Because of the finished work of Christ, John asserts to his readers that you may know that you have eternal life. [14]This is the **confidence** we have in approaching God: that if we ask anything according to his will, he hears us. [15]And if we know that he hears us – whatever we ask – we know that we have what we asked of him (1 John 5).

Imagine with me that you are standing at the exit of your local Wal★Mart Superstore. As people leave with their purchases, you calmly step up, offer to shake their hand, and say, "Did you know that according to the Bible I *know for sure that I have eternal life?* And did you know that if I ask anything according to God's will, *He hears me!?* What do you think about that!?" Some might shake your hand, others might reach for their can of Mace, but a lot of them would hasten their steps to their cars, muttering to themselves, "What a kook! *He* thinks *he* has eternal life! What *arrogance!"*

It is not arrogance to take God at His word. It might not be the height of wisdom to use the approach I have described, but the mere repeating what God Himself says about His children strikes the world as arrogant. We do not want to fall into the sin of *presumption* when we discuss assurance, for our certainty is not based on our performance or on what we think we deserve, but on God's grace.

The fact is, we don't have to know a lot to be sure of something. You may have heard of the woman who called her husband at work and said, "Honey, there's something wrong with our new car." The husband said, "Well, what's wrong?" She said, "I'm sure there must be water in the carburetor." The husband began to laugh. "Honey, you don't even know what a carburetor *is!* By the way, where *is* the car?" "In the swimming pool," she said sweetly.

The biblical doctrine of assurance is not based on our feelings but is tied directly to the work of the Lord Jesus Christ. As both our high priest and the final sacrifice for our redemption, He invites us to draw near in full assurance of faith (Heb. 10:22).

Three Areas of Assault on Assurance

I believe that our culture wants the Christian to languish in doubt and uncertainty, mistaking such for humility. G. K. Chesterton challenged the modern idea of humility when he wrote,

> [W]hat we suffer from today is humility in the wrong place. Modesty has moved from the organ of ambition. Modesty has settled upon the organ of conviction; where it was never meant to be. A man was meant to be doubtful about himself, but undoubting about the truth; this has been exactly reversed. Nowadays the part of a man that a man does assert is exactly the part he ought not to assert himself. The part he doubts is exactly the part he ought not to doubt.... We are on the road to producing a race of men too mentally modest to believe in the multiplication table.[6]

We would hardly be impressed with a surgeon who couldn't tell a kidney from a pancreas, and defended himself by saying he was trying to be humble. The loss of conviction is a symptom of a culture which has so relativized truth that one's man opinion (especially in religious matters) is to be deemed as valid as another's, regardless of its nonsense.

There are three areas which assault the individual believer's assurance in the Lord. We want to notice what the Scriptures have to say on the issues of personal sin and present salvation (what I call "The Failure Factor"), of the private sense of abandonment ("The Forsakenness Factor"), and of the pervasive presence of evil in the world ("The Real Fear Factor").

(1) *The Failure Factor: The Issue of Personal Sin and Present Salvation*

In my files I have a Dennis the Menace cartoon where he is talking with his friend Tommy as Margaret walks by, nose in the air, pushing a baby carriage. Dennis says to Tommy, "Poor Margaret. She never gets a break from bein' around herself." That could be said of all of us, couldn't it?

---

[6] G. K. Chesterton, *Orthodoxy* (Garden City, New York: Image Books, 1959), pp. 31-32.

One writer has declared, "If we were brought to trial for the crimes we have committed against ourselves, few would escape the gallows." How can we maintain a sense of assurance in light of our own efforts to spiritually self-destruct? The Apostle Paul wailed, "O wretched man that I am, who will deliver me from this body of death?" This famous expression occurs in Romans 7 where we read,

> [21]So I find this law at work: Although I want to do good, evil is right there with me. [22]For in my inner being I delight in God's law; [23]but I see another law at work in me, waging war against the law of my mind and making me a prisoner of the law of sin at work within me. [24]What a wretched man I am! Who will rescue me from this body of death? [25]Thanks be to God, who delivers me through Jesus Christ our Lord! So then, I myself in my mind am a slave to God's law, but in my sinful nature a slave to the law of sin.

This kind of spiritual schizophrenia takes place within us all. We have a desire to do what is good, but evil is right there within us. There is an inner delight in the law of God, but a competing law (our sin nature) mounts a full-scale assault on our minds, making us spiritual POW's. And like Paul all we can do is cry out for *rescue!* We need to be rescued from "this body of death." Paul does not abandon his hope or turn away from his assurance. He thanks God for a present deliverance in the very context of the wrestling match between his mind wanting to be a slave to God's law and his sinful nature holding onto him as a bondservant to the law of sin.

The seventeenth century French theologian and mathematician Blaise Pascal hammered hard at this paradox which he saw in human nature. He described both man's glory and man's wretchedness in this familiar quotation:

> What kind of freak is man! What a novelty he is, how absurd he is, how chaotic and what a mass of contradictions, and yet what a prodigy! He is judge of all things, yet a feeble worm. He is [a]

repository of truth, and yet sinks into such doubt and error. He is the glory and the scum of the universe![7]

How can the Christian maintain his assurance of his place in God's family when he falls into sin, jumps into transgression, slips into failure, is overtaken by "mistakes," throws a spiritual temper tantrum at the ways of God, or simply refuses to live as a child of the King? How can that believer still claim to be redeemed, to be "right" with God? Part of the answer is found in the lyrics of a recent Christian song:

Who Am I? by Casting Crowns

> Who am I, that the Lord of all the earth
> Would care to know my name?
> Would care to feel my hurt?
> Who am I, that the Bright and Morning Star
> Would choose to light the way
> For my ever wandering heart?
>
> Not because of who I am
> But because of what You've done
> Not because of what I've done
> But because of who You are
>
> I am a flower quickly fading
> Here today and gone tomorrow
> A wave tossed in the ocean
> Vapor in the wind
> Still You hear me when I'm calling
> Lord, You catch me when I'm falling

---

[7] James Houston's translation, *Mind On Fire: A Faith for the Skeptical and Indifferent* (Minneapolis: Bethany House, 1997), p. 91. Philip Yancey uses the expression that we are "angels wallowing in mud, mammals attempting to fly." (*Rumors of Another World: What on Earth Are We Missing?* [Grand Rapids: Zondervan, 2003], p. 38).

And You've told me who I am
I am Yours, I am Yours

Who am I, that the eyes that see my sin
Would look on me with love and watch me rise again?
Who am I, that the voice that calmed the sea
Would call out through the rain
And calm the storm in me?

Not because of who I am
But because of what You've done
Not because of what I've done
But because of who You are

I am a flower quickly fading
Here today and gone tomorrow
A wave tossed in the ocean
Vapor in the wind
Still You hear me when I'm calling
Lord, You catch me when I'm falling
And You've told me who I am
I am Yours

I am Yours
Whom shall I fear?
Whom shall I fear?
'Cause I am Yours
I am Yours.[8]

The biblical doctrine of assurance has to do with God's promises and not our performance. The question is not who we are or what we've done. In short, the biblical doctrine of assurance rests on *grace*. To not have that assurance is to miss out on the joy which is given by grace.

---

[8] Album: Casting Crowns. ©Club Zoo Music/Swecs music. All Rights Reserved. Used by Permission.

(2) The Forsakenness Factor: The Issue of the Lord's Absence

I have a confession to make. My wife and I sometimes watch the TV show "Without a Trace." Most of the time the stories are well-written and we get to follow the action as the time runs out on those who have been kidnaped. Occasionally, the "victim" has himself chosen to disappear for various reasons which are also intriguing.

Sometimes God seems to have vanished "without a trace." The brutal truth is that occasionally God hides *Himself.* The doctrine of His omnipresence (that He is everywhere) does not rule out the fact that He, at times, conceals Himself from His people for His own reasons. Thomas à Kempis put it this way: "Sometimes Thou dost withdraw Thyself from us that we might know the sweetness of Thy presence." Chesterton had a different slant on the issue when he wrote that "The central idea of the great part of the Old Testament may be called the idea of the loneliness of God." Isaiah clearly says, "Surely God is with you, and there is no other; there is no other god. Truly you are a God who hides himself, O God and Savior of Israel" (Isa. 45:14b-15). How God can be "with you" and yet "hide Himself" is a paradox.

In the book of Genesis we read of Adam and Eve after they had sinned against God: "Then the man and his wife heard the sound of the Lord God as he was walking in the garden in the cool of the day, and they *hid* from the Lord God among the trees of the garden" (Gen. 3:8). The Psalmist prays, "Keep me as the apple of your eye; *hide* me in the shadow of your wings" (Ps. 17:8). He also prays for protection: "Rescue me from my enemies, O Lord, for I *hide* myself in you" (Ps. 143:9). Both hiding from God and hiding in God are real conditions of the believer at various points in life.

But does God ever hide from us? When I was a young Christian, one of the popular sayings was, "If you feel distant from God, who moved?" The *correct* answer was thought to be, "*You* did! You must have sinned or become cold to God, and therefore He feels distant to you."

Sometimes God hides Himself from us because of our sin (see Isa. 64:7). But is it possible that God sometimes hides Himself from His people for other reasons? Isaiah's declaration, "Surely God is with you, and there is no other; there is no other god. Truly you are a God who *hides himself*, O God and Savior of Israel," gives no indication here that He hides Himself because of His people's sin, but perhaps so that His people might seek Him on a deeper and more intimate level.

Many in our world not only deny God's existence, but they insist, almost in the same words as those who crucified Jesus, that He "come down now from [heaven], that we may see and believe" (Mark 15:32). God *has* come down from heaven, demonstrating His love for His wayward creation.

For the believer in Christ, those periods when God seems distant, or when He has removed a sense of His presence from us, *may be* because of our sin. On the other hand, this God who sometimes "hides Himself" may simply be seeking to be sought!

A. W. Tozer understood the need to continually seek the Lord, for he writes,

> Everything is made to center upon the initial act of "accepting" Christ (a term, incidentally, which is not found in the Bible) and we are not expected thereafter to crave any further revelation of God to our souls. We have been snared in the coils of a spurious logic which insists that if we have found Him we need no more seek Him.[9]

When my children were small, I would come home from my night-shift at work, kiss my wife and children hello, and, when their backs were turned, quickly hide in our linen closet. Why

---

[9] A. W. Tozer, *The Pursuit of God* (Harrisburg: Christian Publications, 1968), p. 16. We might take issue with Tozer over his comment that the expression "accepting Christ" is not a biblical expression. We do have texts like John 1:12 and Colossians 2:6 which speak of "receiving" Christ. I think his concern is that of "merely" "accepting Christ," with no heart desire to grow in a knowledge of Him.

would I do such a thing? The kids immediately recognized that Dad was initiating a game of hide 'n seek.

They would ask Mom, "Where's Dad?" [she would lie and say she didn't know – all moms lie], then they would look everywhere for me except that linen closet. Through the wooden slats I could see their little sneakered feet run past. After a while, when the kids were searching some other part of the house, I would slip out and sit at the table, quietly drinking coffee with my wife. The kids would see me, do a double-take, and say, "Where *were* you?" I would, of course, not tell them my secret hiding-place. [I did tell them about the linen closet when they both turned twenty. I thought it was time they knew.]

One morning I came home from work, kissed my wife and children hello, vanished into my linen closet, and heard the kids scampering around trying to find me. After a few minutes, the house became silent. When I came out of hiding, I found them downstairs playing Legos. They had lost interest in finding Dad. They were having a blast. I was devastated.

When God hides Himself from us, He is not playing a game. Those desert-times of the soul present opportunities to seek Him in His Word, through prayer, and by walking by faith. We must not lose our assurance of His presence, for we take Him at His word when He says, "I will never leave you, nor forsake you" (Heb. 13:5).

In his classic *Screwtape Letters*, C. S. Lewis has an arch demon Screwtape writing letters to his nephew understudy demon Wormwood about how to trip up human beings. On the issue of God's apparent absence, Screwtape warns Wormwood:

Do not be deceived, Wormwood. Our cause is never more in danger than when a human, no longer desiring, but still intending to do God's will, looks round upon a universe from which every trace of Him seems to have vanished, and asks why he has been forsaken, and still obeys.[10]

---

[10] C. S. Lewis, *Screwtape Letters*, p. 39.

God's entrance into history in the Person of His Son the Lord Jesus Christ is the foundation upon which we rest our faith. When circumstances cry out "Where is your God?", the believer in Jesus Christ can confidently point back to Calvary and to the empty tomb. And to the promises of Scripture. Although the believer may *feel* forsaken, the reality is that God has not abandoned His child. His child may simply need to do some searching.

(3) The Fear Factor: The Issue of the Lord's Apparent Apathy
"Fear Factor," NBC's self-proclaimed family show, hits homes every Monday night at 8:00 ET. In each "pulse-racing" (according to the network) episode, six contestants (three men and three women) are recruited across the country to battle in three extreme stunts. These stunts are designed to challenge the contestants both physically and mentally. For example, one stunt involved a coffin-like structure filled with twenty-four squirming, writhing snakes ranging in size from 4-feet to a 16-foot boa constrictor. Contestants were told that there are no guarantees against snakebites, but "if you get bit you automatically advance." If a player is too afraid to complete or fails to perform a stunt, the player is eliminated. If they succeed, they are one step closer to the grand prize of $50,000. The "Fear Factor" website adds: "NOTE: These stunts are supervised by trained professionals. They are extremely dangerous and should not be attempted by anyone, anywhere, anytime. Some episodes contain graphic content. Viewer discretion advised."

As the third most-watched program on TV for children under fourteen, it certainly is *not* family-friendly. This season has showcased, as one writer says,

> a variety of specials such as Family Fear Factor, Couples Fear Factor, and Female Fear Factor, each with its own unique twists. The first two put a variety of relationships on the line and often showed competition at its worst. Fear Factor is famous for its well-built, well-manicured women dressed in skimpy bathing suits that, if anything, hinder their ability to compete and Female Fear Factor takes that to the next level. Someone is always sure to remark

on the size of a female contestant's breasts and Joe throws in his fair share of innuendo for good measure. It is pure objectification and totally unnecessary. This week Joe commented that he found watching a woman covered in moldy cheese, eating a grasshopper, and bouncing about with disgust strangely erotic. In a recent phone interview with Ryan Seacrest on "On Air" he said, "We just want to put people on the show that you would want to have sex with. That's our goal." It looks like NBC's definition of family programming is a little skewed.[11]

The show features gross challenges to eat things man was never intended to eat. For example, on Episode 416 (Season 4) during the Couples' Fear Factor, the girls had to lie down in a plexiglass tank, and then were covered with 400 rats. The guys then had to retrieve ten chicken's feet from the tank, using only their mouths! One couple bowed out of the stunt because it was just too gross. The couple who won this stunt won an all-expenses paid trip to Las Vegas.

In Episode 433 (Season 4), the All-Female edition of "Fear Factor" featured one truly gruesome stunt. Contestants were stuck inside a morgue drawer, in a body bag filled with giant hissing cockroaches, flesh-eating worms, crickets and stink beetles. Locked in the pitch black of the morgue drawer, the girls were imprisoned in chains and had to fumble around to find the right key to unlock themselves. [It's important to me to point out to you that I have not watched an entire episode of "Fear Factor." I've gleaned my information from various web-sites. Really.]

The Real Fear Factor

But compared to what I'm going to describe in a moment, all these juvenile TV stunts are like a walk in the park. They involve some risk and some danger, but wait until I tell you the most fearful fear factor that could ever be.

---

[11] www.parentstv.org.

The most fearful fear factor would be that there is no God behind our world, that all the evil that takes place will never be made right, that massive evildoers will get away with "it" (whatever the variety of evil the "it" is). Real fear is to conclude with Jean Paul Sartre that "Life begins on the other side of despair." Or to side with the skeptic Bertrand Russell (who wrote "Why I Am Not a Christian") whose counsel to despair we briefly looked at in Chapter 4,

> That Man is the product of causes which had no prevision of the end they were achieving; that his origin, his growth, his hopes and fears, his loves and his beliefs, are but the outcome of accidental collocations of atoms; that no fire, no heroism, no intensity of thought and feeling, can preserve an individual life beyond the grave; that all the labours of the ages, all the devotion, all the inspiration, all the noonday brightness of human genius, are destined to extinction in the vast death of the solar system and that the whole temple of Man's achievement must inevitably be buried beneath the debris of a universe in ruins – all these things, if not quite beyond dispute, are yet so nearly certain, that no philosophy which rejects them can hope to stand. Only within the scaffolding of these truths, only on the firm foundation of unyielding despair, can the soul's habitation henceforth be safely built.[12]

Because he rejected the Christian gospel, Russell could only fall back on what he called "the firm foundation of unyielding despair." Deep within us all is a sense that things are out of whack, and many believe that there will come a time when God will make things right. If that belief is mere illusion or self-deception, then the Christian gospel is not true, there is no holy God who will judge the world, and believers who hold onto a view that they are redeemed and loved by God are victims of a cruel farce. When C. H. Spurgeon said that "Eternity will right the wrongs of time," he was expressing his assurance that, though He appears absent from a world in pain, God will nonetheless balance the books at the end of time.

Philip Yancey asks the question, "If this is God's world, why

---

[12] Russell, "A Free Man's Worship," pp. 47-48.

doesn't it look more like it? Why is this planet so messed up?"[13] He is merely voicing the agony of sensitive people everywhere who cannot placidly read headlines like the following:

December 26, 2004: A massive 9.0 earthquake and subsequent tsunamis are blamed for 169,752 deaths with 127,294 people listed as missing, including more than 113,000 in Indonesia.[14]

Twenty-four thousand children die each day of preventable diseases and 126,000 more are aborted each year.[15]

Fresno, California: Marcus Wesson fatally shot nine of his children while police waited outside his house and

---

[13] Yancey, *Rumors of Another World*, p. 10.

[14] Jonathan Sacks, the Chief Rabbi of the United Hebrew Congregations of the British Commonwealth of Nations, wrote that "The religious question is ... not: 'Why did this happen?' But 'What then shall we do?' That is why, in synagogues, churches, mosques and temples throughout the world this weekend, along with our prayers for the injured and the bereaved, we will be asking people to donate money to assist the work of relief. The religious response is not to seek to understand, thereby to accept. We are not God. Instead we are the people He has called on us to be his 'partners in the work of creation.' The only adequate religious response is to say: 'God, I do not know why this terrifying disaster has happened, but I do know what You want of us: to help the afflicted, comfort the bereaved, send healing to the injured, and aid those who have lost their livelihoods and homes.' We cannot understand God, but we can strive to imitate His love and care. That, and perhaps one more thing. For it was after an earlier flood, in the days of Noah, that God made His first covenant with mankind. The Bible says that God had seen 'a world filled with violence' and asked Noah to institute a social order that would honour human life as the image of God. Not as an explanation of suffering, but as a response to it, I for one will pray that in our collective grief we renew the covenant of human solidarity. Having seen how small and vulnerable humanity is in the face of nature, might we not also see how small are the things that divide us, and how tragic to add grief to grief" (*Timesonline*, 1/1/05). Rather than renewing "the covenant of human solidarity," we should see life as uncertain and be ready to meet God (as we will see in our study of Luke 13:1-5).

[15] Yancey, *Rumors of Another World*, p. 44.

relatives pleaded for them to intervene.

Joyce, Washington: A 13-year-old boy shot and killed himself in front of his eighth-grade classmates.

New York: A woman apparently collapsed and died while giving her 3-year-old son a bath, and the boy then drowned in the tub.

South Carolina: Because of a failed affair, Susan Smith strapped her three-year-old and fourteen-month-old sons into her Mazda and drove them into a lake and watched them drown.

California: Lyle and Erik Menendez emptied a shotgun into their mother and father, then left the house for more ammunition to fire again into the mother's twitching body.

Jeffry Dahmer not only killed his victims; he cut them up, cooked and ate them, and stored the leftover body parts in his re frigerator.

New York City: Two hijacked airliners slam into the Twin Towers killing over 3,000 innocent people from over eighty different countries.

More than 25,000 Africans are struck down yearly by the AIDS epidemic.

The most powerful king in Israel's history steals another man's wife and has the husband (and many brave soldiers) murdered on the battlefront to hide his sin.

Such news headlines could, unfortunately, be multiplied over and over again. Have we become so insulated to the march of human tragedy, the perpetuation of human misery, the waste of human life and potential, that we are no longer moved? In another context, the Bible commentator William Barclay warns us against such apathy:

> We must remember that indifference ... is a sin, and the worst of all sins, for indifference kills. Indifference does not burn a religion to death; it freezes it to death. It does not behead it; it slowly

suffocates the life out of it.[16]

We dare not become indifferent to the wholesale rebellion of a planet gone mad, for then we lose our humanity. Is *God* indifferent to our human plight? How do we Christians explain His apparent absence in the face of unrelenting terror, atrocities, barbarisms, and abuse? The Scriptures set forth two certainties to which the Christian must cling when God appears apathetic toward a suffering world. These two certainties are the present restraint of sin and the future righteous judgment of God, including the unleashing of God's wrath.

The Present Restraint of Sin

Every Christian generation thinks that its time is "the worst of times." But there remains a civility and a moral underpinning which should be connected directly to the restraining ministry of the Spirit of God. Many Bible scholars take 2 Thessalonians 2:7 as a reference to this work of the Holy Spirit: "For the secret power of lawlessness is already at work; but the one who now holds it back will continue to do so till he is taken out of the way." This "holding back" is a function of the omnipresent Third Member of the Godhead.

How does the Holy Spirit *restrain* sin? He clearly works through human conscience in reminding us of what is right and what is wrong. C. S. Lewis (as we noticed back in Ch. 10) has a classic statement on man's conscience when he says that he wants to make

> [t]wo points: first, that human beings, all over the earth, have this curious idea that they ought to behave in a certain way, and cannot get rid of it. Secondly, that they do not in fact behave in that way. They know the law of Nature; they break it. These two facts are the foundation of all clear thinking about ourselves and the universe we live in.[17]

---

[16] William Barclay, *The Gospel of Matthew* (Philadelphia: Westminster Pr., 1957), vol. 2, p. 14.

[17] C. S. Lewis, *Mere Christianity*, Bk. 1, Ch. 1, p. 21.

Where does this sense of "oughtness" come from? All human beings have been made in the image and likeness of God. Romans 1 makes it clear that sinful men "suppress the truth by their wickedness" (v. 18) and, therefore, "men are without excuse" (v. 20). In some sense sinful men "knew God, [but] neither glorified him as God nor gave thanks to him ..." (v. 21). God gives sinful man over to his lusts, but holds him guilty for His turning away from God. We have, as Romans 2 puts it, "the requirements of the law ... written on [our] hearts ..." (v. 15). Our consciences also bear witness and our thoughts either accuse or defend us (v. 15).

Jesus said that the Spirit to come would actively engage the world:

[8]When he comes, he will prove the world to be in the wrong about sin and righteousness and judgment: [9]about sin, because people do not believe in me; [10]about righteousness, because I am going to the Father, where you can see me no longer; [11]and about judgment, because the prince of this world now stands condemned (John 16:8-11).

The Spirit is at work in this world both in the convicting of sin and in holding back evil. He uses man's conscience to guide him morally.

The Holy Spirit also restrains sin through human governments and authorities which are established by God. Romans 13 says,

Let everyone be subject to the governing authorities, for there is no authority except that which God has established. The authorities that exist have been established by God. [2]Consequently, whoever rebels against the authority is rebelling against what God has instituted, and those who do so will bring judgment on themselves. [3]For rulers hold no terror for those who do right, but for those who do wrong.

Rebellion against what God has instituted will result in judgment. God the Holy Spirit is pleased when justice is upheld, criminals are punished, and the evil which men want to do is deterred by the fear of judgment.

Third, the Holy Spirit restrains sin by the moral influence exerted in our culture by Christians and their churches. We are to be salt and light in our culture. Salt, says the commentator William Barclay,[18] includes the ideas of purity, influence, and flavor. Jesus says to His disciples in Matthew 5:13, "You are the salt of the earth. But if the salt loses its saltiness, how can it be made salty again? It is no longer good for anything, except to be thrown out and trampled by men." Barclay says that salt was viewed by the Romans as the purest of all things (for it came from the purest of all things, the sun and the sea). The Christian must be an example of **purity**. Although he is not to turn his back on the world, he must keep himself from being "polluted by the world" (James 1:27).

When we lose our assurance as Christians, especially as we observe what seems to be God's apathy toward the evil in our world, we need to remember *our role* as salt! We are to have a *purifying* effect on our culture. Could it be that what the world (or even we ourselves) sees as God's absence or apathy is really *our* failure to live as salt in our culture?

A second idea of being salt, Barclay says, is that of **influence**. Because salt was the most common of preservatives, it was used to keep things from going bad, to hold putrefaction at bay. Barclay calls this the Christian's "antiseptic influence on life." Most likely few of us Christians think of ourselves as Listerine to the world, but we are to fight evil by our influence.

R. C. Sproul has a classic statement about the church seeking to become an influence on its surrounding culture:

The church is safe from vicious persecution at the hands of the secularist, as educated people have finished with stake-burning circuses and torture racks. No martyr's blood is shed in the secular

---

[18] William Barclay, *The Daily Study Bible Series*, "The Gospel of Matthew" (Philadelphia: Westminster Press, 1975 reprint, revised edition), vol. 1, pp. 118-122.

west. So long as the church knows her place and remains quietly at peace on her modern reservation. Let the babes pray and sing and read their Bibles, continuing steadfastly in their intellectual retardation; the church's extinction will not come by sword or pillory, but by the quiet death of irrelevance. But let the church step off the reservation, let her penetrate once more the culture of the day and the ... face of secularism will change from a benign smile to a savage snarl.[19]

The third idea of salt, Barclay says, is life, **flavor**! He quotes the apostate Emperor Julian (who came to power after Constantine made Christianity the State religion) who said, "Have you looked at these Christians closely? Hollow-eyed, pale-cheeked, flat-breasted all; they brood their lives away, unspurred by ambition: the sun shines for them, but they do not see it: the earth offers them its fulness, but they desire it not; all their desire is to renounce and to suffer that they may come to die." May I say that we have indeed got *renunciation* down pretty good, don't you think? Oliver Wendell Holmes once said, "I might have entered the ministry if certain clergymen I knew had not looked and acted so much like undertakers." Barclay concludes his discussion of the Christian as salt by saying, "... too often [the Christian] dresses like a mourner at a funeral, and talks like a spectre at a feast."

We Christians need to be life-affirming! We know the God who made all these things – which He has given us "richly to enjoy" (1 Tim. 6:17). When we Christians walk around looking like we've been baptized in lemon juice, when we fail to demonstrate to the world our abundant life, when we look like we're half-dead here and just waiting for our heavenly chariot to take us to glory, then the world has every right to wonder if God exists, and if He does, why don't we who claim to know Him look more joyful?

---

[19] R. C. Sproul, John Gerstner, and Arthur Lindsley, *Classical Apologetics: A Rational Defense of the Christian Faith and a Critique of Presuppositional Apologetics* (Grand Rapids: Zondervan, 1984), p. 4. Taylor expresses this as "allowing ... faith out of its box so that it pokes its nose where it does not belong" (*The Myth of Certainty*, p. 49).

We Christians are also supposed to be **light**. Jesus says in John 3:

> [19]This is the verdict: Light has come into the world, but men loved darkness instead of light because their deeds were evil. [20]Everyone who does evil hates the light, and will not come into the light for fear that his deeds will be exposed. [21]But whoever lives by the truth comes into the light, so that it may be seen plainly that what he has done has been done through God (John 3:19-21).

As **light**, the Christian is to recognize the opposition of evil men (v. 19), to expose the deeds of darkness (v. 20), and to model a God-honoring life before others (v. 21).

We also read in Ephesians 5:

> [8]For you were once darkness, but now you are light in the Lord. Live as children of light [9](for the fruit of the light consists in all goodness, righteousness and truth) [10]and find out what pleases the Lord. [11]Have nothing t o do with the fruitless deeds of darkness, but rather expose them. [12]For it is shameful even to mention what the disobedient do in secret. [13]But everything exposed by the light becomes visible, for it is light that makes everything visible.

Here we learn that as **light** we are to remember what we once were – darkness (v. 8); we are to live as children of light, doing the Lord's will (vv. 8-10); we are to commit ourselves to not participating in the "fruitless deeds of darkness" (v. 11a); and we are to engage in exposing and making visible that which dishonors God (vv. 11-13).

Often we believers simply lack courage to take a moral stand in our culture. John R. W. Stott has well said,

> Speaking personally, I long to see more Christian anger towards evil in the world, and more Christian compassion for its victims. Think of social injustice and political tyranny, of the callous killing of human foetuses in the womb as if they were no more than pieces of tissue, or the cynical wickedness of drug-pushers

and pornographers who make their fortunes out of other people's weaknesses and at the cost of their ruin. Since these and many other evils are hateful to God, should his people not react against them in anger?[20]

Christians are to continue the work which Jesus began, for He said in John 14, "Very truly I tell you, all who have faith in me will do the works I have been doing, and they will do even greater things than these, because I am going to the Father" (v. 12). Just as He was the salt and the light of the world (John 8:12; 9:5), so the believer in Christ is to be the salt and light of the world (Matt. 5:13-16). Believers are to be examples to the world of the power of the conscience (which is molded by the Word of God), the importance of submission to God-appointed human authorities, and the cultural influence of the church in affirming the good and exposing the evil of our generation.

When the world looks at its own suffering, some for which it is responsible and much which comes upon it in its fallen condition, and sees little evidence of God's presence in restraining evil, perhaps it is not God who is absent. God works *mediately* (that is, through His appointed means)[21] through believers to preserve what is good and to expose what is evil. When Christians disengage from their culture, it is not the Creator, but His creatures, who are apathetic to this world's brokenness.

---

[20] John R. W. Stott, *The Contemporary Christian* (Downers Grove, Ill.: InterVarsity, 1992), p. 124. The Christian is not just to do what is right, he or she is to try to fix what is wrong. In contrasting Christianity with other world religions, especially pantheism, Lewis writes: "[Christianity] thinks that a great many things have gone wrong with the world that God made and that God insists, and insists very loudly, on our putting them right again" (*Mere Christianity*, Bk. II, Ch. 1, p. 45).

[21] When we say that God works *immediately*, we are not referring to time, but to directness of action. The opening up of the earth and the subsequent swallowing up of Achan and his family (Josh. 4), for example, would be God's *immediate* action upon unbelief.

The Righteous Judgment of God

The second certainty to which Christians must cling when God appears apathetic toward a suffering world concerns His righteous judgment. Although judgment is God's "strange work" (Isa. 28:21), the Bible is filled with references to His holy wrapping up of history, especially to the *wrath* of God. Someone has said that the great preacher Jonathan Edwards' sermon "Sinners in the Hands of an Angry God" ought to be renamed "God in the Hands of Angry Sinners" today, for many feel that man is too good to be judged and God is too loving to judge. The very subject of God's righteous wrath is both mocked by liberals and minimized by conservative Christians.[22]

A misunderstanding of the concept of God's judgment and wrath may underlie its relatively minor role in much of evangelical theology. Packer's classic volume *Knowing God* describes God's wrath as "never the capricious, self-indulgent, irritable, morally ignorable thing that human anger so often is. It is, instead, a right and necessary reaction to objective moral evil. God is only angry where anger is called for."[23] Pink defines God's wrath as "His eternal detestation of all unrighteousness and the displeasure and indignation of Divine equity against evil."[24]

God is *not* apathetic to the evil in our world. We read in Psalm 7:11 that "God is angry with the wicked every day." Romans 2 says,

> [5]But because of your stubbornness and your unrepentant heart, you are storing up wrath against yourself for the day of God's

---

[22] See my article "Warning a Wrath-Deserving World: Evangelicals and the Overhaul of Hell" in vol. 2, pp. 7-21, of *The Emmaus Journal*, Summer 1993. For a more extensive discussion of remedial versus retributive wrath, please see my *The Other Side of the Good News: Hell According to Jesus* (Fearn, Ross-shire, Great Britain: Christian Focus Publications, 2003), *idem*.

[23] J. I. Packer, *Knowing God* (Downers Grove, Ill., InterVarsity, 1973), p. 136.

[24] Arthur W. Pink, *The Attributes of God* (Swengel, PA.: Refiner Publications, 1967), p. 83.

wrath, when his righteous judgment will be revealed. ⁶God will repay everyone according to what they have done.

Jeremiah records the Lord's declaration against His own people:

> I myself will fight against you with an outstretched hand and a mighty arm in anger and fury and great wrath. I will strike down those who live in this city – both men and animals – and they will die of a terrible plague (21:5-6).

Some liberal theologians perpetuate the myth of a God of wrath in the Old Testament and a God of love in the New Testament, but such a schizophrenic God is not the God of the Bible. There is plenty of love in the Old Testament and plenty of His wrath in the New Testament. After all, the last book of the New Testament declares,

> ¹¹Then I saw a great white throne and him who was seated on it. The earth and the heavens fled from his presence, and there was no place for them. ¹²And I saw the dead, great and small, standing before the throne, and books were opened. Another book was opened, which is the book of life. The dead were judged according to what they had done as recorded in the books. ¹³The sea gave up the dead that were in it, and death and Hades gave up the dead that were in them, and everyone was judged according to what they had done. ¹⁴Then death and Hades were thrown into the lake of fire. The lake of fire is the second death. ¹⁵All whose names were not found written in the book of life were thrown into the lake of fire (Rev. 20:11-15).

We read in John's gospel, "Whoever rejects the Son will not see life, for God's wrath remains on him" (John 3:36).

John Gerstner, the late Reformed church historian, in his book *Repent or Perish*, captures the attitude of many today: "God may not even be," Gerstner hears the unbeliever saying, "but if He is, one thing is sure, He could not send anyone to hell even if He wanted to. His mercy has His hands of holy wrath tied behind his back."[25] In a culture which mocks God's judgment and wrath, we must warn with strong language: "If you hug your sin and reject His Son, He'll do more than rap your knuckles. You will receive only His wrath."[26]

If there is no God of wrath who will righteously judge the deeds of all men, then we might as well side with the sympathies of the writer Jacques Monod who advises that we come to grips with an absent God:

> Man must learn to live in an alien world that is deaf to his music and is as indifferent to his hopes as it is to his sufferings or his crimes.... Man at la st knows that he is alone in the unfeeling

---

[25] John H. Gerstner, *Repent or Perish* (Ligonier, PA: Soli Deo Gloria Pub., 1990), p. 16. Universalists such as Thomas Talbott say that George MacDonald was "fond of pointing out that not one word in the New Testament implies that vindictiveness and wrath are ultimate facts about God, or that Christ's sacrifice was required in order to appease a vindictive God" (Thomas Talbott, *The Inescapable Love of God* [USA: Universal Publishers, 1999], p. 37). Such an opinion is not supported by the biblical data (see my "Warning a Wrath-Deserving World: Evangelicals and the Overhaul of Hell").

[26] Dr. Daniel Fuller makes the same point from a different perspective in his book *The Unity of the Bible*. Arguing from the doctrine of God's glory, Fuller states that "if God uses his great power to work all things together for the good of those who delight in him, then he must direct the full force of that power against people going in the opposite direction." That is, "God could not be loving to those who seek him if he did not vent the power of his wrath against those who remain impenitent. Far from being irreconcilable opposites, God's love and wrath are simply two ways in which he makes it clear that he himself fully honors his name"(Daniel Fuller, *The Unity of the Bible* [Grand Rapids: Zondervan, 1992], pp. 231-232). When a respected scholar like Dr. Marcus Borg (a major player in the Jesus Seminar) expresses his unbelief in the gospel, he needs to be warned of God's judgment: "The notion that God's only son came to this planet to offer his life as a sacrifice for the sins of the world, and that God could not forgive us without that having happened, and that we are saved by believing this story is simply incredible. Taken metaphorically, this story can be very powerful. But taken literally, it is a profound obstacle to accepting the Christian message" (*Meeting Jesus Again for the First Time* [San Francisco: Harper, 1994], p. 131.).

immensity of the universe, out of which he emerged only by chance.[27]

In a relativistic framework which does not turn to the Scriptures for the answer, all we can hope to do is soften the reality we have to endure, says Yancey,

In times of greater faith, people saw themselves as individual creations of a loving God who, regardless of how it may look at any given moment, has final control over a world destined for restoration. Now, people with no faith find themselves lost and alone, with no overarching story, or meta-narrative, to give promise to the future and meaning to the present. To regard nature as beautiful, humans as uniquely valuable, morality as necessary – these are mere "constructs," we are told, invented to soften the harsh reality that humans play an infinitesimal role in a universe governed by chance.[28]

Is that really all there is? Or does the Bible present the picture of a longsuffering God who grieves at the suffering that human beings inflict on one another, uses the pain of the world to "rouse a deaf world" (as Lewis says), and will one day expunge all evil from His presence? Yancey concludes,

What I have tasted of love on this earth convinces me that a perfect love will not be satisfied with the sad tale of this planet, will not rest until evil is conquered and good reigns, will not allow its object to pass from existence. Perfect love perseveres until it perfects.[29]

It is a "fearful thing to fall into the hands of an angry God!" (Heb. 10:31 KJV), says the Word of God. We are presently living in the day of mercy in which Jesus Christ and His forgiveness is

---

[27] Jacques Monod, quoted in Yancey, *Rumors*, p. 20.
[28] Yancey, *Rumors*, p. 20.
[29] Ibid., pp. 172-173.

being offered to sinners.[30] We believers can have the assurance, the certainty, that God is neither apathetic nor absent. He longs for the lost sheep to come home. The believer's assurance should motivate him to join that rescue mission.

---

[30] To the question, why is God delaying His judgment, Lewis writes: "He is going to land in force; we do not know when. But we can guess why He is delaying. He wants to give us the chance of joining His side freely.... God will invade. But I wonder whether people who ask God to interfere openly and directly in our world quite realize what it will be like when He does. When that happens, it is the end of the world.... Now, today, this moment, is our chance to choose the right side. God is holding back to give us that chance. It will not last for ever. We must take it or leave it" (*Mere Christianity*, Book II, Ch. 5, p. 66).

Chapter 13

"The Believer's Anticipation"

"Second only to suffering, waiting may be the greatest teacher and trainer in godliness, maturity, and genuine spirituality most of us ever encounter." (Richard Hendrix)

Richard Leakey, the Kenyan anthropologist and author, was once asked the question: "What happens after death?" To which he replied, "I don't think anything need happen."

"But the day of the Lord will come like a thief. The heavens will disappear with a roar; the elements will be destroyed by fire, and the earth and everything done in it will be laid bare. Since everything will be destroyed in this way, what kind of people ought you to be? You ought to live holy and godly lives as you look forward to the day of God and speed its coming" (2 Peter 3:10-12).

A Brief Review:
In this text we have thought through a number of key issues having to do with living out the Christian life. We began by

looking at the believer's **acceptance**, emphasizing that we have been ransomed, redeemed, reconciled, and rescued. We are now "accepted in the Beloved" (Eph. 1:6). We then examined the believer's **authority** and saw that we should turn away from superstitious views of the Scriptures and focus upon the Bible's nature as a hidden treasure, the believer's food, a collection of case studies, the autobiography of God, and the divine agenda for the Christian. Next we looked at the believer's **anatomy**, asking how we should use our mind, emotions, will, speech, and body for Christ. We discussed the believer's **associations**, seeking to make the point that we need non-Christian friends and we require Christian friendships so that we can practice the four priorities of the Early Church. In Chapter 10, we considered the believer's **attitudes** and in Chapter 11 the believer's **actions**. In our preceding chapter we looked at the believer's **assurance**. We now turn in conclusion to the believer's **anticipation**. [I'll bet you can hardly wait!]

An Attitude of Anticipation?

Even though we've covered the subject of some of the believer's attitudes in Chapter 10, we want to discuss how the Christian should live *an anticipatory life*. This is more than an attitude. It is an orientation, a mindset, an expectation, about both Christ's first and second Comings.

The follower of Christ must not be marked by a defeatist perspective which sees a gray cloud behind every silver lining. He or she should not adopt the cynicism of the world which says that nothing can change in this life, that it all is going to the dogs. The Christian doctrine of hope should sustain the believer in Christ and give courage to live in this world. For what do we hope? Titus 2:13 says that we "wait for the blessed hope, the glorious appearing of our great God and Savior, Jesus Christ...." Our hope is directed toward the Lord Jesus' returning for His people. And that kind of hope can give us courage not only to *wait*, but to **work** for His kingdom. When we say the Christian should be marked by an attitude of anticipation, we do not mean that we can somehow Christianize the world,[1] although we should strive to be salt and light in every area of society. We should not write off the world as if it were simply beyond any redemptive effects of the gospel.

Our Anticipation Aversion

The great "theologian" Carly Simon (former wife of James Taylor) once sang, "Anticipation – It's making me wait! It's keeping me wai-ai-ai-ai-aiting!" Used as a slogan to advertise the slowness and thickness of Heinz catsup, it illustrated one value of waiting. In our instant culture, one which panders to our every craving to have what we want *now*, the very idea of being made to wait seems absurd to us. We want instant dinners, video-on-demand, immediate home loan approval on the internet.[2] We are not a people who wait patiently; we seem to envy the cartoon character RoadRunner's life. We certainly don't see *anticipation* as having educative value. We prefer the "Play" button to the "Pause" button on our lives (often holding down the "Fast Forward" button at the same time). But pausing – waiting – is what every believer in Christ must do.

Richard Hendrix has said that "Second only to suffering, waiting may be the greatest teacher and trainer in godliness, maturity, and genuine spirituality most of us ever encounter." A study by Michael Fortino, the president of the consulting firm Priority Management, discovered that most people spend

---

[1] The theological system known as postmillennialism advances the perspective that we can take the world for Christ, ushering in a kind of Golden Age which will hasten the Lord's Return. Books by John Jefferson Davis present postmillennialism in an understandable way.

[2] Instantaneity has even invaded the men's room where a sensor flushes the urinal for you, water in the sink comes on automatically when you put your hand under the faucet, and the paper towel dispenser grants you a small piece as you wave your wet hands in front of the electronic sensor. I'm reminded of the statement by Stephen Jay Gould who sarcastically said, "If we continue to follow the acceleration of human technological time so that we end in a black hole of oblivion, the Earth and its bacteria will only smile at us as a passing evolutionary folly" (Quoted in Gleick's *Faster*, p. 274).

five years of their lives waiting in lines and six months sitting at traffic lights. In an average lifetime, people spend one year searching for misplaced objects, six years eating, eight months opening junk mail, four years doing housework, and two years trying to return telephone calls to people who never seem to be in. [Fortino's study, by the way, was done years ago when "spam" referred to a kind of canned meat and "RoadRunner" was only a cartoon character.] As a society we *hate* to wait!

Wasted vs. Worthwhile Waiting

There is a difference between wasted waiting and worthwhile waiting. Wasted waiting is when you discover that what you were waiting for was not worth the wait. It is when you realize you were waiting for the wrong thing. Waiting seems to be particularly wasteful when you don't know why you're waiting, when your waiting is unproductive, or when it feels like all you're doing is just standing around. In a culture that doesn't believe it should have to wait for anything, wasted waiting seems like forces outside our control are greedily sucking precious minutes out of our lives.

Worthwhile waiting, on the other hand, has value in and of itself. This kind of waiting produces qualities in you which you otherwise would not have acquired. In worthwhile waiting, the waiting is forgotten when that for which you waited becomes a reality. You know why you're waiting in worthwhile waiting – and you don't mind. There is value to *anticipation*!

In Titus 2 the Apostle Paul writes to Titus:

> [11]For the grace of God that brings salvation has appeared to all men. [12]It teaches us to say "No" to ungodliness and worldly passions, and to live self-controlled, upright and godly lives in this present age, [13]while we wait for the blessed hope – the glorious appearing of our great God and Savior, Jesus Christ... (vv. 11-15).

God's grace is a *waiting* grace. Notice in verse 13 that we are waiting for an event: the blessed hope. But we are really waiting for a *Person*, the Lord Jesus Christ. This is the only time in Scripture that the phrase "the blessed hope" is used. We have other texts that speak of our "hope" in Christ, such as Ephesians 1 where Paul says,

> [17]I keep asking that the God of our Lord Jesus Christ, the glorious Father, may give you the Spirit of wisdom and revelation, so that you may know him better. [18]I pray that the eyes of your heart may be enlightened in order that you may know **the hope** to which he has called you, the riches of his glorious inheritance in his people, [19]and his incomparably great power for us who believe.

We also have Paul praying in Colossians 1:

> [3]We always thank God, the Father of our Lord Jesus Christ, when we pray for you, [4]because we have heard of your faith in Christ Jesus and of the love you have for all God's people – [5]the faith and love that spring from **the hope** stored up for you in heaven and about which you have already heard in the true word of the gospel...

In Hebrews 6 we are told that,

> [17]Because God wanted to make the unchanging nature of his purpose very clear to the heirs of what was promised, he confirmed it with an oath. [18]God did this so that, by two unchangeable things in which it is impossible for God to lie, we who have fled to take hold of the hope set before us may be greatly encouraged. [19]We have **this hope** as an anchor for the soul, firm and secure.

We are waiting for "the blessed hope" (Titus 2:13), "the glorious appearing of our great God and Savior, Jesus Christ...." This expression sounds very much like Peter in 2 Peter where he introduces himself as, "Simon Peter, a servant and apostle of Jesus Christ, To those who through the righteousness of our God and Savior Jesus Christ have received a faith as precious as ours ..." (2 Peter 1:1). We Christians are not waiting for *two* individuals to come back for us, are we? Paul says to Titus, we are waiting for the glorious appearing of "our great God and Savior, Jesus Christ." We Christians are waiting for one individual to come back for us – the Lord Jesus Christ *who is Himself God!* And isn't *God* worth waiting for?[3]

Agnostic Anticipation

Our modern world would prefer not to grapple with the concept of Jesus Christ's second Coming. This makes sense, for it hardly acknowledges His first Coming (except at Christmas when the idea of Christ's Incarnation seems to be in style or, at least, unavoidable). Agnosticism, the position that says "I don't know what to believe – and neither does anyone else, for that matter!", appeals to many. Such a stance might on the surface appear brave and open-minded and humble, but it flies in the face of solid evidence for the truth of the gospel.

In his book *The Journal of a Disappointed Man*, British diarist W. N. P. Barbellion candidly wrote:

> I ask myself: what are my views on death, the next world, God? I look into my mind and discover I am too much of a mannikin to have any. As for death, I am a little bit of trembling jelly of anticipation. I am prepared for anything, but I am the complete agnostic; I simply don't know. To have views, faith, beliefs, one

---

[3] One can't help but think of Samuel Beckett's existential play "Waiting for Godot." The play's theme appears to be how to pass the time in a situation that offers no hope. Godot is a character who never shows up, but waiting for him is the way the actors spend their empty hours. Whether or not Godot exists does not make any difference. The belief in him keeps two people from killing themselves, yet living in a ditch. It keeps them away from the places where they want to go and at the same time, it keeps them together. This belief serves the most important function: it gives purpose to their lives. Beckett is believed to have said that the name Godot comes from the French "godillot" meaning a military boot. Beckett fought in the war and so spending long periods of time waiting for messages to arrive would have been commonplace for him. The popular interpretation that it might mean "God" is almost certainly wrong. Beckett apparently stated that if he had meant "God," he would have written "God" (www.gradesaver.com). Regardless, how good for us believers to literally be waiting for the return of God the Son.

needs a backbone. This great bully of a universe overwhelms me. The stars make me cower. I am intimidated by the immensity surrounding my own littleness. It is futile and presumptuous for me to opine anything about the next world. But I hope for something much freer and more satisfying after death, for emancipation of the spirit and above all for the obliteration of this puny self, this little, skulking, sharp-witted ferret.[4]

The Christian is not "a little bit of trembling jelly of anticipation"! He or she has not "opined" about the next world; he or she has simply believed what God has said in His Word. Although he appears very much the coward, Barbellion has dared turn away from the biblical testimony about life after death, about Jesus Christ being the only way to the Father, about the need to have one's sins forgiven. That sounds not like cowardice, but like incredibly stupid bravery! Perhaps he wants sympathy for his fear of commitment, but he has clearly planted himself in opposition to God's Word and rests in his "hope for something much freer and more satisfying after death." He pretends he has no faith, that he is "prepared for anything," that he lacks the backbone to believe. But he is self-deluded. He *has believed*; he has come to a definite conclusion, a conclusion which turns away from God's proclamation and has substituted his own pathetic opinion about what he *wishes* would be the case.

But what about Barbellion's fear? Revelation 21 tells us in no uncertain terms:

> [8]But the **cowardly**, the unbelieving, the vile, the murderers, the sexually immoral, those who practice magic arts, the idolaters and all liars – they will be consigned to the fiery lake of burning sulfur. This is the second death.

No one will be able to say at the judgment, "I was just a trembling jelly of anticipation." No one will be able to excuse

---

[4] W. N. P. Barbellion (1889–1919), British diarist. *The Journal of a Disappointed Man*, March 2, 1917, Chatto and Windus (1919).

their rejection of Christ by claiming, "I just didn't have the backbone to believe all that stuff about the crucifixion and the resurrection." The **cowardly** will also be consigned to a place of separation from the living God.

A Biblical Optimism

Someone has said that the optimist sees the glass as half-full; the pessimist sees it as half-empty; but the realist sees the water as probably polluted! We are to be *biblical optimists*: that is, our confidence is in God's promises, in His work in and through us, in His fulfilling what He said He would do. He will accomplish His will; the gates of hell will not finally prevail against the building of His church. There is no room for a despairing disciple who has lost sight of Christ's goals and his part in achieving those goals.

Two Categories of Anticipation

I divide the believer's anticipation into two categories: how the Christian should live in light of Christ's first Coming and how the Christian should live in light of His promised second Coming. We will examine each of these briefly.

Our anticipation is not just oriented to Christ's second Coming. We should live anticipatory lives *now* in the sense that we look forward to certain effects of His first Coming on us. There are five responses to His first Coming that ought to be true of every believer.

The Truth of His First Coming: ❶ Let's Apologize!

We do not wait for His first Coming – He has come! That is what Christmas is all about. We are the visited planet. The first response to His first Coming is that we need to defend the true Incarnation of Christ. We must set forth the evidences for Christ's historicity.[5] We don't need to apologize in the common

---

[5] We have excellent resources available to us in this area. Lee Strobel's *A Case for Christ* (Grand Rapids: Zondervan, 1998) is quite helpful here.

understanding of that term (to say we're sorry for being Christians), but we do need to engage in apologetics (providing evidences for our faith). We dare not assume that people accept Christianity's premise that the Savior of the world has been born. "In the midst of a generation screaming for answers, Christians are stuttering," said Howard Hendricks.

Despite the foolish rantings of some postmodern Christians, we are to challenge people to believe the gospel *because it is true!* The undermining of truth and its pursuit is probably the biggest set-back to the cause of Christ in the history of Christianity.

For the believer in Christ, recapturing the truthfulness of the truth of Christ's first Coming means that our work for Him is not "in vain." Because of Christ's victorious sacrifice and triumphant resurrection, death has lost its sting (1 Cor. 15:55). Paul explodes in praise as he says, "But thanks be to God! He gives us the victory through our Lord Jesus Christ." He continues,

> Therefore, my dear brothers and sisters, stand firm. Let nothing move you. Always give yourselves fully to the work of the Lord, because you know that your labor in the Lord is not in vain (v. 58).

We must recover the place of biblical apologetics if we are going to set forth Christianity as *the* answer to modern man's lostness.[6] We must not give up, abandon ship, bail out, or drop out when it comes to arguing the case for Christ. Abraham Kuyper said, "When principles that run against your deepest convictions begin to win the day, then battle is your calling,

---

[6] In his important text, John G. Stackhouse, Jr. focuses on Christian arrogance and apologetic dogmatism. He says that all we can do is lead someone to an actual encounter with Jesus. Humility, rather than an effort to win religious arguments, is the key. (*Humble Apologetics: Defending the Faith Today* [New York: Oxford University Press, 2002]). I'm reminded, however, of the ditty that although you can't argue someone into the Kingdom of God, if we Christians are always losing arguments, we won't win people either!

and peace has become sin; you must, at the price of dearest peace, lay your convictions bare before friend and enemy, with all the fire of your faith."[7]

We anticipate that God will use our apologetic efforts in presenting the evidences for the Lord Jesus Christ. We seek to persuade[8] and we look forward to the Holy Spirit bringing conviction of sin to those who listen to a defense of Christianity's truth.

The Truth of His First Coming: ② Let's Cooperate!

The Apostle Paul prays for the Philippians in chapter 1:

> I thank my God every time I remember you. [4]In all my prayers for all of you, I always pray with joy [5]because of your partnership in the gospel from the first day until now, [6]being confident of this, that he who began a good work in you will carry it on to completion until the day of Christ Jesus.

This "good work" in us which Christ will bring to completion is our sanctification, our becoming holy like the Lord Jesus. It was Christ who *began* that good work in us; it will be Christ who will *carry it to completion*. But we are not automatons or robots in that process. We *cooperate* with the sanctifying work of Christ through the Holy Spirit. We submit to God's Word, we allow our lives to be changed by prayer, we progressively turn away from sin, we commit ourselves to His priorities, etc.

A serious study of Scripture is how we attune our hearts to His will. Daily, committed, strategic prayer is how we become motivated to live for Him and not for ourselves. Listening to the counsel of godly advisors is how we break out of our myopia, our near-sightedness, and gain some perspective on our lives.

---

[7] Quoted in Colson, *Against the Night*, p. 163.

[8] As much as I appreciate Billy Graham and his ministry, I wish he had named his ministry's magazine something like "Persuasions" instead of "Decision," for the book of Acts shows us the early Christians' efforts in *persuading* people to believe the gospel.

When I was in high school I distinctly remember the day Mrs. McGillicutty substituted in biology. Needless to say, we students drove her crazy with our antics. [It is common high school student policy that subs are to be tormented]. We all agreed ahead of class that if Mrs. McGillicutty asked any of us any questions having to do with biology, we would all answer, "Would the answer be '*osmosis*,' Mrs. McGillicutty?" In biology and chemistry, osmosis refers to a process by which molecules of a solvent pass through a semipermeable membrane from a less concentrated solution into a more concentrated one. A second definition of osmosis is "the gradual assimilation of ideas." We high-schoolers were neither permeable nor concentrated. We just thought the word "osmosis" sounded good, and so we tortured our teacher. I'm pretty sure she became an insurance agent the next year.

Many Christians think that spiritual growth happens as a result of *spiritual* osmosis. They make sure they are seated in their respective pews at the appointed hours of church services so that they can soak in truth. But there is no such thing as spiritual osmosis. We are only fooling ourselves if we think that mere attendance is how we grow in the Christian life.[9] Of course, not attending the services of a good local church won't help either. But we grow not just out of attendance, but by *paying attention* to what is being taught, by opening our hearts to the divine substitute teacher the Holy Spirit (whom we had better not abuse!), and by choosing to do God's will with our lives. In speaking of how the Christian grows, C. S. Lewis' archdemon Screwtape writes his nephew understudy Wormwood:

> Desiring their freedom, He ... refuses to carry them, by their mere affections and habits, to any of the goals which He sets before them: He leaves them to "do it on their own."[10]

---

[9] In my tradition I often heard Christians refer to church attendance as "being under the sound of the Word." But hearing alone is not enough, as the epistle of James makes abundantly clear.

[10] C. S. Lewis, *Screwtape Letters*, p. 13.

Our "doing it on our own" involves anticipating God blessing the choices we make to become more like the Lord Jesus Christ. We give in to His grace; we submit to the transforming process. He does not co-opt us; He awaits our cooperation.

The Truth of His First Coming: ❸ Let's Infiltrate!

This was my burden in Chapter 11 on the believer's actions. We have no biblical justification for developing godly ghettos or staying in our Christian cocoons. We are to be salt and light in our culture, a challenge which I have discussed in our previous chapter. Daniel Taylor says, "Christians should be getting dirt under their fingernails in almost every area of interest to human beings."[11] I agree with his challenge when he adds,

> The Christian who is inclined and equipped should make the greatest contribution possible to the wide range of human activities. We should be the first to do many good things, not the ones dragged reluctantly into the modern world. We also should expect to learn much of value from nonbelievers in the process. They too, it is rumored, are made in the image of God.[12]

We are to have a savory effect on society. We dare not *isolate*; we must *infiltrate*! We Christians should be productive members of PTA meetings, local neighborhood associations, members of sports teams, volunteers for charity organizations, fellow peaceful protesters in Pro-life rallies, etc. We need to have committed Christians as philosophy professors in *secular* universities, religion teachers in local junior colleges, ethics instructors in business schools, lawyers who refuse to compromise their morals, plumbers who do honest work at a fair price, and car mechanics to whom we can recommend our own grandmothers when their cars need repairs. Our lives should be our advertisements, not quarter-page ads in a Christian Yellow Pages. Our reputations should precede us, not

---

[11] Taylor, *The Myth of Certainty*, p. 46.
[12] Ibid., p. 54.

massive mailings with little fish symbols on the card advertising that we are *Christian* realtors, etc. We should not wear our religiosity on our sleeve. But when people find out that we are committed to Jesus Christ, they should not be surprised.

Infiltration is vastly different than isolation or assimilation. Isolation is when we separate ourselves from our culture, stand back and criticize it, and wait to be fetched off the planet by angelic escort. Assimilation is when we become so like our surrounding culture that we become indistinguishable from it. We share its fundamental assumptions about life and we lose our identity and our message. Are you seeking to *infiltrate*?

We anticipate God's using us in our culture to make a difference for His kingdom. In light of His first Coming, we are to be examples of John the Baptist's advice to believers in secular positions. We read in Luke 3,

> [12]Even tax collectors came to be baptized. "Teacher," they asked, "what should we do?" [13]"Don't collect any more than you are required to," he told them. [14]Then some soldiers asked him, "And what should we do?" He replied, "Don't extort money and don't accuse people falsely – be content with your pay."

The Epistle to Diognetus apparently was an effort to explain second century Christianity to one who was examining its claims. The letter describes the early believers:

> They dwell in their own countries but simply as sojourners. As citizens, they share in all things with others, and yet endure all things as if foreigners. Every foreign land is to them as their native country, and every land of their birth as a land of strangers. They marry, as do others; they beget children; but they do not destroy their offspring. They have a common table but not a common bed. They are in the flesh, but they do not live after the flesh. They pass their days on earth, but are citizens of heaven. They obey the prescribed laws, and at the same time surpass the laws in their lives. They love all, and are persecuted by all.... They are poor, yet they make many rich; they are completely destitute, and yet they enjoy complete abundance.... They are reviled, and yet they bless....

When they do good they are punished as evildoers; undergoing punishment, they rejoice because they are brought to life.[13]

Please notice: The early Christians did not isolate themselves from their surrounding culture. Nor did they treat this world as their final home. They engaged in marriage, had children, but did not practice abortion. They shared their meals but not their spouses. They obeyed earthly laws, enriched the communities where they lived, and suffered persecution patiently. In light of Christ's first Coming, so should we.

The Truth of His First Coming: ❹ Let's Propagate!

One of my all-time favorite Christian radio hosts was a young woman we will call Mary. She worked at our local Christian radio station and would occasionally have a "slip of the lip." During Pastors' Appreciation Month, she wanted to encourage her listeners to do something *creative* for their pastors. She also wanted to challenge them not to miss the opportunity to express their thanks to their pastors, so she thought they needed to be encouraged to be *proactive*. You guessed it. What she said on air was, "This is Pastors' Appreciation Month. So go out and do something *procreative* for your Pastor this week!"

We *are* to be procreative as believers. We're to seek to "be fruitful and multiply." We are to sow the seeds of the gospel wherever we can. We cannot bring people to Christ; we cannot make them believe. However, we can sow seeds and trust God to water them and bring them to fruition. We read in Psalm 126:5-6, "Those who sow in tears will reap with songs of joy. He who goes out weeping, carrying seed to sow, will return with songs of joy, carrying sheaves with him." This Psalm's theme is "songs of joy" (see vv. 2, 3, 5, and 6). We are to care enough about the lost that we will weep, we will sow, and, by God's grace, we will reap! Isaiah 55:10-11 says,

---

[13] Epistle to Diognetus (about AD 130), accessed at http://www.gospelcom.net/chi/quotes/quote003.shtml.

¹⁰As the rain and the snow come down from heaven, and do not return to it without watering the earth and making it bud and flourish, so that it yields seed for the sower and bread for the eater, ¹¹so is my word that goes out from my mouth: It will not return to me empty, but will accomplish what I desire and achieve the purpose for which I sent it.

We anticipate God blessing the sowing of gospel seeds. I recently invited an unsaved friend of mine (we'll call him John) to consider coming to a Bible study my wife and I were starting. "It's based on the best-seller *The Purpose-Driven Life* by Rick Warren. We'd love to have you and your wife come," I said. I loaned him a copy of the book and he said he would get back to me.

A week later I asked John if he and his wife were going to be able to come to our Bible study. "No, I don't think so," he said. "It's just not something for us." I was disappointed. When he and I played tennis later that week, he gave me the book back. I said, "John, if you change your mind, you and your wife are invited to come whenever you would like to." I thought that was the end of the discussion.

After a few games, we took a break and John volunteered why they would not be coming to the study. "It's just ... just that the book is way too *specific!*" "What do you mean?," I asked. "Well, my wife's background is Lutheran; mine's Catholic. We're both on our second marriage. And I've done too much reading in other religions to be that specific. You know, Larry, Christ never claimed to be God." "So you've kind of given up on a pursuit of truth?", I asked. "I didn't say *that!*," John responded. "But you can make the Bible mean anything you want it to mean. All that is really important is to be good to one another and live a good life." "Man" (I thought to myself), "I *love* sowing seeds!"

The Truth of His First Coming: ⑤ Let's Be Ready to Meet the Lord!

In thinking about how we Christians can live anticipatory lives in light of the Lord's first coming, one passage of Scripture comes to mind which is rather shocking. Jesus has some reporters bring Him some extremely disturbing – and tragic – news. How He responds to their report is both surprising to them and helpful to us in preparing us for the end of this life. Let's look at Luke 13:

> Now there were some present at that time who told Jesus about the Galileans whose blood Pilate had mixed with their sacrifices. ²Jesus answered, "Do you think that these Galileans were worse sinners than all the other Galileans because they suffered this way? ³I tell you, no! But unless you repent, you too will all perish. ⁴Or those eighteen who died when the tower in Siloam fell on them – do you think they were more guilty than all the others living in Jerusalem? ⁵I tell you, no! But unless you repent, you too will all perish.

This is a highly significant passage for many reasons, not the least of which is that it presents some insight into Jesus' *theodicy* (His defense of the justice of God in the face of evil's reality). The text breaks down nicely into two sections: (1) verses 1-4 deal with what I call *victims of a vicious crime*, and (2) verses 5-6 discuss *victims of a violent accident*.

In the first section, the report is brought to Jesus about some of His Galilean countrymen who are massacred by Pilate while they were in the midst of worshiping God. We don't know what their offense was; we simply are told that they are executed and that their blood was mixed with their sacrifices (a despicable act of desecration).

Jesus asks a question in verse 2 to uncover the motive of the reporters: "Do you think that these Galileans were worse sinners than all the other Galileans because they suffered this way?" Why had they reported this event to Jesus? Perhaps their motive was political; that is, they wanted to incite Jesus against the Roman authorities so that He would lead a rebellion. A second possible motive might have been theological. Maybe their underlying question was, "How could something this horrible happen to God's people when they are in the act of worship?! How can God let something like this take place?!"

I believe that their motive was probably theological, for Jesus' question ("Do you think that these Galileans were worse sinners than all the other Galileans because they suffered this way?") seems to challenge the idea that these victims of this vicious crime somehow "deserved" what happened to them. Jesus answers His own question by saying, "I tell you, no! But unless you repent, you too will all perish" (v. 3). Jesus' answer implies that they had not been executed because of their exceeding sinfulness. He then quickly challenges the reporters with the words: "But unless you repent, you too will all perish." Was Jesus saying that Pilate would be coming for them next? Or was He teaching that life is risky, evil rulers do evil things, even to God's people? And God's people need to be ready to die, if it is God's permitted will, at the hands of others.

What I find particularly engaging about this text is what happens next. In verses 4-5 *Jesus* is the reporter and *He* brings up a contemporary tragic event to be considered. He refers to the death of eighteen when a certain tower fell on them. Jesus makes it clear that this group also did not deserve their fate – they were not more guilty than all the others living in Jerusalem. They were simply victims of a violent accident. Jesus answers His own question about comparative sinfulness by saying, "But unless you repent, you too will all perish" (v. 5). I do not think He is saying, "Beware! A tower might fall on you!" Rather, He is saying that life is dangerous. And even God's people can become victims of a violent accident. So God's people – all people – need to be ready to meet God![14]

Christians die every day as a result of vicious crimes or violent

---

[14] By the way, Jesus provides us here with a model of how we should deal with human tragedy. If you are like me, when a major earthquake happens or some other tragedy results in the loss of human life, you tend to hide from your pagan friends, fearful that they will bring up these events to you and ask, "How could a God of love let this happen?!" According to Jesus, *we* should be bringing these catastrophes to the attention of others – and then clearly speaking about the brevity of life and the cruciality of being right with God.

accidents. We believers are to be ready to meet the Lord, affirming the biblical truth that we do not know what a day might bring forth. Our lives should reflect the truth of James 4,

> [13]Now listen, you who say, "Today or tomorrow we will go to this or that city, spend a year there, carry on business and make money." [14]Why, you do not even know what will happen tomorrow. What is your life? You are a mist that appears for a little while and then vanishes. [15]Instead, you ought to say, "If it is the Lord's will, we will live and do this or that."

When the film director Woody Allen says, "It's not that I'm afraid of dying; I just don't want to be there when it happens," Christians respond to such mockery with a readiness to meet the Lord. We do not seek death, but want to honor the Lord when in His providence He decides to take us home.

Dorothy Sayers put into words the sentiment of many in our culture when she wrote:

> The sin of our times is the sin that believes in nothing, cares for nothing, hates nothing, finds purpose in nothing, lives for nothing, and remains alive because there is nothing for which it will die.[15]

We, on the other hand, blend our voices with the Apostle Paul's who said, "For me to live is Christ, and to die is gain" (Phil. 1:21).

The Reality of His Second Coming: ❶ Let's Not Speculate!
Jesus Christ clearly taught regarding His second Coming, "But about that day or hour no one knows, not even the angels in heaven, nor the Son, but only the Father" (Mark 13:32). Christians have categorically ignored those words throughout history and have played "can-you-top-this?" in setting dates for the second Coming, even though Jesus Himself said He did not know the day or the hour of His return.

Two scholars specializing in mass hysteria report the following event which occurred in 1806 in Britain.

---

[15] Quoted by Charles Colson in *Against the Night*, p. 93.

In that year a panic spread through Leeds and the surrounding communities that the end of the world was at hand. The "panic terror" began when a hen from a nearby village was said to begin laying eggs inscribed with the message, "Christ is coming." Large numbers flocked to the site to examine the eggs and see the "miracle" first-hand. Many were convinced that the end was near and suddenly became devoutly religious. [One scholar] states that excitement then quickly turned to disappointment when a man "caught the poor hen in the act of laying one of her miraculous eggs" and soon determined "that the egg had been inscribed with some corrosive ink, and cruelly forced up again into the bird's body."[16]

All Christians want Jesus Christ to return, but that was a bit extreme, don't you think?

Another researcher tells the story of Edgar C. Whisenant, a retired NASA rocket engineer from Little Rock, Arkansas, who published a book entitled *Eighty-Eight Reasons Why the Rapture Will Be in '88*. The publisher claims they sold or gave away over six million copies. Whisenant's book predicted that the rapture would occur on September 11, 12, or 13, 1988. When the rapture did not occur, Whisenant said he found a slight error in his calculations and moved the date to September 1, 1989. As one scholar says,

When that date also proved wrong, Whisenant decided henceforth to keep his mouth shut. He told a reporter he was under medication to control paranoid schizophrenia, but that his mental condition had no bearing on his calculations.[17]

[On a personal note: I own a copy of Whisenant's book. I have always found it amazing that such date-setting books never come with a money-back guarantee. After all, if they are

---

[16] Robert E. Bartholomew and Erich Goode, "Mass Delusions and Hysterias: Highlights from the Past Millennium," *Skeptical Inquirer*, May, 2000, vol. 24, i3, p. 20.

[17] Martin Gardner, "The Second Coming of Jesus," *Skeptical Inquirer*, Jan. 2000, vol. 24, i1, p. 9.

wrong, they ought to refund your money. And if they are right, no refund is necessary.]

One particularly unfortunate example of date-setting comes from South Korea. In 1992, Lee Jang Rim, the head of one of some 200 Protestant churches in that country, announced that the rapture would take place on October 28, 1992. Based on a vision of a sixteen-year-old boy, twenty thousand Korean fundamentalists in South Korea, Los Angeles, and New York City took the prediction seriously. Hundreds quit their jobs, many left their families, some women unfortunately even had abortions (presumably to make their own raptures easier). Rim's church bought costly ads in the Los Angeles *Times* and the *New York Times*. They urged readers to get ready for the rapture and to refuse to have 666 imprinted in bar code on their foreheads or right hands. On October 28, one researcher says,

> Riot police, plainclothes officers, and reporters crowded outside Korean churches, flanked by fire engines, ambulances, and searchlights. Believers took the failure of the prophecy calmly, and there were no reported riots. Only sadness. In December 1992 Rim was arrested and sentenced to two years in prison for having bilked $4.4 million from his flock. He had invested the money in bonds that didn't mature until the following year![18]

Another example will hopefully suffice to show that date-setting is injurious to the spiritual health of the believer – and an embarrassment to the cause of Christ. Harold Camping, President of Family Radio (thirty-nine radio stations nationwide), published in 1992 his book *1994?* which predicted that the second Coming would occur in September of that year (what *is* it about *September*?!). Camping followed *1994?* in 1993 by a sequel titled *Are You Ready?* These two books totaled 955 pages. This non-ordained Bible scholar conducts a nightly call-in radio talk show which he hosts from his headquarters in Oakland, California. When September came with no sign

---

[18] Ibid.

of the Lord's return, Camping adjusted his date to October 2. When that passed uneventfully, he stopped setting dates, but he soon began teaching something that is far more injurious than a bad date for the second Coming.[19]

The *Left Behind* series of fictional novels, written by Tim LaHaye and Jerry Jenkins, depict a pre-tribulational rapture and its after-effects, and have sold over 40 million copies. One researcher says of this series that,

> Novels and films are churning out an intricate set of narratives that blend fundamentalist orthodoxy and conservative politics in a nightmarish vision of the world's imminent demise. Given that a recent Time/CNN poll showed that 59 percent of Americans believe that the events in Revelation are going to come true, the extraordinary popularity of the apocalyptic *Left Behind* series is something to be taken seriously indeed.[20]

---

[19] Ibid. In 2002 Camping, octogenarian founder and head of Family Stations Inc., began teaching that Christians are in the Great Tribulation and should depart from their congregations. "No longer are you to be under the spiritual rulership of the church," Camping wrote in a 2001 tract, "Has the Era of the Church Age Come to an End?" He cites the injunction of Jesus for believers to flee a "Jerusalem" that has been "compassed with armies" (Mark Kellner, "Camping: 'Leave Church': Family Radio founder's latest teaching prompts church defections", *Christianity Today*, May 21, 2002). Christian recording artist Steve Camp writes: "Heresy is always a stealing of some Christian rags to cover heathen nakedness! Harold Camping is sewing a new fig leaf to cover his abhorrent privates by trying to establish a new Romanism with Family Radio as the cathedral and he the self-appointed new Pope. But careful, biblical examination reveals that 'this Emperor has no clothes.' After his failed prophecy that Christ was returning in 1994 – he has resorted to another Edenistic pursuit – the demise, dismantling, and extinction of the local church. This is pure folly – Christianity by Howard Stern – and is comical except for the thousands who have unwittingly adopted it as orthodox." (http://www.familyradioiswrong.com/camping_most_dangerous.htm).

[20] Melani McAlister, "An empire of their own: how born-again Christians turned biblical prophecy into big-time profit," *The Nation*, Sept 22, 2003 v277, i8, p. 31.

Randall Balmer, an evangelical who has written a series of influential studies on the fundamentalist movement, says that the focus on prophecy emerges out of a "theology of despair" based on a "slavishly literalistic" reading of Revelation. He describes the *Left Behind* series as "camp fiction," and calls it both triumphalist and self-righteous. Other commentators aren't nearly so generous: *Christian Century* magazine described *Left Behind* as simple-minded "beam me up theology."[21]

According to author D. Parvaz in an issue of *Christianity Today*, the arrival of the new millennium isn't the first time some people thought the world was going to end. History is littered with failed prophecies and false alarms. He then gives a short list from the past 1,000 years:

999: Christians aware of the calendar count that began with the birth of Jesus believe the Second Coming will occur at the end of the first millennium.

March 21, 1843, to March 21, 1844: Led by William Miller, the Millerites, a sect of more than 50,000 based mostly in Massachusetts and New York, abandon their material possessions and take to the hills, where they wait for the world to end.

1844: Again the Millerites wait for Armageddon. Miller sets the date as October 22. The apocalpytic no-show is dubbed "The Great Disappointment."

1891: In 1835, Mormon leader Joseph Smith predicted the Coming of the Lord fifty-six years later.

1914: Jehovah's Witnesses (an offshoot of the Seventh-Day Adventists, who are an offshoot of the Millerites) await the Second Coming. They believe Christ returned in 1884 but chose to remain invisible.

---

[21] Ibid.

April 22, 1959: In Texas, the Branch Davidians believe they will be killed and resurrected.

1975: Word of the impending apocalypse spreads through the Jehovah's Witness membership, though the church never confirms the prediction.

1984: The Jehovah's Witnesses suffer another unfulfilled prophecy of doom.

October 2, 1985: The Jesus of Burien (a.k.a. William E. Peterson) claims Armageddon came on this day and he is already well into his reign as Christ returned.

April 19, 1993: The Branch Davidians, now led by David Koresh, think the world will end this year. The cult's standoff with government agents ends in a fiery tragedy, resulting in eighty deaths.

March 26, 1997: The Heaven's Gate cult carries out a mass suicide. The thirty-nine members believe that hidden in the tail of comet Hale-Bopp is some sort of self-aware life form coming to prepare us for what they call a "galactic evolution."

October 23, 1997: Archbishop Ussher, a seventeenth century archbishop of Armagh in Ireland, calculated that God created the world on October 23, 4004 BC, and that the end of the world would come on this date 6,000 years later.

March 31, 1998: A Taiwanese UFO cult, Chen Tao, anticipates God's return – in human form – in Garland, Texas. The leader, Hon-Ming Chen, claims the Lord's return will set off a series of events leading to the world's end in August 1999.

September 1999: Nostradamus' prophecies include a meteor hitting the Earth sometime this month, – according to those who translated his predictions to our current calendar – setting off a chain of disasters (earthquakes, hurricanes, famine, etc.) leading to the end of the world.

September 1999: Shoko Asahara, leader of the Japanese Aum Shinrikyo cult, predicts the world's end this month.

Illustrations abound of Christian families who sold all their property, took their kids out of school, donned ascension robes and waited on a high hill for the Lord's return. Follow-up reports show that the father lost his job, the children were remanded to the State, the bank foreclosed on the house, and the church was embarrassed by well-intentioned but misled Christians who thought that Jesus' statement "no one knows the day and hour of the Son of Man's return" (Mark 13:32) did not apply to them. We're not to waste our lives in speculation, but to invest our lives in preparation. We are to be active in His work until He comes.

The Reality of His Second Coming: ❷ Let's Not Spectate!
This response is similar to the first response of empty speculation, but here we are referring to a problem worse than the misuse of our minds (in setting a date for the second Coming). Here we are speaking of the misuse of our *lives*, failing to become involved in our culture, standing back and simply watching our world go to hell in a handbasket. We believers are to get busy in Christ's work in the world. When Martin Luther was asked, "What would you do if you knew Jesus Christ was coming back tomorrow?", he replied, "I would still plant my apple tree today and pay my bills on time!"

Recently one of the ugliest events in NBA history took place. The Detroit Pistons, 2004s world champions, were playing the Indiana Pacers at home. The Pacers were creaming the Pistons and, with less than a minute left in regulation, Ron Artest of

Indiana fouled Ben Wallace as he drove for a lay-up. Wallace shoved Artest. As Artest unwisely lay down on the media table, a fan threw a cup of beer on him, and Artest charged into the stands. Fights broke out. More players rushed into the stands. Jermaine O'Neal threw a haymaker at a fan who had come out onto the basketball floor. The game had to be called because of the violence. A number of the players were suspended; criminal charges were filed against the spectators who stopped their spectating and took out their frustrations by hurling beer and at least one chair at the Pacers' players.

While those players should not try to defend themselves for going into the stands, the spectators should have stayed just that – spectators! No doubt alcohol contributed to the incident.

We Christians, on the other hand, must stop being spectators. We are to be fully involved participants in the game of life. We have no right to sit on the sidelines, becoming so heavenly-minded that we are of no earthly good. John Stackhouse encourages Christians to so infiltrate society that our Christianity becomes *latent* in culture by the excellence of our Christian engagement.[22]

God wants us to be full participants in this broken world. But somehow we have convinced ourselves (for various reasons)[23] that God wants us to focus solely on our individual, spiritual lives. The Bible's definition of true religion in James 1:27 brings both realms (personal purity and social concern) together:

> Religion that God our Father accepts as pure and faultless is this: to look after orphans and widows in their distress and to keep oneself from being polluted by the world.

A case could be made that we Christians have succeeded in

---

[22] *Humble Apologetics*, p. 215.

[23] Some of those reasons include: a reaction to the Fundamentalist/Modernist controversies of the 1920s and 1930', a strong division between the secular and the spiritual realms of life, a misunderstanding of Jesus' statement "The poor you will always have with you" (John 12:8), etc.

keeping ourselves from being polluted by the world,[24] but what about the orphans and widows?

Micah 6:6-8 also makes it clear (as we saw in Ch. 5) that we are not to be just standing around as believers, but are to engage ourselves with the needy of the world:

> With what shall I come before the Lord
> and bow down before the exalted God?
> Shall I come before him with burnt offerings,
> with calves a year old?
> Will the Lord be pleased with thousands of rams,
> with ten thousand rivers of oil?
> Shall I offer my firstborn for my transgression,
> the fruit of my body for the sin of my soul?
> He has showed you, O man, what is good.
> And what does the Lord require of you?
> To act justly and to love mercy
> and to walk humbly with your God.

This passage is crystal clear that God will not accept sacrifices (no matter how numerous) as a substitute for ourselves. He will not settle for our dedicating our firstborn to Him while we give our fidelity to another god (even the god of self). Micah reminds Israel of the truth they should have already known, that God has declared what He considers good – and that is a life lived in justice, mercy, and humility. All three of those qualities require a commitment to *others*. Justice is seeking practical righteousness in our society. Mercy involves the withholding of punishment of the guilty for a higher goal. Humility (as we noticed in Ch. 10) requires putting others before ourselves,

---

[24] The subject of worldliness is a broad one, but often misunderstood by Christians. Both John 17 and 1 John 2:15-17 emphasize that worldliness is more an attitude, a spirit, than a list of things Christians don't do. A case can be made that believers have *not* kept themselves "unspotted" from the world, that all they have done is stick to their cultural "lists." For a humorous depiction of Christians and their fight against worldliness, see Garrison Keillor's *Lake Wobegon Days*.

seeking the welfare of those around us.

We are to "*act* justly," to "*love* mercy," to "*walk* humbly." Why those three verbs? *Justice* which is not seen is justice which is not done. We are not to simply profess righteousness; we are to practice it.

Mercy is to be loved. Many in our culture consider mercy to be weakness, for ours is not a culture committed to compassion. Jesus had to say to the Pharisees in Matthew 9: "It is not the healthy who need a doctor, but the sick. But go and learn what this means: 'I desire mercy, not sacrifice.' For I have not come to call the righteous, but sinners" (vv. 12-13). In Matthew 23:23 Jesus declares the "more important matters of the law" to be justice, mercy, and faithfulness. Mercy is one of the spiritual gifts mentioned in Romans 12:8. God is "rich in mercy" (Eph. 2:4). We learn in James 2:12 that "Mercy triumphs over judgment." The little epistle of Jude challenges us to: "Be merciful to those who doubt; save others by snatching them from the fire; to others show mercy, mixed with fear – hating even the clothing stained by corrupted flesh" (vv. 22-23).

Humility ought to mark our walk with the Lord. Although we are to make our boast in Him (Jer. 9:23-24), we must not walk in pride, for such pride He will judge. The Lord expects us to defend the defenseless, to respect the secular authorities, and to be model citizens in our culture.

Perhaps you've heard the following story:

A very wealthy man took his son on a business trip out in the country. The purpose of this trip was to show his son how poor people can be. They spent a couple of days and nights on the farm of what would be considered a very poor family. On their return from their trip, the father asked his son, "How did you enjoy our trip?" "It was great, Dad." "Did you see how poor people can be?" the father asked. "Oh, yeah," said the son. "So what did you learn from the trip?" asked the father. The son answered, "I saw that we have one dog and they had four. We have a pool that reaches to the middle of our garden and they have a creek that has no end. We have imported lanterns in our garden and they have the stars at night. Our patio reaches to the front yard and they have the whole horizon. We have a small piece of land to live on and they have fields that go beyond our sight. We have servants who serve us, but they serve others. We buy our food, but they grow theirs. We have walls around our property to protect us; they have friends to protect them." With this the boy's father was speechless. Then his son added, "Thanks, Dad, for showing me how poor *we* are."

We believers are not poor, but extremely wealthy in the Lord. We dare not hoard our wealth, idly sitting by as the world falls apart.[25]

The Reality of His Second Coming: ❸ Let's Strive to Imitate!

When we look with anticipation towards the second Coming of the Lord Jesus, it is not enough simply to not speculate or spectate. We must take a positive and proactive approach, responding to His coming back for us in the ways which the Word lays out. For example, we read in 2 Peter 3,

> But the day of the Lord will come like a thief. The heavens will disappear with a roar; the elements will be destroyed by fire, and the earth and everything done in it will be laid bare. Since everything will be destroyed in this way, what kind of people ought you to be? You ought to live holy and godly lives as you look forward to the day of God and speed its coming (vv. 10-12).

---

[25] The Old Testament character of Jonah leaps out as one who brazenly overlooked the city of Nineveh, waiting for God's judgment, refusing himself to repent of his callousness. Although he reluctantly preached God's message, his heart did not change. He is found in the end of his short book longing for God to avenge his [Jonah's] enemies. He becomes angry when he loses his comfort. His apathy is met by God's question, "You have been concerned about this vine, though you did not tend it or make it grow. It sprang up overnight and died overnight. But Nineveh has more than a hundred and twenty thousand people who cannot tell their right hand from their left, and many cattle as well. Should I not be concerned about that great city?" (Jonah 4:10-11).

Peter makes it quite clear that the "day of the Lord" will be unexpected (it will come "like a thief") and cataclysmic (it will mean the disappearance of the heavens, the fiery destruction of the elements, and the laying bare of the earth and everything done in it). This language of complete upheaval should not lead the believer into a life of complacency, resignation, or despair, but should motivate him or her towards a life of godliness and holiness. Eschatology (the study of end-time events) should drive us to sanctification (the pursuit of becoming more like the Lord Jesus Christ).

A similar passage which encourages the believer to holiness in light of Christ's second Coming is that of 1 John 3 where we read,

> [2]Dear friends, now we are children of God, and what we will be has not yet been made known. But we know that when Christ appears, we shall be like him, for we shall see him as he is. [3]All who have this hope in them purify themselves, just as he is pure.

There is much that we do not know about our future condition as believers in Christ. What will be the nature of our glorified bodies? Will we forever have the appearance of the earthly age at which we died (or were taken to heaven at the second Coming)? [I certainly hope not. I'm not all that enthralled with being in my 50s. Perhaps we'll be able to choose our age-appearance. I kind of liked twenty-three.] What *do* we know about what we will be? We know, according to 1 John 3 that we shall be like Christ when He appears. Theologians sometimes use the term the "beatific vision" in discussing the seeing of God face-to-face. John indicates that when that happens, when we look upon the One who gave Himself for us, the transformation process of our being conformed to His image will be complete and we will "be like Him." However, the practical focus in this third chapter of 1 John is verse 3 which says, "All who have this hope in them purify themselves, just as he is pure." In light of His second Coming, we should be engaged in the process of self-purification.

I recently read a somewhat lengthy study of the Orson Welles' production "The War of the Worlds" which raises some interesting questions for Christians living in anticipation of Christ's second Coming. A researcher wrote:

> On Halloween Eve 1938, a live fictional radio drama produced by Orson Welles was broadcast across much of the United States by the CBS Mercury Theatre. [The program] depicted an invasion by Martians who had landed in Grovers Mill, New Jersey, and soon began attacking with heat rays and poison gas. Princeton University psychologist Hadley Cantril (1940) concluded that an estimated 1.2 million listeners became excited, frightened, or disturbed. However, subsequent reviews of Cantril's findings by sociologists David Miller (1985), William Sims Bainbridge (1987), and others, concluded that there was scant evidence of substantial or widespread panic. For instance, Miller found little evidence of mobilization, an essential ingredient in a panic. Hence, it was a collective delusion and not a true panic. Cantril also exaggerated the extent of the mobilization, attributing much of the typical activity at the time to the "panic." **In short, many listeners may have expressed concern but did not do anything in response, like try to flee, grab a gun for protection, or barricade themselves inside a house.** Either way one looks at this episode, it qualifies as a collective delusion. If, as Cantril originally asserted, many listeners were frightened and panicked, it is a mass delusion. Conversely, if we are to accept the more recent and likely assessments that the "panic" was primarily a media creation inadvertently fueled by Cantril's flawed study, then erroneous depictions of a mass panic that have been recounted in numerous books and articles for over six decades constitute an equally remarkable social delusion.[26]

We Christians have not fallen prey to a "remarkable social delusion." Jesus really *is* going to come back for us!

But I wonder if many Christians do not respond to the

---

[26] Robert E. Bartholomew and Erich Goode, "Mass Delusions and Hysterias from the Past Millennium," *Skeptical Inquirer*, May 2000 v24, i3, p. 20. Emphasis mine.

promise of Christ's second Coming much like those who heard "The War of the World's" broadcast on October 30, 1938. They may express concern, but *they do not do anything in response.* What are we to do in response? We're not to try to flee, grab a gun for protection, or barricade ourselves inside a house. We are to "occupy" (keep busy) until Christ returns. We are not to worry about what others do, but are to personally choose to follow the Lord (John 21:22).

One day our walk of faith will give way to sight. He is worth the wait and all the effort which we can expend in becoming like Him here.

Other books of interest
from

Christian Focus Publications

LARRY DIXON

DOC TALK

A FAIRLY SERIOUS SURVEY OF ALL THAT THEOLOGICAL STUFF

Doc-Talk

A Fairly Serious Survey of all that Theological Stuff

Larry Dixon

People ask for the strangest things in Christian books – a *pocket-sized*, large print Bible or a profound leader's guide for *instant* Bible studies! Half a moment's thought would make us realize just how silly we can be…. does a really interesting book on Christian doctrine come into the same category?

God is the most interesting person you could know, so why did you ever doubt it could be done?

'Whenever Larry Dixon writes about doctrine, it's very understandable AND practical. He writes in a way that not only satisfies your intellect, but warms your heart and motivates you to action.'

George W. Murray,
Columbia International University, South Carolina

'Larry Dixon has a marvelous facility with words, making profound concepts appear straightforward. Covering the entire scope of Christian theology as he does, the reader is teased along to richer territories effortlessly. For Christians who want a primer on the basics of Christian theology, this is the book to read.'

Derek W. H. Thomas,
Reformed Theological Seminary, Jackson, Mississippi

'Dr. Dixon is a systematic theologian, and his material is well organized. Hence the ease with which a reader makes his way through the book. I recommend the book to Christians who want to know what to believe - and to theologians too!'

C. Donald Cole,
Moody Broadcasting Network

ISBN 1-85792-729-X

THE OTHER SIDE OF THE GOOD NEWS

universalism   annihilationism   postmortem conversion   eternal damnation

CONTEMPORARY CHALLENGES TO JESUS' TEACHING ON HELL

LARRY DIXON

The Other Side of the Good News

*Confronting the Contemporary Challenges to
Jesus' Teaching on Hell*

Larry Dixon

It is a time of Christian confusion and, therefore, uncertain witness. *Is there a* biblical doctrine of hell or are Christians free to hold a variety of viewpoints on this issue? If so, does it matter which one?

Larry Dixon examines current theories and encourages you to take the Bible's teaching on hell as seriously as Jesus did. If he came to give us the Good News then we don't want people to spend eternity on *the other side of the Good News.*

Three alternative views to the traditional doctrine of hell are examined; universalism, annihilationism and post-mortem conversion. In a thought-provoking final chapter Larry summarizes how different views affect our interaction with non-Christians and the extent of our freedom to hold different views.

Is there some very bad news to the good news of the Gospel?

'This is a book which every serious student of the Bible and theology must read.'

Millard J. Erickson, Truett Seminary, Waco, Texas

'...capably defends the church's historic position on hell... respectfully interacts with opponents and writes in a manner that is at once attractive, passionate and accessible to ordinary believers.'

**Robert A. Peterson,
Covenant Theological Seminary, St. Louis, Missouri**

'A thoughtful, provocative, and fair-minded treatment of a controversial theme in Christian doctrine.'

**Thomas Oden
Drew University Graduate and Theological School,
Madison, New Jersey**

ISBN 1-85792-804-0

HOW THE DOCTRINES OF
GRACE CHANGE YOUR LIFE

TERRY L. JOHNSON

WHEN GRACE
COMES HOME

*'Whether evangelicals know it or not, their future as a viable movement
depends upon the rediscovery of such God-honoring theology.'* James M. Boice

When Grace Comes Home

How the doctrines of grace change your life

Terry Johnson

How does 'Grace' become a part of your life so that God becomes real to you in every situation?

'Terry Johnson has provided a splendid work on how right theology bears upon our worship, character, suffering, witness and growth in the Christian life. Whether evangelicals know it or not, their future as a viable movement depends upon the rediscovery of such God-honoring theology.'

The late James M. Boice,

'Rarely can the vitamin content of sweet, strong, classic pastoral Calvinism have been made so plain and palatable as it is here.'

J. I. Packer,
Regent's College, Vancouver

'Terry Johnson… enriches our understanding of the difference that the doctrines of Grace not only make to the way we do theology, but also for the ways in which we serve God and love our neighbors.'

D G. Hart,
Westminster Theological Seminary,
Philadelphia, Pennsylvania

'This fine book proves for Christians something that they should already know, but often miss: theology matters! With much practical wisdom and help for Christian thinking and living, this book makes good application of good theology.'

W. Robert Godfrey,
Westminster Seminary in California, Escondido, California

Terry Johnson is the Senior Minister of the historic Independent Presbyterian Church in Savannah, Georgia

ISBN 1-85792-539-4

BEGINNING
THE CHRISTIAN LIFE
RICHARD BEWES

'I really don't think there is a better guide
to give to a new Christian'
RICO TICE

Beginning the Christian Life

Richard Bewes

In this world 100,000 people a day are becoming Christians, in some countries the number outstrips the birth rate. Each week 1600 new congregations are formed.

This is not a story you will be familiar with through your news media!

For you who have become one of those new believers, and also for those curious at such a phenomenon, Richard Bewes, was, until his retirement in 2004, the senior pastor of one of the largest churches in London, England, guides you into becoming a mature believer.

Richard is a regular broadcaster on BBC religious slots and a best-selling author but also his Anglican church has been one of those caught up in the amazing growth that occurs where people still teach the life-changing story of Jesus of Nazareth.

If you want to move forward in your life as a Christian start reading now!

'This book is full of humanity, color and above all Bible wisdom. It wonderfully beckons us into a life of following Christ, and I really don't think there is a better guide to give to a new Christian'
Rico Tice, Author, Christianity Explored.

Until his retirement in 2004 Richard Bewes was Rector of All Souls church in London, an accomplished broadcaster, best-selling author and popular conference speaker.

ISBN 1-84550-017-2

Christian Focus Publications

publishes books for all ages

Our mission statement –

STAYING FAITHFUL

In dependence upon God we seek to help make His infallible Word, the Bible, relevant. Our aim is to ensure that the Lord Jesus Christ is presented as the only hope to obtain forgiveness of sin, live a useful life and look forward to heaven with Him.

REACHING OUT

Christ's last command requires us to reach out to our world with His gospel. We seek to help fulfill that by publishing books that point people towards Jesus and help them develop a Christ-like maturity. We aim to equip all levels of readers for life, work, ministry and mission.

Books in our adult range are published in three imprints.

Christian Focus contains popular works including biographies, commentaries, basic doctrine and Christian living. Our children's books are also published in this imprint.

Mentor focuses on books written at a level suitable for Bible College and seminary students, pastors, and other serious readers. The imprint includes commentaries, doctrinal studies, examination of current issues and church history. *Christian Heritage* contains classic writings from the past.

Christian Focus Publications, Ltd
Geanies House, Fearn,
Ross-shire, IV20 1TW, Scotland, United Kingdom
info@christianfocus.com

For details of our titles visit us on our website
www.christianfocus.com

OPP 3:4-5. In this opposition formed by a polemical dialogue, the subjects Jesus and Nicodemus are almost exclusively qualified by their sayings, that is, by the different kinds of knowledge they display. Jesus is qualified as having "true knowledge" (as expressed by "Truly, truly") and Nicodemus as having a "false knowledge." True knowledge involves taking into account the activity of the divine (Spirit) and religious matters (in 3:5 "water" certainly refers to baptism); false knowledge is limited to human matters (3:4; the "flesh," 3:6). Having this true knowledge gives Jesus a special ability to teach Nicodemus, as expressed by the emphatic "I say to you" (3:5; cf. 3:3, 11).

A comparison with the preceding positive subject (Jesus as described by Nicodemus in 3:2) shows that Nicodemus was right in calling Jesus a teacher. He was also right in viewing him as characterized by a special ability. But he did not perceive that this special ability is not primarily an ability to do signs (miracles), but rather an ability to teach (to communicate a knowledge).

Further examination of the contrast between Jesus and Nicodemus shows what is so special about Jesus' knowledge. It is knowledge concerning people (believers or religious leaders such as Nicodemus)[28] and their ability to enter the kingdom ("one cannot enter the kingdom," 3:5; cf. the repetition of "can" in Nicodemus's statement, 3:4; cf. also 3:3). In order to be able to enter the kingdom (3:5) and to "see" it (3:3), one must be "born anew" (and/or "born from above"), a view that Nicodemus rejects (see 3:7). But in order to be born anew, one needs to receive a specific ability: one needs to be enabled by the "Spirit" and not by the "flesh" (3:5-6).[29] This ability provided by the Spirit is underscored since it is contradicted by Nicodemus who only takes into account human abilities (the ability of an old person and a mother's womb as a necessary means for being born). If we put these qualifications in their hierarchical order, we note that (1) the Spirit needs first to enable people to be born anew/from above, (2) then, as born anew/from above, people are enabled to see and enter the kingdom. Thus, one of John's convictions is that the Spirit must intervene in people's lives (making them born anew/from above) before they can see and enter the kingdom. This conviction is about believers (since, in 3:15, all believers are promised "eternal life," a phrase that seems equivalent to kingdom of God).

28. Note that in Jesus' statement in 3:7, "You must be born anew," "you" is plural in Greek, yet it encompasses Nicodemus, "a ruler of the Jews."

29. In 3:5, the text associates "water" with the "Spirit" as that which enables people to be born anew. Yet, since the text establishes a contrast between Spirit and flesh (as is explicit in 3:6), water is not part of the convictions the author underscores. The role of water in this passage is discussed in step 6 (chap. 3).

OPP 3:6. This opposition does not demand much explanation, since it simply underscores the preceding point. The Spirit (the divine) is unlike the flesh (human beings) in that it has the special ability (power) to cause people to be born anew. This is why one can also say that true believers are "born from above,"[30] the point underscored by the contrasting effects upon receivers (see below, step 4).

OPP 3:9-10. Once again, Jesus and Nicodemus are opposed in a polemical dialogue; thus, they have different kinds of knowledge. More specifically, Nicodemus is qualified as lacking knowledge, as expressed by the fact that he asks a question,[31] "How can this be?" and by Jesus' rhetorical question, "You do not understand this?"[32] This is a lack of knowledge concerning the ability ("can") of the Spirit to cause people to be born anew (cf. 3:5-8). This lack of knowledge disqualifies Nicodemus from being a true teacher of Israel. Why is Nicodemus lacking this knowledge? In order to answer this question, we must take note that 3:11 refers to *two kinds* of knowledge.

True teachers (such as Jesus *and others*, "we")[33] "bear witness to what they have seen" (3:11). By setting this phrase parallel to "we speak of what we know," John specifies the type of knowledge one needs as a true teacher. It is knowledge that one acquires by "seeing." Nicodemus is disqualified as a true teacher because he does not see, and thus lacks this knowledge. As a true teacher of Israel, he would understand "how this can be," because he would see that people are born of the Spirit, and thus could bear witness to this. But he is unable to see, and thus cannot bear witness. This is lacking the kind of knowledge that one needs to have in order to be a true "teacher of Israel." But the end of 3:11 expresses that Nicodemus and others like him (plural "you") lack another kind of knowledge, because they do not receive the testimony of one who knows, Jesus or others ("we"). Through Jesus' teaching, Nicodemus is given the

---

30. The Greek word *anôthen* means both "anew" and "from above."

31. When someone asks a question, this person concedes that he or she lacks knowledge about something.

32. A rhetorical question implies an answer, and therefore amounts to a statement.

33. Regarding the first-person plural, note that, in the process of reading the first part of the verse "we speak of what we know, and bear witness to what we have seen," readers think that the "we" refers to Jesus and (an ideal) Nicodemus. But when reading the end of the verse "but you [plural] do not receive our testimony," the readers are led to correct this preliminary interpretation. Jesus is speaking in general terms, contrasting Jesus and other people like him who are true teachers with Nicodemus and people like him who are not true teachers. When these two plural forms are noted, one cannot interpret the we as a majestic we. Other people can bear witness to what they have seen, even though Jesus is unique in that he is the only one who is in a position of witnessing about "heavenly things," because he is the only one who has been into heaven (3:12-13). For the various proposals regarding the interpretation of the we, see Schnackenburg, *John*, 375–76 and notes.

means (ability) to have this knowledge, but he refuses this teaching. This lack of knowledge is rooted in a *lack of will* to listen to Jesus.[34]

How is this knowledge that one can have by receiving Jesus' testimony related to the knowledge that a true teacher must have? One thing is clear: these two kinds of knowledge do not have the same function. A true teacher bears witness to what he or she *has seen*, and thus needs *firsthand knowledge*; one cannot bear witness on the basis of secondhand knowledge! Therefore, *secondhand knowledge*, knowledge received from those who bear witness to what they have seen, must have another function. Since a true teacher also needs to have this secondhand knowledge, we have to assume that one needs this knowledge in order to be able "to see." This is confirmed when we keep in mind that all this is said by Jesus in the context of his dialogue with Nicodemus. Thus, in the case of Nicodemus, the testimony that is not received is Jesus' saying concerning "being born of the Spirit." If Nicodemus had received this teaching, he would have been able to see (recognize) that people are born anew, and that this is made possible by the role of the Spirit. Then, he would have been in a position to bear witness to these things that happen on earth ("earthly things," 3:12).

From this opposition, we have learned much about what characterizes true religious leaders, but not much about Jesus, except that Jesus presents himself as "like" a true religious leader, since he says "we" (3:11). Thus, one can deduce that Jesus has been enabled "to see," so as to be able to bear witness and teach (as is emphasized by OPP 3:4-5).

OPP 3:13.   This new opposition concerning Jesus specifies what gives Jesus the ability "to see." According to John's convictions, Jesus is unlike any other person in that he has descended from heaven and ascended into heaven.[35] This is what enabled him to see not only "earthly things" but also "heavenly things," and this knowledge enables him to bear witness. Bringing together the convictions about Jesus expressed by the discourse up to this point, it appears that, for John, *Jesus is set apart from any other person in that he is a teacher who has a special ability to communicate true knowledge regarding the role of the divine in human experience ("earthly things," 3:12) and regarding "heavenly things," because he alone has been in heaven from where he came.*

---

34. Since Jesus rebukes Nicodemus for not receiving his testimony, and since receiving is a reflexive action (appropriating for oneself), I concluded that it is a matter of lack of will, rather than a lack of ability. Despite this argument, on the basis of this opposition by itself, one cannot completely exclude that it is a lack of ability (that Nicodemus was unable to receive Jesus' teaching). OPP 3:18 and 3:19 will confirm that it is a lack of will.

35. Allusion to the incarnation and to the resurrection-exaltation.

OPP 3:11-12, 15. This is the first of a series of oppositions that have unidentified believers as their positive subjects. Because the positive subject, "whoever," is not qualified in any way, there is no contrast of the subjects. But since Nicodemus is now contrasted with believers, rather than with Jesus, previous points concerning Nicodemus as a religious leader also apply to believers. True believers are like an ideal Nicodemus in that the will to receive Jesus' teaching is also necessary for them to see the activity of the Spirit. Since "receiving Jesus' testimony" and "believing his teaching" are equivalent phrases in 3:11-12, we have to conclude that true believers are people who are "willing" to receive Jesus' teaching.[36]

OPP 3:16 and 3:17. These two oppositions with God as positive subject can be treated together, since the convictions that they express are clear. For John, the true God is qualified as loving the world, as the one who sent Jesus, the only Son, and as having the will that people receive eternal life and be saved. A god who would have the will that people be condemned or perish is, for John, a false god. God's love for the world establishes God's will to save the world.[37] Jesus, the only Son, is delegated by God to perform this action. A son who would go into the world to condemn it would be the son of a false god.

These oppositions also express additional convictions about Jesus: namely, that he is sent by God and acts in the name of God, carrying out God's will. Jesus' special ability to communicate true knowledge about the role of the divine in human experience and about heavenly things is, therefore, the means through which God's will to save the world is carried out. This implies convictions regarding the world (i.e., people who are to be saved): without the knowledge that Jesus alone can communicate, people cannot be saved.

OPP 3:18 and 3:19. These two oppositions express convictions about believers (positive subjects). To be saved, people need to be believers, that is, to believe in Jesus as the Son of God (3:18). The following opposition spells out what characterizes such believers, namely, their positive response to the coming of Jesus: loving the light rather than darkness. As

---

36. One should not be misled by the Revised Standard Version translation of 3:12b, "how can you believe." The Greek text can be rendered literally "how will you believe," or with the New English Bible, "how are you to believe." Nothing emphasizes ability in the text.

37. God wants to save the world, because of a positive inclination toward the world (God's love). This illustrates the general rule that someone's will to do something is always established on the basis of the perception of a value in a situation—technically, a "proprioceptive" evaluation of the situation. Whether it is positive as here (envisioning a potentially euphoric situation) or negative (envisioning a potentially dysphoric situation), such an evaluation leads someone to want to act in certain ways. Thus, when a text underscores a subject's will, it signals that this subject has made an evaluation of a situation. We can then look for clues about the specific kind of evaluation that took place, and strive to discern the convictions about what is viewed as good (euphoric) or bad (dysphoric).